PART OF THE PATTERN

PART OF THE PATTERN

A PERSONAL JOURNEY THROUGH THE WORLD OF CHILDREN'S BOOKS, 1960–1985

• • •

ELAINE MOSS

THE BODLEY HEAD
LONDON

British Library Cataloguing
in Publication Data

Moss, Elaine
Part of the pattern: a personal journey through
the world of children's books, 1960 to 1985.
1. Children's stories, English—History and criticism.
2. English Literature—20th century—History and
criticism
I. Title
823'.914'099282 PR990
ISBN 0-370-30860-3

 Thanks are also
due to Quentin Blake for permission to reproduce a cartoon of himself and the
author, to Lothrop, Lee & Shepard Books, The Bodley Head and the artist
for an illustration from Shirley Hughes' *Up and Up*, to Coward-McCann, Inc.,
Hamish Hamilton and the artist for an illustration from Raymond Briggs'
Father Christmas, and to Kaye Webb and the Puffin Club for the postcard
designed by the late Jill McDonald.

Printed and bound in Finland for
The Bodley Head Ltd
30 Bedford Square, London WC1B 3RP
by Werner Söderström Oy
Photoset in Linotron Ehrhardt by
Rowland Phototypesetting Ltd
Bury St Edmunds, Suffolk
First published 1986

IN MEMORY OF

BERYL NORTON

WHO GAVE ME THE

FIRST SCRAPBOOK

CONTENTS

Preface

The articles and interviews reproduced in *Part of the Pattern* are culled from my fieldwork in children's books in the twenty-five years from 1960 to 1985. Though a large part of that work was in the form of reviews of children's books for a wide assortment of newspapers and journals and for the National Book League's *Children's Books of the Year* (my responsibility for the years 1970 to 1979) very few reviews are included in this collection. Reviews of books no longer in print or even remembered might be of interest to the researcher (who can find them in libraries) but they are of little moment to the general reader involved, or becoming involved, in children's books in the late 1980s.

The point of *Part of the Pattern* is to stimulate such a person, be he or she a parent, an author, an illustrator, a teacher, a librarian, a television producer, a bookseller, a computer software manufacturer. So the limelight here is on the background people who set the stage on which children's books appear and from which they work their magic. How children's books are written and illustrated, published and sold, used in schools or by the child alone, drawn into social and political debate—these are the subjects discussed.

Because the book is arranged chronologically it to some extent charts the journey of a greenhorn who became first an enthusiast, then what the media people like to call an 'expert' in the field (though there is really no such thing: one becomes experienced and experience enables one to offer informed comment; that is all). It also pinpoints certain developments in the field of children's books in the period 1960–1985 as and when I was drawn by such developments into the fray. But it is neither an autobiography nor is it a history of children's books over twenty-five years—merely a record of the haphazard way life throws a person and an area of interest into productive collision.

In order to give some shape to the material, I have divided it into three sections. This might tempt the casual observer, looking at the Contents page, to jump to the conclusion that my life has been neatly parcelled up in the same way. Not at all! Though the pieces in *Freelance Forays* only come from the period 1960 to 1970, I went on freelancing through the 1970s and still do so. Similarly, I started writing for *Signal* in 1970 and I still write for *Signal*—but the 1980 pieces have been set aside. Life isn't tidy, but books have to be. Always a reluctant speaker, however, I shied away from giving public lectures until 1979; so *Recorded Deliveries* does represent the sum total of my more formal talks.

I would like to take this opportunity to thank the many editors, especially Nancy Chambers of *Signal*, who have given me space in their journals over the past twenty-five years; Julia MacRae, formerly of Hamish Hamilton, currently of Julia MacRae Books who took on the annual publication, with the National Book League, of the *Children's Books of the Year* catalogues; but above all my husband John and daughters Valerie and Alison whose patience, forbearance and encouragement made my two lives under one roof possible.

Elaine Moss
June, 1985

Beginnings

Four bulging scrapbooks lie scattered on the floor of the little garden room—cool in summer, ice-cold in winter—that I use as an office. They are on the floor because they are huge and heavy, and my desk is smallish and, as always, crammed: a filing basket of (unfiled) letters and articles; my notebooks; a card index or two; a row of reference books; a jar of assorted pens, pencils, scissors, staplers, glue-sticks; paperweights; a bottle of ink (I hate ball-point pens); a typewriter, a telephone and a pair of thick yellow socks—because I am writing this in the winter and will get colder as the morning draws on. I have cleared enough space in the middle of the desk for a large lined writing pad—and I have conquered the worst moment. I have filled my pen and started to write.

This makes me sound like a professional and that amazes me. Because when I began to write about children's books and their authors and illustrators twenty-five years ago I did not even have a desk—just a kitchen table—and I was surrounded not by shelves full of picture books, myths and legends, poetry, novels, bibliographies (collected over quarter of a century) but by saucepans, washing-lines, children's toys. Working time was intermittent and much interrupted—but often, all too often, there was no work to do. I remember with some nostalgia watching the van with the parcel post draw up each morning outside the block of flats we then lived in. Was there a package of books for review, a manuscript from a publisher to report on? The bell did not ring. The van drew away. There was always tomorrow.

The tomorrows have succeeded one another all too fast; and without much planning on my part—just a few opportunities offered and seized upon—a life in and around the work of children's books has developed and I have lived it with something approaching delight.

How did it all begin? What were the factors in my childhood and the years before 1960 (when my first article in *Books & Bookmen* appeared) that nudged me towards becoming 'part of the pattern' of the development of children's books and reading in Britain in the ensuing twenty-five years?

Books have always been 'part of the pattern' of my life, an inestimable source of comfort, stimulation and companionship. Personal. Unique. Yet many children grow up without them. As a middle-class child born in 1924 I was fortunate. We had books around the house; books were given to us as presents: the *Joy Street* annuals, the pony books by 'Golden Gorse', *Alice*, *Puck of Pook's Hill*, Mrs Osborn Hann's 'Peg' series, Dorita Fairlie Bruce's 'Dimsies'—and later on Henty (my father's favourite) and Margaret Irwin and D. K. Broster (mine). We were read to at home on Saturday mornings, and at school whilst doing needlework. *Old Peter's Russian Tales* will for ever be associated, for me, with pricked fingers and a rough canvas bag on which I clumsily stitched a brown patchwork camel, a green palm tree, an orange sun. I remember borrowing avidly from classroom libraries where I hated the fact that the books were caged up behind glass and I longed to release them, and buying, with my own pocket-money, the *Schoolgirls' Own Library* 'Bessie Bunter' series of yellow and black booklets that I collected, read and re-read until the thin paper with its over-inked type disintegrated into ghost confetti. So I suppose my eclectic approach to children and reading has its seeds in my own childhood.

It was my parents' intention that I should be formally educated. I would go on from St Paul's Girls' School to a university—but World War II interrupted all that. Fifteen when it broke out, at sixteen I found myself an evacuee with my family in Hertfordshire where all the schools were already full to overflowing. Innocent, ankle-socked and half-way through *How Green Was my Valley* (there were no specially tailored series for teenagers in those days) I was sent along by my mother to be interviewed for my first job in Letchworth Public Library where I was taken on as a Junior and paid 17s 6d (87½p) a week. A child still, I was given the Children's Library to look after—among other chores like filing issues and writing overdue notices. But sometimes I would be sent to guard the Reference Library where I was allowed to spend time studying for 'Inter' (the equivalent of present-day A levels) by correspondence.

Looking back I can see that an interrupted education was a boon for me. When I did finally arrive at London University (Bedford College was evacuated to Cambridge for most of the war) I was an independent learner—'self-winding' as Russell Hoban would say—whereas most of my contemporaries were accustomed to being spoon-fed at school. Libraries were already part of my life, so the Cambridge University Library, bewildering to the uninitiated, became not only a home from home for me but a place of worship. Miles of catalogue, acres of shelves, Robert Frost a fellow reader in the Reference Room. That was inspiration, pure and heady. Yes, I would become a Chartered Librarian. But only after taking a teacher's training (at the Institute of Education in London with the buzz bombs flying, becoming eerily silent just before dropping around us). And after teaching, too, at a school that defies classification, no longer exists, but must have been the most daunting initiation imaginable. Yet I was not daunted; being twenty-one is wonderful. I grew up fast at Stoatley Rough school. My job was to teach English and History up to what would today be O level to an assortment of by then English-speaking boys and girls from many countries who had been refugees in the 1930s; and also to teach English as a foreign language to the children—Polish, German, Czech, Dutch, French—who were in 1945 newly arriving, in a physical and mental disarray that is indescribable here, from the Nazi concentration camps. The luxurious concept of mounting pressure campaigns for books for ethnic minorities would have been laughable pie-in-the-sky to us in those dark and terrible times. We used imaginatively whatever we could lay hands on; and because the young human spirit is a phoenix the occasional miracle was accomplished.

It was seeing how stories and poetry could be used, in that school, to open young minds to hope, that was the practical foundation of all that has followed for me; it was taking a special paper in Library Work with Young People as part of my subsequent library qualifications that *afterwards* gave me the theoretical base. Accidentally I had discovered that practice before theory gives roots to and makes sense of the ideal.

But it was working for Grace Hogarth, in the early years of my married life, that finally plunged me into the twin streams of writing about children's books and working, as and when opportunity arose, with parents, teachers and children. Though my job as part-time secretary and reader for Grace Hogarth, then a publishers' agent in London for four American publishers, had nothing or almost nothing to do with children's books (we were looking for British novels, travel books, biographies, the US rights of which our American publishers might buy) Grace Hogarth was a children's book enthusiast to the core. She had worked for the Oxford University Press in New York and London in the 1930s and had been the publisher of Edward Ardizzone's *Little Tim and the Brave Sea Captain*, a book that was to revolutionize the concept of children's picture books. She maintained her friendships with American children's editors and it was one of these, Margaret McElderry then of Harcourt Brace, who, reading an editorial report I had written on a children's novel for Grace, remarked 'that girl should have a future in children's publishing'. Librarianship, yes. Teaching, yes. But publishing? I had never really thought of that.

Well, it did not happen quite that way. But during our daughters' early years I read and reported on many manuscripts of children's novels for a wide assortment of publishers, which was why I would wait for the parcel post so anxiously. I wonder, now, if I did those manuscripts justice. I certainly hope so, because writing is a hard and lonely task and a manuscript is an extension of the person behind it, a laying bare of part of the psyche.

What I do know, however, is that reading and assessing those children's novels-in-embryo gave me the third experience, after teaching and librarianship, that completed the groundwork for what was to follow.

By 1960 I was equipped—by the greatest good fortune—for the life of a freelance writer and broadcaster, special interest: children and their books.

PART 1
FREELANCE FORAYS
1960–1970

Illustration from *Up and Up*, © Shirley Hughes

When Antonia Ridge, novelist and a BBC *Woman's Hour* producer, invited me, after my first nervous broadcast (on adoption, I think it was), to become a contributor to the programme on any subject that interested me, I chose children's books. My Christmas round-up for 1957 was apparently well received; and from that began a twenty-year association, apart from the occasional break, with *Woman's Hour*.

At the time I did not realize that *Woman's Hour*'s awakening curiosity about children's books was symptomatic of the late 1950s and early 1960s. But it was.

Children's book publishing had flourished in the 1930s—Edward Ardizzone, J. R. R. Tolkien, Arthur Ransome, Alison Uttley, Noel Streatfeild, Ursula Moray Williams were its stars—though not as an independent branch of publishing. It had been damped down, with a few glowing exceptions such as the beginning of the Puffin list, by World War II and its aftermath of shortages of which paper was but one. In the 1950s, however, the flames again broke through; first novels by new authors such as Rosemary Sutcliff, Gillian Avery, Philippa Pearce, William Mayne and Lucy Boston, picture books by V. H. Drummond and William Stobbs claimed critical attention. Publishing houses began to appoint full-time children's editors part of whose job would be to find new authors and artists whose work would appeal to children. And they offered these new authors (and, at a later date, artists) not down payments for a book, as had been common in the past, but contracts with royalty clauses that would give them their due interest in the success of their work.

The doors were opening wide. But how was the reading public (bringing books to the notice of the vast *non*-reading public was to become a later preoccupation) to hear about these books? As Marcus Crouch has remarked, 'The vast annual output of British publishers became a matter of real anxiety . . . It was increasingly difficult to keep track of worthwhile books, and the existing reviewing journals became quite inadequate.'*

Editors of programmes like *Woman's Hour*, specialist magazines such as *Books & Bookmen*, newspapers like *The Times*, weeklies such as the *Spectator*, all of these in the 1960s became

* *Treasure Seekers and Borrowers*, Library Association, 1962, p. 113.

keen to give space to children's books—if they could find the people to write the articles. I happened to be one of the people who was ready at the right time.

So, with what now looks like youthful over-confidence, in 1960 I set off, commissioned by *Books & Bookmen*, to do my first interview—with Rosemary Sutcliff. An historical novelist with a growing reputation, she had that year been awarded the Carnegie Medal for *The Lantern Bearers*.

ROSEMARY SUTCLIFF
A LOVE OF LEGEND

Rosemary Sutcliff's passion is the continuity of history. 'History,' she says, 'is not a collection of isolated set-pieces. It is a continuous process and very much alive.' So she sets her books at times of upheaval and change—Roman conquering Briton, Saxon overcoming Roman, Norman ousting Saxon and so on—and her theme is not death, but survival.

This theme is never bolder or more striking than in *The Lantern Bearers*. It is the story of a young Roman officer, Aquila, who, when the last legions were withdrawing from Britain, leaving the land open to the invading and plundering Saxon, deserted the Eagle and stayed behind in the land which his family, though Roman, had known as 'home' for generations.

Aquila is symbolic of the light and culture of Rome which he carries forth into the Dark Ages. He is the personification of Rosemary Sutcliff's conception of living history and it is therefore fitting that the Library Association should have had the prescience to wait for this novel in order to bestow upon its author the Carnegie Medal for the best children's book of 1959.

Rosemary Sutcliff does not come from a literary family: when I asked her if writing was hereditary she said drily, 'Well, my father used to write Admiralty sailing instructions and his only advice to me has been, "Never use two words if one will suffice".' Neither can she draw from her own childhood experience since Still's disease has held her in its thrall since the age of two; yet the children in her books spring free; they run with the air of Devon (or the Downs or the Lakes) fresh in their nostrils, climb, swim, ride, with joy and vigour. They are touched by the wand of a wizard.

Rosemary Sutcliff lives with her father in a long, low white house near Arundel in Sussex. 'It was probably the stables and still-room of the old rectory,' she says, 'and I suppose our garden was the paddock.' She works in a room with windows on three sides, her table piled high with books of reference, the telephone right by her. Writing is a way of life for her and she takes it quite calmly; if the telephone rings ('this is the room where everything goes on,' she says) it disturbs her for a moment 'but I'm soon away again in my work.' I asked her if she ever worked in her lovely garden. 'No,' she said, 'I cannot concentrate. I'll see a bird or an insect and spend my time watching it.' This acute sensitivity to nature and joy in the outside world is reflected in the superb background drawing of countryside, birds and animals which gives a satisfying wholeness to Rosemary Sutcliff's novels.

How many hours a day does Rosemary Sutcliff work? 'I start when I'm ready and finish when I'm tired.' How much does she write in a normal day? 'About 1,800 words,' she said, 'a page like this.' And she indicated a foolscap sheet covered with elfin writing. I asked how many drafts she made before sending her manuscript to the typist (she is unable to type) and she said, 'Four.' This immense labour is worthwhile because the result is a book for which the foundations have been carefully laid ('I'm not one of those people who can start writing without knowing what the end is going to be,') and subsequently cloaked, a seemingly effortless work of art.

But sensitivity and a capacity for hard work cannot alone make a writer of Rosemary Sutcliff's calibre. Imagination is the spark which has ignited the flame, an imagination richly fed in childhood by her mother who read to her tirelessly—Kenneth Grahame, Lytton, but mainly Kipling: the *Just So Stories* (her sense of humour is exactly attuned to the Elephant's Child whose first act with a newly acquired trunk is to spank all his insufferably interfering relations), *Puck of Pook's Hill*, *The Jungle Books*, *Stalky and Co.*

Her love of legend, her compassion for animals, her deep sense of comradeship and intense interest in Roman times are, of course, personal, but they were undoubtedly nurtured by Kipling. Her first writing venture, in fact, was a collection of legends. Were these rejected, then? 'Well, yes and no. They were passed from hand to hand at a regimental dinner and ended up at the Oxford University Press who didn't want legends but on the strength of them commissioned *Robin Hood*.' 'And have taken everything you've offered them since?' 'Yes,' she answered simply, as though every author may place his outpourings simply at the cost of posting the manuscript.

Rosemary Sutcliff did not begin to write until she was twenty-five. 'It seemed unlikely when I was a child that I should ever succeed at anything,' she said. 'I hated school and was hopeless at everything.'

'Not English and History, surely?' 'Oh yes, I loathed them *and* Nature Study *and* Latin and all the things that interest me now. But I loved drawing, so at fourteen—one could leave mercifully early in those days—I was taken away from school and sent to Bideford Art School where I was thoroughly happy painting in oils.' A chance question brought to light the surprising information that this modest young woman, she is thirty-nine, became an expert miniaturist whose work has been shown at the Royal Academy and has brought her membership of the Royal Miniaturist Society.

She gave up painting after she began to write, 'because I found it was becoming more of an exercise than an art. My writing became my art and I'm glad because people bought my miniatures and I never saw them again whereas I can keep my books by me.'

The note of affection in her voice prompted me to ask which of her books was her favourite. Unhesitatingly she chose *The Eagle of the Ninth*, the first of her Roman novels. And whilst on the subject of favourites I also asked her whether she read adult historical novels and if so which authors she admired. 'I don't have time for much reading outside my work,' she answered, 'but I'm devoted to T. H. White (though I've given up recommending him to people because I never seem to be right about who is going to like him). I admire Mary Renault tremendously and,' she added shyly, 'I enjoy Josephine Tey.'

As miniaturist and children's author, Rosemary Sutcliff has the honours in her pocket. But she is certainly not resting on her laurels. This autumn has seen the publication of no less than three new books by this versatile author for children (who, incidentally, has also written two highly successful novels for adults).

To the Batsford 'History' series Rosemary Sutcliff has contributed a volume which will bring delight to the lover of English country houses, *Houses and History*. She has written a monograph on *Rudyard Kipling*, which is an intensely revealing personal appreciation, a miniature in print. And there is her new children's novel, *Knight's Fee*, the story of a half-Breton, half-Saxon dog-boy at Arundel Castle who, by strange fortune, becomes a knight in Norman England. Here again is the insistence on race overlaying rather than superseding race. *Knight's Fee* is in small compass compared with some of Rosemary Sutcliff's more ambitious projects, but because of its vividness and warmth it yet adds to the stature of this courageous and remarkable author.

There follows, in my scrapbook, page upon page of reviews from *Books & Bookmen*, *The Times Literary Supplement*, the occasional piece for the *Sunday Telegraph*, *The Sunday Times* and so on, reviews of books now for the most part forgotten. But in 1962 Margery Fisher's *Growing Point* had come on the scene, the first of the post-war flowering of journals devoted to the reviewing and discussion of books for children. Written, published, distributed and financed by Margery Fisher single-handed, it has survived for twenty-three years, a monument to its creator's passion, industry, steadfastness and literary taste. Outsiders' contributions to *Growing Point* are rare, so it was astonishing to be asked to write for it an article on new developments in series publishing. But Margery Fisher, knowing that our daughters were seven and five by this time and therefore likely consumers of the burgeoning series for 'beginning readers', must have thought that I was in a good position to comment on these for her. Some of the stories, like *Little Black Sambo* and *Rufty Tufty*, would not be likely to find themselves in such an article today. But they were blithely recommended in 1964, and to excise them from this 1985 reprint would have been to falsify the evidence of children's book history.

VARIETY IS ALL

Is publishing just like any other business? This question may, at first sight, seem a long throw from beginning-to-read books but in fact the answer to it has a direct bearing upon the flood of material with which the bewildered parent of young children is faced in the bookshop.

Once upon a time, in the United States, a man by the name of Seuss dreamed up a new approach to reading. He realized that children at the very early stage of reading badly need confidence in their ability to make sense of words on a page. He also realized that short words need not make dull sentences. 'The cat sat on the mat' became, overnight, *The Cat in the Hat* and suddenly, learning to read was FUN.

In Great Britain one publisher thought this 'Beginner Book' series worth a trial. *The Cat in the Hat* was launched quietly; runaway sales did not follow. Collins, however, were prepared to take the whole Beginner Book series and back it with a mammoth sales campaign. Publishing *is* like any other business and that is why every parent who is interested in books for the very young has seen, borrowed or even bought the zany *Cat in the Hat*, *Sam and the Firefly* or, one of the newest, *Snow*. That is why, despite the garish, sprawling illustrations, this series is now more in vogue than Angela Banner's *Ant and Bee* series and H. A. Rey's *Zozo* both of which, in a quieter manner, also ease the child over the early hurdles.

Unfortunately, because publishers cannot resist exploiting a made market, we are now experiencing the results of a rush to jump on the Beginner Book band-wagon. Scores of publishers are producing series ostensibly catering for the early stages of reading. Are these series really necessary, or do they succeed just because we, the public, are too lazy to search the shelves of the libraries and bookshops for books (real books, not books written to order for a series), which our young children will not only enjoy reading but will profit mentally from reading?

It is only natural, when time is short and a toddler is methodically unpacking the shopping from the string-bag, that one should dive for a book which, by a series title, proclaims its suitability for beginning readers—'I Can Read' series, 'Beginning to Read' series, etc., but take heed! Promotion is beginning to take precedence over production; standard is being sacrificed to sales. Some of the books in all of the series are good, but a great number are worthless.

How can one tackle for oneself the early reading years? It has been my experience that at the stage when a child has just learned to read he is prepared to go back two years in subject matter in the books he reads to himself provided that an older person reads to him books which are at his own level or preferably a little in advance of that level. For instance, a child who listens avidly at bedtime to *The Lion, the Witch and the Wardrobe* by C. S. Lewis will happily read Helen Bannerman's *Little Black Sambo* to himself, or to a younger member of the family, before breakfast.

Between the ages of five and eight this double approach to reading is of vital importance especially if, as is often the case, an intelligent child is a slow reader. One can stimulate a sense of book magic by reading aloud from Mary Norton, Eleanor Farjeon, Lewis Carroll, Andrew Lang, Kingsley, Kipling, Alison Uttley, Rumer Godden to a child who can only cope, for himself, with quite elementary material.

The important features of first books for a young child to read to himself are simple sentence structure, clear print, short chapters (or, preferably, short stories); a plot that moves, details which intrigue, pictures which break up the text. Edward Ardizzone is an author-artist who can create books which embody all these requirements and which, in addition, create a rich fantasy mood. His 'Little Tim' stories appeal equally to boys and girls and have time and again provided the enchanted bridge from deciphering words to reading stories.

Just as the very young child enjoys hearing stories in which sounds, phrases and sentences are repeated, sometimes with variations, so the older child who is starting to read gains confidence when he meets a familiar line. Folk tales (such as 'Chicken Licken', 'The Gingerbread Man', 'The Three Little Pigs') and fairy stories, in suitable editions, make excellent tooth-cutters in this respect. They invariably have entrancing plots and colourful characters and their appeal is over a wide age range. The important thing is to ensure that the child is given a book of tales which is well but simply written.

There are many modern writers who successfully combine simplicity with style and are therefore good food for the early reader. Hilda van Stockum in *Jeremy Bear* and other books; Helen Morgan whose *Meet Mary Kate* has many stories about one little girl; Leila Berg whose *Little Pete* has a number of stories about one little boy; and Ruth Ainsworth whose *Rufty Tufty* stories never fail to hold a child's attention. Eileen Colwell's *Tell Me a Story* and Rosalind Vallance's *The Youngest Omnibus* are two collections of good stories and rhymes taken from many authors and sources, books which the diligent parent would do well to take as a signpost to other fruitful byways.

From libraries, or for very special presents, there is a wealth of large picture books some of which, like Wanda Gág's *Millions of Cats* are for the very young; others such as Philippa Pearce's *Mrs Cockle's Cat* and V. H. Drummond's *Mrs Easter and the Storks* make nutritive reading for children up to the age of nine to whom pictures are a stimulus.

The largest pitfall on the road to reading is boredom, the '*another* one of *those*' reaction which may set in if the series habit is over indulged. Variety is all.

As part of my freelance journalism I had been writing the occasional children's book review article for David Rees, then Literary Editor of the *Spectator*. But when, in 1965, he offered me the chance to edit and lead the Children's Book Review supplements, twice a year, this was a real break. My brief was to choose the books and topics I wanted to write about, make comments on prizewinners, take a broad view of a field that was flowering fast. My audience would be complementary to that of *Woman's Hour*, bringing in more fathers and, I hoped, signalling to the politically and artistically aware readership of the *Spectator* that children's books were an important ingredient in family life.

One topic then being debated was fiction for over-twelves. Did these readers need to be specially considered by publishers? Kaye Webb of Penguin thought so. She founded the Peacock list (damned as quite unnecessary by Marghanita Laski whose experience of teenagers appeared to be limited to those who could find their own literary nourishment) and reprinted in it the work of Gerald Durrell, D. K. Broster, Enid Bagnold, Stanley Weyman. I see that I supported this initiative with adjectives that would today sound the death knell of such a series: 'morally sound, middle-brow, straightforward'!

Despite, or perhaps because of, this climate, Josephine Kamm's *Young Mother* was recognized as the barrier-breaker it was to become.

Pat, the central character of Josephine Kamm's *Young Mother*, far from coping with the very human predicament in which she finds herself, is buffeted by the prevailing winds of society's prejudices and brought back into line by its machinery for dealing with unmarried mothers and their babies. Pat is no Regency lass with a dashing beau to tumble her; she is a grammar-school girl working for A levels and she cannot even remember what the man who fathered the child she carries looked like—because her drink, at 'one of those parties', had been spiked. Mrs Kamm's courageous book is remarkable in many ways: it is clear; it is unsentimental; it is sympathetic; it is factual. Everyone with whom Pat is associated, her mother (the home is a broken one), her sister who is engaged, her brother who is still at school, suffers. Pat herself, pregnant in a job as mother's help, in the mother-and-baby home and in the agony of having to part with her child for adoption, suffers most of all. This is not a study in depth, but it is a skilful and honest sketch of a bad situation—required reading for headstrong girls, and for parents who think it 'square' to stay in the house when their teenage children give parties. For those parents, at the other end of the scale, who may consider this subject unsuitable for older girls' reading, I quote Anne Carroll Moore, a pioneer in the field of children's literature, who once said, 'Tragedy lies . . . not in knowing too much but rather in not knowing enough to think things through.'

It was three years before Pan/Macmillan 'Topliners' were to hit the headlines and focus attention on teenage reading for the less literary child (see p. 32) but unquestionably the main talking point in between was Maurice Sendak's then controversial (now classic) picture book, *Where the Wild Things Are*. In the *Spectator* I was able to give it a column review to itself; there was also space for a long review of Bettina Hürlimann's important historical (and prophetic) study of children's books; and an opportunity (such as one could not get today) to explore the way Rumer Godden in *The Kitchen Madonna* speaks eternal truths about the human condition to children of all backgrounds through a subtle study of two emotionally deprived children who happen to be middle-class. Another signpost towards future battlegrounds.

WHERE THE WILD THINGS ARE by MAURICE SENDAK

Maurice Sendak's *Where The Wild Things Are* has been an American *succès de scandale* since it won the Caldecott Medal (awarded annually to a distinguished American picture book) in 1964. With its publication here, in four other European countries and in Japan it seems likely to become a world-wide talking-point. Most picture books flower and fade peacefully in their own field. Maurice Sendak's has become a battleground, not among small children, who by and large find it intriguing, funny and a great opportunity to release their own animal spirits, but among the grown-ups, who are split into two camps: some triumphantly acclaim it a landmark in the history of literature for children; others fear it may give nightmares to the young. For the Wild Things, fanged, beaked, winged and hairy (but fat and cuddly, too), 'gnash their terrible teeth, roll their terrible eyes and show their terrible claws' as ferociously as any child in a temper. And this is what the book is all about.

Because Max, the boy hero, is in disruptive mood his mother calls him 'Wild Thing!' and sends him off to bed without any supper. Wild Thing indeed, thinks Max. Perhaps I am, and if so I'll go to the land Where the Wild Things Are. Gradually, through the magic blend of text and picture, we feel Max's real world slipping away and a fantasy world of forest, sky and ocean taking its place. Max sails off in his private boat (every child *has* his private boat) to the land of the Wild Things where he is greeted by them and crowned King. 'Let the wild rumpus start!' says Max, imperiously—three double pages of pictures with no text invite small boys with percussion instruments to provide a ringing, banging accompaniment to the beasts rampant. But when Max says 'Stop!' the Wild Things subside—and are sent off to bed (parents, please note) without *their* supper; and when Max wants to leave these projections of himself behind and return 'to someone who loves him best of all,' he firmly says 'No!' to their entreaties that he should stay. Max is in control of these Wild Things throughout and this is why five-year-olds who identify with Max do not feel threatened by the Wild Things, as they sometimes will by a menacing, destructive Walt Disney creation.

Because it is a work of art, a valid interpretation by a gifted writer and illustrator of an intense child experience, *Where the Wild Things Are* can be extolled by artists, lyricised by poets and analysed by psychiatrists to their hearts' content. But it is not, primarily, an intellectual exercise; it is a book for young children and parents to read, act out and enjoy together, and as such it must stand or fall. So many picture books have an instant appeal which diminishes; Sendak's is a shock at first but delight in it grows as the pages are turned—and they surely will be—again and again.

THREE CENTURIES OF CHILDREN'S BOOKS IN EUROPE
by BETTINA HÜRLIMANN,
translated and edited by BRIAN W. ALDERSON

In Stockholm in the year 1900 an extraordinarily prescient book appeared under the (then) astonishing title *The Century of the Child*. What are we, the children of that century, doing with the opportunities that have been given us? Bettina Hürlimann's review of children's literature in Europe from 1650 to the present day is no dry-as-dust history: it uses the historical method to bring modern trends into perspective.

Based on the author's warm and intelligent response to children and their books, her lively interest in the place of the child in European society, and her own experiences among artists and teachers, *Three Centuries of Children's Books in Europe* is both an absorbing commentary on the past and an urgent plea that we should look at the slippery slopes children's books are beginning to tread before we reach the edge of the abyss. For in every technological development which can enrich our children's lives there lurks the peril of misuse. The tale-spinning record may bring expert storytelling to the bedside but it is no substitute for the mutual involvement of mother and child in a book; photography can extend a child's vision or it can freeze his imagination; colour printing brings us beautiful picture books—and the comic.

But should the comic be considered at all in a book about children's literature? The frightening answer is, yes. Mrs Hürlimann throws her weight behind that of John Steinbeck (who predicts that bubble-talk literature is in the process of supplanting real literature) when she writes of the devaluation of words in the face of picture worship and warns that parents who buy nothing but comics for their offspring may suddenly become aware of the inconceivable fact that their children are no longer either capable of reading, or willing to read, any book which makes a demand on their intelligence.

Yet this author is no gloomy Cassandra; she experiences joy and happiness in literature and life and communicating this to her readers is her personal contribution to the war against canned culture. She is illuminating on *Struwwelpeter*, penetrating on the two levels of *The Little Prince*'s appeal and cogent in her argument that children's authors are simply good writers (Perrault, the Grimms, Twain, Stevenson) whose work appeals to the young. But nothing in this timely book is more heart-warming than the author's profound belief that *Babar*'s Utopian kingdom can set children on the right civic road and that *Ferdinand the Bull*, *The Happy Lion* and *Dr Dolittle* can help to stem the growth of violence.

An idealist? Perhaps. But we need more watchdogs like Mrs Hürlimann if John Steinbeck's nightmare vision is not to become our grandchildren's reality.

THE KITCHEN MADONNA by RUMER GODDEN

Many people believe that background in children's books is a divisive element (out-with-pony-club, in-with-'pop') and so it can be if it is merely a sterile backcloth to a superficial plot. But an impassioned writer capable of using background as an organic force which is working in her characters, a writer who has a sound understanding of children and their relationships, can set her story in Burma or Bermondsey, have as her hero a prince or a pedlar and still command a broad audience. For emotion, sensitively explored, is a vast and unifying common ground.

Rumer Godden's *The Kitchen Madonna* is set in the immaculately planned home of an architect couple in a London square, yet the feelings which flood through Gregory, their shy, clever nine-year-old son, when he arrives home from school to a dark empty house—mother on a building site, the latest *au pair* still at classes—will strike familiar chords in a dockland latch-key child or in the son of a globe-trotting millionaire.

When Marta, a middle-aged Ukrainian, comes to the Thomas family as mother's help, Gregory feels a kinship for this sad, uprooted homely woman who brings him the security he so badly needs. ('"I'm afraid Marta's not very tidy," said Mother, but Gregory and Janet, especially Gregory, liked the kitchen far better now.') Secretly, in his loft, Gregory makes a Ukrainian-style Kitchen Madonna for Marta, from millinery scraps, a *Times* photograph, beads, doll's hair, toffee papers. The boy and the Kitchen Madonna, which grows under his loving hands, emerge in silent unison.

Rumer Godden's sure, light touch, her deep respect for children (she is as good on Gregory's extrovert little sister as she is on the withdrawn hero), her consummate literary craftsmanship and her underlying theme—that modern children need warmth, love and a measure of disarray to counteract the cold efficiency of the planned society which threatens to engulf them—make *The Kitchen Madonna* a masterpiece of our time. Carol Barker, illustrating brilliantly in line and colour, has adapted the author's technique to her own medium.

The reader is shown the background and trimmings to the story but he is left to visualize the characters which grow from these for himself. A book for under-tens—and for their parents, too.

My scope was further broadened when *The Times* inaugurated its 'Saturday Review' pages in 1967, and Michael Ratcliffe, who was the editor of this section, asked me if I would contribute children's book reviews on a fortnightly basis. The amount of space he gave to the subject was extraordinary. Today *The Times*, in common with other national newspapers, is comparatively niggardly in its apportionment of space to children's books. Here are three review pieces published within a five-week period!

The Tolkien piece is a brisk salute to a recognized master; the Dahl an opening round in a controversy over this writer that was to grow in intensity as his success with young readers increased; the article on fantasy is included because, rooted in the period of the now revered 'landscape fantasy' of the 1960s, it also foreshadows today's plethora of books (for young people as well as for adults) on nuclear disaster.

SMITH OF WOOTTON MAJOR by J. R. R. TOLKIEN

Smith of Wootton Major is a pocket-sized allegory. On the surface it presents a fairy story about a village, a Master Cook who doesn't believe in fairies, a magic star baked once every generation in a children's Festival Cake and a kindly boy, Smith, who, having swallowed the star (inner light) can roam at will in Faery (the land of heightened sensibility). But the book is so much more than a mere story. Through this potent fantasy Tolkien urges the rationalist to respond, while there is time, to the spiritual springs within him, to travel, like Smith, from Dawn to Eventide, awake to love and beauty, to life and death, to terror and compassion but above all to mystery. Here is a well of wisdom for each reader to dip into with his own bucket, then study his reflection in the pure water he draws up—if he dares. *Smith of Wootton Major* is handsomely decorated in medieval black-line style by Pauline Baynes.

The Times, 1967

CHARLIE AND THE CHOCOLATE FACTORY *and* JAMES AND THE GIANT PEACH by ROALD DAHL

Humour has few classics but unless I am very much mistaken Roald Dahl's *Charlie and the Chocolate Factory* is destined for the roll of honour, junior section. It is the funniest children's book I have read in years; not just funny, but shot through with a zany pathos which touches the young heart.

Charlie Bucket, the hero, is the poorest boy imaginable (one bar of chocolate a year and two helpings of cabbage as a special treat on Sundays). His four grandparents, all over 90, 'as shrivelled as prunes and as bony as skeletons', lie huddled and hungry in their one bed 'two at either end dozing away the time with nothing to do'. But Charlie's visit to the mysterious Wonka Chocolate Factory, a land of mint grass and chocolate rivers, changes the Bucket family fortunes.

Mr Willy Wonka, the imperious chocolate wizard, is looking for a protégé he can trust; he disposes of Charlie's rivals (greedy Augustus Gloop, disobedient Violet Beauregarde, spoilt Veruca Salt, brash Mike Teevee) and chooses skinny, wide-eyed Charlie as the heir to his secret recipes—which include sugar-coated pencils for sucking, luminous lollies for eating in bed, and stickjaw for talkative parents. Faith Jaques, illustrating, catches every mood, sad, mad, and vulgar (why not?) of this bubbling fantasy.

James and the Giant Peach, Roald Dahl's earlier book for children, has taken six years to cross the Atlantic. It tells how James, an orphan, escapes the guardianship of two monstrous aunts, the wicked Aunt Spiker and the dastardly Aunt Sponge. One day 'this disgusting beast', 'this filthy nuisance' (the Aunts never call James by his real name) spills a bag of magic ('Miserable creature!') near the roots of a peach tree.

A peach swells to enormous proportions and James goes to live inside it. With a set of captivating and resourceful insects as crew, James and the Giant Peach roll, float and waft from rural England to a New York ticker-tape reception, squashing the Aunts flat *en route*. Dahl's dialogue in these two books smacks of Carroll, his verses of Belloc. But he is a great original in that he gives modern children the humour they appreciate—in style.

The Times, 1967

THE FANTASTIC LIVING FORCE OF LANDSCAPE

The Sixties will go down in the history of English children's literature as the years in which the power of landscape was developed as a living force in fantasy: William Mayne is one of the two major writers (the other is Alan Garner) who has brought the past into the present in his books, not through a child's experiences in an old house or garden, but through the age-old mystery of the hills, an organic mystery that works through the imagination of the children who belong to Welsh mountain or Yorkshire moor. For we are all, these authors remind us, part of our natural environment.

For William Mayne, as for T. S. Eliot, 'all time is eternally present'. In his new story, *The Battlefield*, the past is active both under the soggy soil by the ancient look-out tower in the old battlefield and in the livcly curiosity of Lesley and Debby, the innkeeper's daughters. The two sisters are drawn by features of the moorland landscape, by odd bits of local history and by wisps of overheard conversation about supernatural portents, into a hair-raising adventure in which they, as part of the natural universe, redeem a past wrong.

Mayne is a subtle writer with a wonderful ear for Yorkshire dialogue and the *non sequiturs* of family conversation which are often so revealing; but above all he is a craftsman, building up his story with a carpenter's care. Gradually, innocently, the ordinary small happenings (a frozen pipe, a picnic) suffuse with the inexplicable phenomena (blood-red water in the beck, a flame in the field) and grow to a tremendous climax in which a landslide carries the two terrified children downhill in the uprooted look-out tower to crush the restored stone cross newly erected on the village green, a cross which rightfully belonged to the dead beneath the battlefield. The old shepherd sleeps by the bar-parlour fire and wakes to comment, 'Upset nature, and nature rights itself' . . .

In *The Plug at the Bottom of the Sea* Robert Lamb tells a most improbable story with total conviction. Some children will read this novel as a weird and entertaining tale about a shipwrecked boy and girl who are marooned at night on a rock in mid-ocean and wake to find all the water gone because, by accident, they have set in motion a mechanism which pulls out the plug at the bottom of the sea, leaving boats, fish, gulls and mermaids high and dry. But the perceptive child will realize that Mr Lamb is seriously concerned with civilization's blindness to the dangers of nuclear warfare.

'Now I am a peaceful man and we are a peaceful land,' said Geiges, King of the West, 'but we have decided to build the plug which of course we shall never use because it is too dangerous to even talk about.'

'But what if we are forced to use it?' asked all the wise men.

'That is too terrible to even think about so we cannot discuss it,' said the King.

Out of place in a children's book? I don't think so, because Mr Lamb allows the child to digest or pass over his implications; he never rams them home.

Henry Treece, in a book published posthumously, pursues the same theme. *The Dream-Time* presents a kaleidoscopic picture of man at the dawn of his consciousness, a dream sequence in which his nobleness and creative powers are seen struggling to overcome his capacity for destruction. Though fully illustrated, by Charles Keeping, this strange, haunting book is surely only meant for children insofar as we are all children threatened by extermination—as the author makes clear—from within.

The Times, 1967 (extract from long review article)

By 1968 children's books were not only news, they were big business. National newspapers appointed children's book editors—Margery Fisher on *The Sunday Times*, John Rowe Townsend on *The Guardian*, Naomi Lewis on *The Observer*, Brian Alderson on *The Times*. I continued to write the occasional piece for *The Times* for a few years, sometimes looking at new developments ('Reluctant at Fifteen'), sometimes summing up the contribution of a leading figure in the field. But I was becoming more interested in the wider audience for children's books at a time when differing views about the purpose of children's book reviewing were beginning to surface; was it an occupation for literary critics or for people whose main concern was that children from all backgrounds should be able to find books to enhance their lives? Did one have to turn one's back on the highest forms of children's literature in order to bring children's books to a wider audience? I did not think so. It was at this stage that I learned 'The Peppermint Lesson' and wrote about it for the National Book League's journal, *Books* (p. 33).

RELUCTANT AT FIFTEEN

What do teenagers read? The answer to this question is pretty short: everything, or almost nothing.

Academic fourteens nourish themselves on Dickens and the Brontës, Golding and Orwell, with Ian Fleming as a snack between meals. Libraries and bookshops attract them the way coffee bars and record shops draw their less intellectual contemporaries. Yet reading in adolescence is just as important for the non-academic young who constitute a large percentage of the secondary-school population, the section the school-leaving controversy is all about. These children mature faster than their more bookish friends; their need to identify themselves with adults is more urgent. Ostentatiously, they spurn 'kids' stuff' (which includes children's books in the library) in favour of mod gear and a pop culture in which books play no part.

But they lack stories, so they attempt to satisfy their hunger by watching television, unaware that their true need is not just for the story but for an exploration of the emotions which are the mainspring of the action. Only books can give these young people the opportunity to test their own feelings and new experiences against those of a fictional character, privately and at a moment chosen for themselves.

But what can they read, these youngsters who have been taught by society to expect instant entertainment? The classics are too difficult, many modern novels too advanced in technique, the story in the teenage weekly too synthetic to fulfil any real function. They need books which are basically adult and serious, which throw some light upon the human situation and which tell a story vividly, briefly and in some depth.

Is there a place for special paperback fiction publishing for adolescents? Probably yes, though distribution of any series that is neither adult nor juvenile, through outlets geared only to these two categories, presents problems, as Peacock, a series of reprints for in-betweens, has discovered. A best-selling Peacock is Beverly Cleary's *Fifteen*, which covers a year in the life of an American teenage girl: her first boyfriend, her efforts to appear sophisticated, and those awful moments when parents behave like—parents. This is a book of considerable charm, sensitive, funny and dead on target but it tells only half the story the adolescent of today wants to hear.

Sam and Me, by Joan Tate, from Pan/Macmillan 'Topliner' tells the other half. It is concerned with teenage insecurity. Jo, the heroine, is a girl with an institution background and she finds herself, in adolescence, almost incapable of making a positive contribution to the relationship which is maturing between her and Sam. For Jo, it is enough to be Sam's slave: but Sam, who is an intelligent young man, needs Jo to be a real person. A moving story, in which physical and emotional problems are skilfully and imaginatively handled. *Sam and Me* is surely a book that the reluctant teenage reader will seize upon and devour because it throws a clear beam of light on to some of the sexual problems modern youth has to face.

Sam and Me was written for original paperback publication. These Pan/Macmillan 'Topliners' are edited by Aidan Chambers with the needs of the reluctant teenage reader in mind. Mr Chambers is a secondary-modern schoolmaster, dedicated to the teenager who, he believes, needs to be specially provided for, in literature and in life. Mr Chambers is certain that the teenage non-reader is really an avid reader deprived, and he hopes to prove his point with 'Topliners'.

Despite evidence from America that books written for a defined audience tend to become lifeless formula-novels, Mr Chambers thinks he can attract genuinely creative talent; his book jackets will look adult and these paperbacks should find their way into newsagents and station kiosks, as well as bookshops and schools.

Joan Tate says that the only difference between herself as a teenager and her three children at that age is that they talked about things she only thought about. If Aidan Chambers does find original imaginative and responsible authors whose work, like Mrs Tate's, reflects just this difference, the teenage reader may soon cease to be reluctant; the way is now open for light, yet emotionally sustaining, literature.

The Times, 1968

THE 'PEPPERMINT' LESSON

Don't go looking round the bookshops for *Peppermint*. Though this was probably the most important book in my younger daughter's early life, to your child it would probably mean very little: just another story and not a particularly good one at that.

Why, then, did mine clamour for it so often? Why, when it was falling to pieces, did I have to glue it together? Why was it never scribbled on, thrown out of bed, lent to a friend or given away with the jumble? I had no idea—for years and years.

Then one day, when Alison was about eleven, out of the blue came the revelation. How could I have been so blind—but yet, was it really so obvious? Before I give the game away I must describe *Peppermint* in some detail. If only you could see it—but you can't.

Peppermint is by an author whose name is Dorothy Grider. Dorothy Grider is also the illustrator. From the copyright matter I deduce that Miss Grider is an American and my guess is that she sold the story and pictures for an outright small sum (no royalty) to the Whitman Publishing Company, Racine, Wisconsin, who subsequently did a deal with Raphael Tuck and Sons, London, enabling them to put *Peppermint* on the market in the UK for about two bob a copy. It is a cheap book in every sense of the word, yet to one child it was, and still is in a way, pure gold.

Heaven knows how *Peppermint* got into our house—a visiting aunt must have given it to one of the children instead of a packet of jelly babies, I should think. For then, as now, I was knee-deep in review copies of new picture books and story books from the good publishing houses—the only books I bought were the great classic picture books (early *Babars*, *Clever Bill*, *Little Tim*) 'without which', as blurbs are so fond of saying, 'no nursery bookshelf is complete'.

So of one thing I am certain. With the yardsticks I was already making for myself as standards by which to judge the steadily increasing flow of high quality picture books for children in general (only the parent can tell whether a particular book 'takes' with his own child), I would never have forked out a penny, let alone a florin, for a book like *Peppermint*.

Peppermint has a shiny red cover from the front of which a white kitten face, sad-eyed, pink-eared and bewhiskered, looks soulfully (the adverb is important, as you'll see later) out. The word 'peppermint' is trick-printed in red and white twisty-candy-sticks above the pussy. On the back cover the series stamp (*Tell-a-Tale*) is surrounded by a cavorting pig, rabbit, lamb, goose, pony and squirrel—all loosely linked by a painted blue 'framing' ribbon. The spine, now merely desiccated Sellotape, was probably once a thin strip of red paper.

The story of *Peppermint* is simply told in undistinguished (and un-Anglicized) flat American prose: Peppermint, the frail little white kitten, is the fourth of a litter of kittens born in a candy store. Is she sick? No, she's just thin and pale and nobody buys poor Peppermint—though Lollipop, Chocolate Drop and Caramel, her sisters, are all gleefully acquired by young customers. One day a little girl cries in the candy store because there is to be a Cat Show at school and she has no kitten—and no money to buy one. The candy store owner gives her Peppermint. Peppermint is taken home lovingly; she is bathed, 'blued', brushed and combed; she wins first prize in the Cat Show and she lives happily with the little girl for ever after.

Like the words, the pictures are totally without distinction. Comic-style kids and cats, blobby colours, accentuated sashes and splashes. Totally expendable, one would have thought: a watered-down, vulgarized *Ugly Duckling*. Where, oh where did *Peppermint*'s special appeal to this one child lie hidden?

I'm ashamed to say that its appeal was not hidden at all. It was as clear as daylight—but I was looking in the wrong direction. Alison is an adopted child; her hair is pale straw, her eyes are blue; she was taken home, like Peppermint, to be loved and cared for and treasured. It was a matter of identification not just for the duration of the story but at a deep, warm, comforting and enduring level.

So we still have *Peppermint*. Its place on the family bookshelf is assured and no longer questioned, not only because it is precious to Alison—in a way that the technically efficient and typographically superior *Mr Fairweather and his Family* (written by Margaret Kornitzer for the express purpose of explaining adoption to pre-school children) has never been but because it taught me an invaluable lesson. The artistically worthless book—hack-written and poorly illustrated—may, if its emotional content is sound, hold a message of supreme significance for a particular child. If it does, it will be more important to that child's development than all the Kate Greenaway Medal-winning books put together.

For a book by itself is nothing—a film shown in an empty cinema: one can only assess its value by the light it brings to a child's eye.

NBL 'Books', 1970

Promotion of children's books directly to children was a further step in the right direction at that time, bringing fresh air into the somewhat enclosed atmosphere of the children's book world. Kaye Webb of Penguin, editor of the Puffin list, was exactly the person to initiate it. A brilliant journalist with a passion for stories and poetry, she has an immediate rapport with children that sparks off a creative response from them. She dreamed up the Puffin Club and gave bubbling life to its literature—*Puffin Post* and later *The Egg*—its annual exhibitions, and its excursions. On its third birthday in 1970 I went, on behalf of *Children's Book News*, to interview it.

MANY HAPPY RETURNS PUFFIN CLUB

A bespectacled young man, sleeves rolled up, walks into the Puffin Club office at Harmondsworth carrying a small hand-printing press.

'How *super*, Colin!' (even Kaye Webb, the founding genius of the Club, doesn't actually *say* 'p'super'). 'Can we *really* borrow it for the Exhibition?'—the Third Birthday Exhibition, that is. Colin nods. Rosemary, the Club Secretary, clears a space on one of the littered tables. Sylvia, Rachel, Dorothy, Sally and Yvonne (you know them all if you read *Puffin Post*) crowd round, and Glyn, the youngest member of this team of enthusiasts, moves the coffee mugs to safety.

'Could the kids actually use it, do you think?'

Colin says why not? It's safe, so long as it's facing—this way: and he turns it round.

There is a rare moment of silence. Then someone says: 'Couldn't we set up the type for a Certificate of Attendance so that Puffineers who come to the Exhibition can print themselves one?'

'Yes, and fill in their own names.'

'Perhaps we could make a Puffin to perch on this handle.'

'Yes, and photograph it for the next *Puffin Post*.'

'No, let's get Jill' (Jill is Jill McDonald, the *Puffin Post* artist whom Kaye found in New Zealand) 'to draw a Puffin printing his own Certificate of Attendance at his Third Birthday Party . . .'

And so—an idea is born, promoted and ready to fly, an idea that is fun, that is original, that is bookish, that will have direct appeal to children. Whose idea? Well, everyone's really. Because the Puffin Club staff work as a team. The atmosphere in that office is exhilarating.

Across the window, which stretches the length of the room, a streamer declares, quite truthfully, that 'There's nuffin' like a

Puffin'. Four desks are snowed under with the mail which arrives each morning in two enormous cartons—new members to be enrolled (between 75 and 100 a day); entries for competitions; orders for diaries, new badges, book-plates, bookworms, note-paper; decisions about prizes ('Could I have a Puffin Tee-shirt, do you think?'); requests for tickets for the next excursion ('I was wondering, where is the Geffrye Museum? You see, I am an American and do not know my way around quite yet . . .'); letters of thanks, 'your firework party was fabulous'; friendly letters 'because I like writing letters and getting answers'; letters asking for pen friends ('please may I have a frind in astralia?'); and hundreds of letters about the Puffin books that members of this extraordinarily lively and articulate Club are reading. (From Taupo in New Zealand 'I am reading at the moment a book called "The Prinsess and the Goblin" witch I am injoying'; from Darien, Connecticut, USA 'I have read your books about Narnia. I think they are very good. The one I like best is "The Magician's Nephew". Aslan is nice and I would like to ride on his back . . .' from Broadstone, Dorset 'I have just read "Earthfasts" and I think it is William Mayne's best book yet. I think that it has a really good blend of "supernatural" and normal everyday life. "Earthfasts" is well worth the "£o££y".'

By midday the four waste-paper baskets are brimming with envelopes and the out-trays on the desks are beginning to fill with the answers each child gets to his letter or enquiry. Sometimes it's a preliminary McTavish type all-purpose postcard printed in shocking pink. This imaginative and humorous card (absurdly evocative!) must have given delight and satisfaction to thousands of children because (and in this it is typical of the Club) enormous care has been taken to ensure that it hits exactly the right note. But very often, as the random fragments I quote in this article show, the letters call for personal answers from the Club staff: 'Dear Rosemary, I have knitted these bootees for your baby . . .'

Sylvia, who writes hundreds of letters a week, says she feels more in touch with children and able to help them sitting here in Harmondsworth than she did in her many years as a children's bookseller. Why? Because, and this is another factor which makes the Puffin Club unique and wonderful, contact with children is direct. Although the postbag contains numerous side-references to parents' interest—'I found my father reading MY *Puffin Post*'—parents and teachers, whose support, as intermediaries between child and book, so often has to be wooed by blurb-writers and reviewers, are extraneous to the relationship between the Puffineer and his Club, a

relationship which develops spontaneously into something rich and rewarding, both ways.

For the Puffin Club wants not just Puffin readers but active members who take part in the many outings and holidays that are planned for them up and down the country: Bristol, Cheltenham, Maldon, Norwich, Exeter, York, Dunfermline, London. The 'Spree Book', an enormous scrap book kept in the office, is chock-full of photographs of ecstatic Puffineers sailing, camping, singing, acting;

autographs of all who go anywhere with the Club dance and sprawl in vari-coloured felt-pen on adjacent pages. And all this fun because you are a book-lover! The idea is revolutionary. As Kaye says, 'We bring outsiders into contact with one another and from the moment they meet they begin to exchange ideas about books and authors, their common ground. After that, things go swimmingly for them . . .'

Fifty children, for instance, from all over the UK turned up at Featherstone Castle, Northumberland, on Boxing Day for a ten-day holiday. The organizer from Colony (who collaborate with Puffin Club over residential holidays) went to meet them at the station, leaving Kaye Webb behind in the great, cold, stone castle in the valley. 'I was determined the castle should look like a magic castle,' says Kaye (who is the great great granddaughter of the inventor of the Toy Theatre) 'so when he'd gone I switched on every light in the place so that the kids would see it glowing. And it did look *marvellous*. But half an hour later the whole castle fused—so we had to tell stories by candlelight!' Disaster into triumph.

On this holiday, as on all others, Puffin authors turned up and joined in. At Featherstone it was William Mayne who was 'planned'—but Ursula Moray Williams came unexpectedly ('Just luck,' says Kaye. 'I ran her to Paddington one night and before she knew what she was doing she'd promised to come all the way from Cheltenham to Northumberland after Christmas. She was a god-send: wonderful with the kids. She swept the stage, made them up for the play, helped cut sandwiches, resuscitated a child who fainted *and* she's coming again to Malvern in the summer.')

Whilst on holiday Puffineers read Puffins and enter their comments—'just marks out of 10 if they're too busy to write much'—in a large book the Club provides for the purpose. There's no boot-licking in these pages. 'Couldn't be bothered to go on after Chapter 2,' said one. 'Babyish,' said another. But most of the remarks are favourable, intelligent and interesting.

Day outings include visits to zoos, to Drama Clubs, to concerts, to museums—and wherever the outing is to be, there the local Puffineers will meet the indefatigable Club personalities whom they already feel they know intimately through *Puffin Post* and correspondence.

Puffin Post, the magazine of the Puffin Club (available to members only), is the focal point for all Puffineers. A glorious hotchpotch of new stories by Puffin authors, of poems, competitions, reviews and interviews, jokes and recipes and photographs, it is printed on paper which is white or green or yellow or blue and bound in a multi-hued cover designed by Jill McDonald to include all manner of puffins doing deliciously exotic things and making pithy 'balloon' comments in their own unique p'style. ('Jill is a marvel,' says Kaye. 'Whatever idea you give her she makes it a thousand times better.') The reading matter in *Puffin Post* is vibrant and attractive; Jill gives the magazine its modern, jaunty visual image—an un-stuffy image which may well have been responsible for drawing hundreds of not-so-devoted readers into the Club.

The competitions in the magazine are mainly literary and artistic. The literary entries—poems, stories, crosswords—come in droves in neat envelopes, but the artwork, often collages on huge sheets of sugar paper thick with cotton wool and doylies, twigs and feathers, pen-nibs and bottle tops, arrive boxed and sealed like gifts from a luxury store—and are unwrapped as lovingly and carefully, with the same sense of suppressed excitement. The top half of the wall opposite the window is given over to art competition entries—so that the office has the festive look of a lively classroom, year in, year out. Puffineers themselves can see the winning pictures when they visit the Annual Birthday Exhibition—at the NUT Headquarters in London during the Easter holidays, at other times in the provinces.

Not all Puffineers of course, for many, like the self-styled 'Upside-down Puffineer' who sent in, for the autumn nature competition, a collage of Australian *spring* flowers, live half a world away. A flick through the membership stencils—now nearly 50,000 of them—brings the worldwide aspect of the Club quickly to light: Fatima Alhaji Kem Selem, Lagos, Nigeria; Pupa Chinai, Bombay, India; Gul Faik Inan, Ankara, Turkey; Timothy Metcalf, Brisbane, Australia; Jan Eckert, Washington, USA; Maki Yamada, Yokohama, Japan. 'Oh yes, and I'm just about to enrol a group of Lithuanian children,' says Rachel. 'I met their teacher at a party in London and she's wild about the idea.'

The size of membership varies tremendously from county to county in the UK. Is it the same pattern, I asked, as the sales of Puffin books? No one knows because Penguin don't break down their sales figures to give this picture. But the most touching, and heartening, letter I read (from a ten-year-old boy on the outskirts of Glasgow) shows better than anything else how the tentacles of the Club are creeping into the philistine territory:

> 'My friend Michael Kelly asked me how can he join the puffin club and I told him that you have to buy a puffin book with a joining form inside* but there is only one problem. where Michael and I

*Not quite accurate, even in 1970.

> live the shops dont sell puffin books so he wont be able to get a book. and to go into Glasgow would be out of the question because he has a very bad leg and cant travel. so would it be allright if he just sent you his 5/- in an ordinary envelope and would you please send your reply to Michael's house . . .'

Michael is now a member. How long will it be before he can buy Puffin Books in Kirkintilloch?

What makes this Puffin Club so phenomenally successful? The limitless flow of ideas from Kaye Webb, the boundless energy, enthusiasm (and professionalism) of her staff, the determination to please and help and stimulate every Puffineer who writes to the Club or comes to the outings.

The sixties saw many welcome innovations in the world of children's books but the birth of the Puffin Club, on March 23rd 1967, was, I think, the brightest of the new stars because this Club provides hot lines between reading child and reading child, between child and book, between child and author and between child and publisher.

Many Happy Returns, Puffin Club! P'skol.

Children's Book News, 1970

The Sixties: A Perspective

During the 1960s the upsurge of talent in authorship and illustration so evident in the previous decade had continued.

The picture book, revolutionized by technological developments in the field of colour reproduction, extended its scope as a medium for the communication of ideas. Brian Wildsmith's *ABC* in 1961 was the first children's picture book in which the artist was given the freedom to use the full range of the palette without having to make laborious colour separations by hand for the printing of his work. (This was made possible by the Klischograph, an invention of the post-war period which separated artwork electronically into the four colour printing plates.) John Burningham's *Borka* soon followed. Raymond Briggs blossomed into prominence with the huge *Mother Goose Treasury* ('408 Rhymes and 897 Illustrations' as the cover proudly proclaims). Pat Hutchins's *Rosie's Walk* used a new storytelling technique that allowed the child listener to know from the pictures a great deal that the text forebore to disclose. Maurice Sendak's *Where the Wild Things Are* (published in the United States in 1963 and turned down by every publisher in London before The Bodley Head finally took the plunge) threw open the boundaries of experience within which picture books had hitherto contentedly operated. Charles Keeping's *Charley, Charlotte and the Golden Canary* explored the emotional warmth engendered by close-knit urban communities, communities that were under threat in the sixties from high-rise developments. Papas exposed the underbelly of twentieth-century 'progress' in *Tasso* and other picture books for the Oxford University Press. The world of the picture book in Britain was thriving; and the picture book world—in which rights of picture books were being sold internationally through the Bologna Book Fair (which began in 1964)—had come into existence.

Authorship too went from strength to strength in the 1960s. Authors of the 1950s—Gillian Avery, Lucy Boston, Rosemary Sutcliff, William Mayne, Penelope Farmer—were being published steadily (whilst Philippa Pearce slowly gestated immaculate short stories such as *Mrs Cockle's Cat*). Many of the new authors of the 1960s were, like their predecessors, primarily interested in the past. Joan Aiken wrote wild witty adventure stories set in the non-existent, but definitely historical, reign of King James III; Leon Garfield's *Smith* was a vivid and racy re-creation of life for the underdog in eighteenth-century London; Hester Burton wrote careful, sober historical novels of a romantic nature; K. M. Peyton's *Flambards* stories grew into a family chronicle of absorbing interest. Pauline Clarke in *The Twelve and the Genii* used the fantasy technique to take her readers back into another time, another place—the Brontës' nursery at Haworth. Alan Garner brought one of the ancient myths of Wales into the modern world of teenage love and jealousies when, in *The Owl Service*, his present-day young people found themselves acting out in their own lives a powerful story from the Mabinogion. All these were winners of the Library Association Carnegie Medals. Meanwhile, Michael Bond's 'Paddington', Roald Dahl's 'Charlie' and E. W. Hildick's 'Lemon Kelly' were winking at children from the wings.

It was a heady period. Authors and illustrators of talent were welcomed by publishers whose lists were expanding. Publishers of quality books had no difficulty in selling to a public and school library market whose funds increased, in mid-decade, at a rate of ten per cent per annum. No wonder series began to flourish: Acorns and Antelopes, Beginners and I Can Reads, Pied Pipers and Read Alouds and all manner of career books rolled off the presses.

No wonder, either, that observers in the field felt that this was a time to take stock of the state of children's literature. Margery Fisher's *Intent Upon Reading*, Marcus Crouch's *Treasure Seekers and Borrowers* and John Rowe Townsend's *Written for Children* were all published during this decade, as was a new edition of Geoffrey Trease's immensely enjoyable *Tales Out of School.*

It was at this period too, as we have seen, that review space for the new flowering of children's literature was being found in national newspapers and journals.

Since Woodfield and Stanley, the Huddersfield booksellers, had initiated *The Junior Bookshelf* (1936) there had been no new specialist children's book review journal (apart from the reviewing, mainly of information books in the early numbers, in *School Librarian*) until in 1962 Margery Fisher began to publish *Growing Point*; then came Naomi Lewis's annual *Best Children's Books*

(1963–1967) which was also to cover the output of children's publishers from a literary standpoint. But Eric Baker's *Children's Book News* (1965–1970), under the editorship of Nancy Lockwood (Chambers), began to commission articles and reviews from teachers and librarians who used books with children: new perspectives. And Anne Wood's *Books for Your Children* (1964) was a magazine designed not for professionals but for parents; it was to be the seed-bed for the Federation of Children's Book Groups, a nationwide pressure group of parents enthusiastic about reading in the home.

So the 1960s, despite the literary and artistic excellence of the books being published for children, marked the beginning of an unrest in the world of children's books. The age, some called it 'a second golden age', was producing great books—but were the ones most praised, some teachers and librarians began to ask, the kind of books that were likely to appeal to the vast numbers of children they met in their day-to-day work in library or classroom? Was it right that library shelves were stacked full of books bought with public money that most children would not or could not read, that the Carnegie Medals and the newly created *Guardian* Award seemed to go exclusively to authors whose so-called 'children's' books only touched the lives of advanced, often teenage, readers? Would authors, publishers and above all critics (who were thought to set the fashion in publishing) please spare more thought for the young readers or would-be readers who were at present rather neglected and who also needed writing of excellence but of a less demanding nature?

Anne Wood, a parent and primary-school teacher herself, attacked the élitism of the established children's book world in her magazine, *Books for Your Children*. Aidan Chambers who taught English in a Secondary Modern school made a special plea in *The Reluctant Reader* for books that would, by their relevance to the reader's own experience, attract the teenager who could read but was disenchanted by what was on offer. Janet Hill, Children's Librarian of Lambeth in London, was one of the first people to draw attention to the need for children's books that reflected the cultures of newly arriving families from the Commonwealth and of older established minority groups.

A split was developing between the purists in the children's book world ('The Irrelevance of Children to the Children's Book Reviewer' was the title of an article by Brian Alderson in a 1969 issue of *Children's Book News*) and the pragmatists. To many of us at that time, what seemed important was that the split should not become an uncrossable ravine. Anyone who has worked with children and books knows that with time, patience, knowledge of the field and of children much that is of excellence can reach most of the young. There is a huge middle ground that must be held if the inspired and overworked teacher is to be able to rely on the specialist children's book critic for guidance. What was needed was a change of emphasis.

In 1969 Sidney Robbins, at Exeter University's Department of Education, initiated the annual Exeter conferences. Bravely, he tried to bring critically acclaimed authors and practising teachers face to face in the hope that the gap between them would be bridged. They met. They clashed. And as often as not each came away affronted by the demands made on his professionalism by the other.

Print, which is more enduring and less emotive than speech, might be a cooler way of doing the same thing. Eclectic and unaligned common-sense publications seemed now to be called for.

And in 1970, they came.

PART 2
'SIGNAL' CONTRIBUTIONS
1970–1980

Quentin Blake being interviewed by the author, © Quentin Blake

By 1970 my family was teenage so I had more time for active involvement in work with children and books. I have described how in the 1960s, by the greatest good fortune, I was ready to write about children and books just at the moment that editors were looking for correspondents on the subject. The same fortuitous timing was to make the 1970s a period of excitement and exploration for me as the pattern of comment on and information about children's books changed radically—towards experience in using them with the young.

1970 was an extraordinary year in the history of children's books in Britain. Four initiatives emerged, the first three of which were to involve me to a lesser or greater extent as the decade developed.

In 1970 the National Book League decided to abandon its annual touring exhibition that had been called *New Children's Books* and to replace it with *Children's Books of the Year*, an exhibition selected from the whole field of children's publishing which would have an annotated printed catalogue and, in due course, a London summer showing. The first four *Reading for Enjoyment* booklists were published by the bookseller Eric Baker from the Children's Book Centre in Kensington Church Street. The first issue of *Signal*—a periodical whose purpose was to 'provide a voice for writers whose ideas about, and interests in, children's books cannot be contained in brief reviews or articles'—arrived unheralded from its editor, Nancy Chambers. And *Children's Literature in Education* came into being, originally as a vehicle for the publication of the papers given at the annual conference on children's literature organized by the University of Exeter—though it was to develop differently as the years went by. These were the starting points of an unusually hectic and innovative decade during which the reviewing and promotion of children's books diversified and mushroomed.

Children's Books of the Year was to be entrusted entirely to me—since, called in for three weeks to help choose all the fiction for *New Children's Books*, I had been extremely critical of the haphazard methods of selection, only possible because the list that accompanied the exhibition on its rounds was unannotated and therefore no good reason had to be given for the inclusion of this or that title. For the *Reading for Enjoyment* booklists I wrote

Reading for Enjoyment with 2 to 5 Year Olds whilst fellow *Times* reviewers, Brian Alderson, Jessica Jenkins and Aidan Chambers, covered books for the 6 to 8, 9 to 11, and 12 and over readers respectively. *Signal*, under the generous and eclectic editorship of Nancy Chambers, was to become a home base from which I could explore in articles the various fields that make the children's book world so fascinating to me.

I have called this part of my book '*Signal*' *Contributions* not because during the 1970s I wrote exclusively for *Signal*—far from it—but because *Signal*'s editor gamely published articles by me throughout that period (and indeed on into the 1980s) that both reflected the passing scene and its developing concerns and also drew together the threads of my working life.

'Signal' Contributions falls into three sections. The first contains interviews with authors and artists; the second, 'In My Experience', contains light-hearted articles about such subjects as my book experiments in a Primary School library, and selling books in a street market. The third, a long essay entitled 'The Seventies in British Children's Books', is for those readers most concerned with the overall development of children's book publishing in Britain and the influences, financial, multicultural and from television, with which publishers had to contend in the 1970s.

Interviews with Authors and Artists

Looking at the articles I wrote for *Signal* during the decade 1970 to 1980 there is a discernible pattern which I can now see was a mirror of my determination to learn more at first hand about children's books and about children-*and*-books, concepts that were drawing apart at this period. Nancy Chambers, though a firm editor with a beady eye for the unthought-through statement and a heavy pen for the grammatical misconstruction, gave me an open brief. So I wrote about whatever interested me and that changed as the decade progressed.

Having written hundreds of review articles in the 1960s and being already embarked upon the reading and annotations for *Children's Books of the Year*, not surprisingly I felt an urge to know something more, at this juncture, about the creative process that brought about the novels, stories and picture books, review copies of which now flooded into my house.

Who were these authors and artists? How did they work? Why did they write, or paint, for children? What was their own view of their activities? I could re-read all their books and make what I hoped would be inspired guesses; or, far better, I could follow up my reading with an interview, always an illuminating and educative experience.

I began with authors.

NINA BAWDEN
AN AUTHOR FOR TODAY

One of my first articles on an author for 'Signal' was about Nina Bawden, which will seem a fairly obvious choice to readers in the 1980s—but in 1971 she had written neither 'Carrie's War' nor 'Rebel on a Rock' which, together with an historical novel, 'Peppermint Pig', were to bring her critical acclaim. Many people admired her work in 1971, but she had not, at that date, been generally recognized as 'an author for today'.

At a social gathering of children's book people I once said to a fellow reviewer that Nina Bawden was the kind of writer I should like to see brought into the limelight: her adventure stories are accessible to a wide readership, her characters deeply but unfussily observed, her themes contemporary and her background vivid and various. He looked at me with amazement, granted all I said, took a sip of red wine and then dismissed my championship of Miss Bawden with the remark, 'But her books are so poorly produced—no illustrations.'

I was dumbfounded. Was he right? Were the books poorly produced? I couldn't remember: those I knew had been so good to read. And unillustrated? Was it possible that I had created in my mind's eye the terrifying picture of the flood in Kenya—'great chunks of red mud, trees, huts being thrown up into the air then gobbled up by the water' (this was the starting point for Ben Mallory's adventures in *The Secret Passage* and *On the Run*)? Had I really never seen an artist's drawing of Polly-Anna, the informing five-year-old twins ('We *saw'd* her, Simon') with their funny round faces and blobby noses (minor but memorable characters who bob up, from time to time, in the pages of *The Runaway Summer*)? Did I conjure up for myself so clear an idea of the cosmography of the sleasy suburb which is the setting for Miss Bawden's most compelling novel, *A Handful of Thieves*? I left my drink untouched and rushed home to find out.

True, true . . . Nina Bawden's books (apart from *The Witch's Daughter*) are unillustrated. But badly produced? Five lively jackets by Shirley Hughes outweigh one undistinguished effort (for the author's first children's book) by Alan Breese. Paper, print and margins? Reasonable. An occasional example of poor proof-reading, I'll admit, but no child, once drawn into a Bawden story, will care a fig that there isn't a picture to be seen, because her words create such vivid images; and if, here and there, inverted commas fail to close themselves . . . ? My friend the expert will mark it up (quite rightly, for we are nothing if not guardians of standard) against the book, but the young reader will already be at the end of the next paragraph and over the page. . .

In the best Bawden stories, adults are not whisked off at a moment's notice on lecture tours to Australia or (who will be the first in on this one?) hijacked in Jordan so that a family is left to its own resources with dire but thrilling results. The children in Miss Bawden's books are always aware that Mum will wonder where they've got to; they ring up (albeit with cock-eyed excuses) to keep faith with their parents. Their adventures are within the framework of family and neighbourhood and because of these boundaries—which readers experience in their own lives—the stories are more real, the heroes easier to identify with and root for.

Nina Bawden is as concerned with the fears and emotions and small pleasures of Grans and maiden aunts (so often dismissed as comic characters) as she is with the relationship between children. And they are not exceptional Grans and aunts either. They use irritating quotations and phrases *ad nauseam*: 'as old as my tongue and a little older than my teeth'; 'by the time that happens I'll be ready for my box'. They fuss about manners and they tend to keep themselves up tight. But they are lonely, ordinary people with qualities of heart and understanding to which the children respond, each in his own fashion. In *The Secret Passage* and its sequel *On the Run*, the way Aunt Mabel is seen to develop (slowly and painfully, like an iceberg subjected to the unfamiliar attentions of the thawing sun) from spinster boarding-house-keeper, all spit-and-polish, to wise, sympathetic protective mother-figure (capable of passionate defence of Ben when he's in trouble) as the orphaned Mallory children increasingly become 'her family', is truly remarkable; no less remarkable than the way Ben, in the same two books, grows from protected youngest child (whose mother was swept away in that Kenyan flood) into a resourceful, independent, determined, self-sacrificing, adventurous boy whose loyalty and directness get him both into, and ultimately out of, a sticky situation. For he becomes self-appointed protector of an exiled African princeling whose life is threatened by the rebels who overthrew his father's regime in Tiga.

Groups of children have their own identity, but it is an identity which is a composite of the individuals belonging to the group. Because Miss Bawden carefully explores each individual she is able to create groups whose aspirations and conflicts spring not from arbitrary ideas or superficial pressures but from deep-seated characteristics and passions. Her best group, the five children who form the Cemetery Committee (so called because it meets in a junk yard) in *A Handful of Thieves*, is as real to me as are my own children's friends. See with what ease Miss Bawden suggests their characteristics and throws light on their families. In the following piece they are discussing where they can have their firework party: Aristotle is the guy who has become dismembered in a battle between the Cemetery Committee and the nightwatchman at the junk yard.

> Algy had to be home by seven on Saturdays, so we started back along the path. None of us felt much like talking, and Rosie was particularly gloomy. From time to time she sighed and said, 'Poor Aristotle . . .'
>
> To cheer her up Sid and I began to discuss where we should build the bonfire on Firework Night. Rosie had the biggest garden of all, and the best-tempered mother, but we couldn't light a fire there, because it would frighten all the animals. Sid hadn't got a garden, nor had Clio. Mine was too tidy for bonfires, and as for Algy—well, it would have been easier to ask the Queen if we could light a small fire in the front of Buckingham Palace, than to ask Algy's mother.
>
> 'It's not going to be much fun anyway, now Aristotle's gone,' Rosie said drearily. 'There's no point in doing *anything*, if we haven't got a guy.'
>
> 'Well even if we haven't,' I said, 'we can light a pretty good fire in my Gran's back yard. I'll ask her if you like, she never grows anything there, she says there isn't enough sun, and it's full of good rubbish we can burn.'

Who would believe that this decision to use Gran's yard would be the factor that was to transform the Cemetery Committee into a Handful of Thieves? For it is during the firework party that Fred discovers that Gran's new lodger, Mr Gribble—'a thin man with a fat man's voice'—has run off with Gran's savings, the forty pounds that she always kept in a teapot on the shelf. The Committee is determined to bring Mr Gribble—an Alastair Sim character who chats up old ladies and enlists their sympathies in his 'good causes'—to justice. After tracking him down, Fred and the 'dim, but decent and dogged' Algy—against Sid's sober advice—break into Gribble's new lodgings to try to recover Gran's money, thus becoming, in the eyes of the law, a 'handful of thieves'. Here Miss Bawden uses the adult background she has carefully built up round the 'Thieves' to make the point that no one must take the law into his own hands and that the police, despite their calm, slow, ponderous manner, act like lightning when necessary.

Violence threatens: Mr Gribble nearly kills Algy who, intoxicated by the chase, acts with foolish bravado. When the adults step in, the 'Thieves', far from being resentful, are relieved. Because the reader knows them all so well he shares their understanding that some things are too hot for kids to handle.

But few topics, in Miss Bawden's view, are too difficult for children to understand if the approach is right—that is to say if these topics slide naturally into a realistic and fast-moving story. In her books she introduces, with minimum fuss and sentimentality but with deep feeling (as often expressed in 'covering up' as in displays of emotion), the death of the Mallorys' mother (*The Secret Passage*), the remarriage of their father (*On the Run*); a disturbed child of divorcing parents—'Nice people are so *boring*' (*The Runaway Summer*); and a blind child—'Do be *quiet* or I can't see' (*The Witch's Daughter*). World political events provide the mainspring for two of the books—and why not? African rebellion is behind *On the Run*, and the plight of the Kenyan Asians forces itself, in the person of Krishna Patel, an illegal immigrant found on the beach, to be felt by sad and selfish Mary, heroine of *The Runaway Summer*.

Nina Bawden, through her humorous, lively, unpretentious adventure stories, both entertains her young readers and opens their eyes to the world around them. In her best books—*On the Run*, *A Handful of Thieves* and *The Witch's Daughter*—(a book in which a wild girl on the lonely island of Skua learns the meaning of friendship—and a blind child outwits a jewel robber)—adventure 'creeps up from behind' and its course is dictated not by superficial coincidence but by the reactions of each character, child and adult, to every new circumstance as it occurs. Because Miss Bawden delights in bringing together in her stories children from widely different backgrounds (the three children in *On the Run* are middle-class Ben; Liz, a street-urchin 'wanted by the Welfare'; and Thomas, an African prince in exile) the readership for her books is bound by neither class nor colour. Nina Bawden is an author for today. To claim more for her would be an extravagance. It is enough.

Signal, 1971

URSULA MORAY WILLIAMS
and 'ADVENTURES OF THE LITTLE WOODEN HORSE'

I know exactly why I wanted to meet Ursula Moray Williams. It was because 'Adventures of the Little Wooden Horse' had been read to tatters in our family, wept over, suffered with, loved whilst many suppers burned and baths went cold. The same was true of 'Charlotte's Web' but E. B. White was inaccessible in the United States, whilst Ursula Moray Williams said she would be delighted, when she next came up to London from Tewkesbury, to drop in for a chat.

Ursula Moray Williams began writing for children in the early 1930s—those distant pre-war days which we tend to think of as a literary desert so far as books for the young are concerned.

Yet the ten years before the outbreak of World War II saw the publication of a select few books for children which we can fairly say—almost two generations later—have stood the test of time: Arthur Ransome's *Swallows and Amazons*, Eleanor Farjeon's *Martin Pippin in the Daisy Field*, Noel Streatfeild's *Ballet Shoes*, Ardizzone's *Little Tim and the Brave Sea Captain* and Tolkien's *The Hobbit* were all published in the thirties. One of the outstanding books of that fruitful but misjudged decade was unquestionably Ursula Moray Williams's *Adventures of the Little Wooden Horse*. But among the fat bumper books and annuals which were clogging the soil, doing their best to stifle the few healthy green shoots, how did *Adventures of the Little Wooden Horse* find its way through to the sunlight? Who published it? What did the first edition look like? Was it recognized by reviewers (were there any?) as the classic it was to become?

Talking to Ursula Moray Williams, handling the first edition of *Adventures of the Little Wooden Horse*, and looking through the odd assortment of so-called reviews, much became clear that I had hitherto not understood.

Ursula Moray Williams belongs to the old school of children's writers who have never been forced into the public gaze. They stayed at home (like Uncle Peder, the old toy-maker in *Adventures of the Little Wooden Horse*), whilst their books (like the little wooden horse himself) went out bravely into the alien world, made friends and had adventures.

Married to Conrad Southey John (a descendant of the Lake poet), mother of four sons, grandmother five times over, Ursula Moray Williams was more than a little surprised that in 1971 the limelight should suddenly have descended on her and the book she published thirty-three years ago. Surprised, and rather pleased, though obscurity had never troubled her—'I've not made much of a name as a writer but it doesn't worry me because I've had so much of everything else.'

How refreshing! She began to write in the early years of her marriage before her first son was born; in 1937 she became pregnant with him—and, almost simultaneously, with the urge to write *Adventures of the Little Wooden Horse.* Where did the character come from? Until we had talked a little she seemed to have no idea, had never even thought about it. 'It just exploded inside me and took over. I write compulsively: during the war years I was cooking for ten of us but I *had* to write, just as my twin sister had to paint and design. Anyway, I find it easier to write against the clock.'

Were her parents creative people? 'Not at all. My father was a classical scholar, my mother had a Froebel training. We lived in a crumbling folly in Hampshire which we rented for £80 a year. And it *was* crumbling. My sister and I had a beloved governess who gave us lessons, and we moved from room to room (there were hundreds of them) as the ceilings fell in on us.' What sort of person had the governess been? 'Marvellous; she didn't interfere with our *childhood* at all.' Did she read to them? 'No; my mother did that. Always something a little in advance of what we would read to ourselves. *The Cloister and the Hearth* at eight; Scott at ten; we never managed Dickens—struck him at the wrong time, I suspect.' 'And fairy tales?' I asked, because *Adventures of the Little Wooden Horse* has so much of the feel of good folklore about it. 'We read those to ourselves. I adored *Pinocchio*' (no pause here, but this made me sit up) 'and I can remember we always wanted to borrow books from any children we visited. Once my sister filled her bloomers with a friend's books—but it was no good. Mother noticed, and back they had to go.'

We reverted to the topic of Pinocchio—a wooden doll made by Gepetto the carver, a doll that had adventures and came to life. Had it ever occurred to Ursula Moray Williams that the little wooden horse (he is so humble a creature that he never dignifies himself with capital letters) fashioned as a toy by Uncle Peder—the toy which unexpectedly begins to weep at the prospect of being sold, but in a moment of need is able to summon up enough courage to kick up his little wooden wheels and embark on hazardous adventures in order to save the life of the old man—had it ever occurred to her that her childhood passion for Pinocchio might have been partly responsible for the creation of the little wooden horse? Clearly it hadn't.

Did she ever have a little wooden horse of her own? 'No, never. But we had hobby horses made from sticks and stuffed stockings which went with us everywhere. We even rode to a local meet on them once and I can remember the scornful remarks of a well-turned-out little rider on her smartly groomed pony: "Those silly children think they can go hunting on their hobby horses. They think they're *real*!"' (The little wooden horse is always being laughed at by big flesh-and-blood horses and braying donkeys.) 'But to us, you see, they *were* real. The thin line between fantasy and reality isn't so thin if you believe in the fantasy, is it.'

The little wooden horse himself is an example of that thin line broadened by a total conviction and belief.

> So he never closed his little wooden eyes at all, but lay with his wooden ears a-prick . . .
> His little heart nearly jumped out of the hole in his neck . . . They filled him up with marbles which were very heavy and uncomfortable, rattling about in his inside like stones, till for the first time in his life the little wooden horse had a stomach ache . . .

In the course of his adventures the little wooden horse suffers mishap after mishap after mishap.

> Now here am I, a quiet little horse . . . having escaped death by the axe of a little old woman, and by overworking at the hands of a wicked farmer, and by suffocation in the mine, going to be burned in the fire and have all my money taken away! Oh master! Oh master! I shall never see Uncle Peder again.

And this is less than half-way through the story! Even in the penultimate chapter when the tired little wooden horse is at last homeward bound through the familiar forest on his way to the cottage, uplifted by the thought that Uncle Peder will be there to welcome him with open arms, his hopes are dashed once more.

> So the little wooden horse trundled on, counting fifty as he went, till he had turned the corner and was in the well-remembered glade.
>
> 'Now I will open my eyes,' said the little wooden horse. He opened them wide and looked about him: but now they grew round with surprise and fear for there was no cottage in front of him, no blue smoke coming out of the chimney, no cabbage patch, no Uncle Peder sitting before the door, no shed, no garden, no cowhouse! Everything was in ruins, with the weeds rambling in and out of the bricks as though for a long time there had been nobody there.

I asked Ursula Moray Williams how she could bear so relentless a tragedy. 'I know, I know. I was in tears when I wrote it but by that time the story had so taken charge of me that I wasn't really writing it any more. I just couldn't do a thing about it.'

All ends well for the little wooden horse in a final chapter which is pure joy for the reader (or listener) because he and the little wooden horse gleefully share the knowledge that the little wooden horse and Uncle Peder are in fact reunited long before Uncle Peder realizes it. For Uncle Peder is sitting, with the little old woman whom he has just married, inside the coach which, unbeknown to them, is being drawn away from the church by the little wooden horse himself. The little wooden horse hears Uncle Peder sigh, 'I shall never find him now. He would have come back long ago if he'd been alive.' And when the little wooden horse, unable to contain his excitement a moment longer, jumps out of his shafts and presents himself to his old master—what a reunion, what happiness, what joy!

But in the course of this epic fantasy violence, death and evil are looked straight in the eye, much as they are in the world's folk stories. No Freudian excuses here. Wickedness is wickedness. Terror is terror. Evil is evil. The little wooden horse, who is a compound of all the human virtues—he is good, loyal, quiet, resourceful, honest and determined—overcomes them. Did Ursula Moray Williams have a strongly religious upbringing? 'Yes, of the most conventional kind.' Was she taught to believe in the power of good and evil? 'Utterly. Utterly.'

Adventures of the Little Wooden Horse is a long book. Today's children's editors, publishing in a vastly different scene where the demands of specialists in schools and libraries have to be taken into account, where life moves fast and parents are often hard put to it to find time to read to their children, might have been tempted to ask the author to cut and trim. But in 1938 there were no standards for children's books to conform to. Indeed, there was no such thing as a children's editor or a children's list (as the separate entity it now is) in most publishing houses. There were men like Jonathan Cape, Stanley (later Sir Stanley) Unwin and George G. Harrap who were passionate about books. Books. Any book that had quality.

These men were, as Miss Moray Williams pointed out to me, craftsmen making books in the same sense that Uncle Peder was a craftsman making wooden toys. Jonathan Cape found Arthur Ransome; Stanley Unwin's eye lit on *The Hobbit*; and George G. Harrap immediately sensed the classic qualities of *Adventures of the Little Wooden Horse*. He lovingly commissioned illustrations (from Joyce Lancaster Brisley) and sent letters of warm recommendation to some thirty buyers of children's books. 'I am, of course,' he wrote to the author, 'very chary of writing such personal letters. I rarely do it, on principle.' When he died, in 1939 just after the book was published, his photograph was put in the firm's window surrounded by copies of *Adventures of the Little Wooden Horse*.

It was C. S. Lewis who once remarked that a children's book which is only enjoyed by the children is a bad children's book. *Adventures of the Little Wooden Horse* is universal in its appeal; parent and child are as spellbound by it now as an earlier generation was in 1938. Re-illustrated by Peggy Fortnum it is still the favourite bedtime reading of thousands of children, bearing out the prediction of the only reviewer in 1938 who spotted its potential. Inept and unperceptive comment abounded, but Eleanor Graham, writing in *The Sunday Times* on 16th October that year, said, 'I believe this story will find a permanent place among books for the six to nine year olds, and will be loved by generations of children.'

She was right. No one, it seems, is more surprised by its success than its progenitor. 'I like people to like what I write, but I don't particularly feel they will. Writing, like education, is very much your own business, isn't it.'

It is. It is.

Signal, 1971

JANET McNEILL
and 'THE BATTLE OF ST GEORGE WITHOUT'

I went to Bristol when I wanted to write about Janet McNeill, because 'The Battle of St George Without', one of the best, most deeply felt yet fast-moving adventure stories for children written in modern times, is a Bristol book to its core. Bristol, a sea-port looking West, has always been a melting pot for many races. Janet McNeill's calm acceptance of this made her book the distinguished forerunner, along with some of Nina Bawden's, of later more self-conscious efforts to be multicultural.

Janet McNeill's *The Battle of St George Without* struck me when I first read it, and strikes me still, as the most natural and easy and warm and real of all those stories for older children which grow from the rich soil offered by a lively but materially poor group of kids, the epitome of a neighbourhood. As Charles Keeping draws the deprived city child in his great picture books—*Charley, Charlotte and the Golden Canary; Through the Window*—so Janet McNeill, with a deep respect and understanding, tinged with compassion and leavened by a rippling sense of humour, writes of him.

How does it happen that an author whose prose has the classical balance of a scholar's, whose similes ('The footsteps stopped like a thread cut by scissors') are mathematically precise, and whose wit ('"Don't get excited old boy or your whiskers will short"') is as sharp and effective as Cuchulain's spear, can inhabit so easily an ordinary slum boy like Matt McGinley, her hero in *The Battle of St George Without*, and produce street dialogue ('"He's loony as they come, plain bats, but everything he says is true"') of such unerring accuracy?

An hour spent with Janet McNeill provides all the answers.

Janet McNeill is a tall, thin, white-haired Belfast woman with mild, kind, quick eyes and a firm chin, held high in defiance of ill-health and the limitations it imposes on a naturally lively and vigorous person. Her heart is torn by the troubles in Ulster—'Poor . . . old . . . Ireland,' she sighs; but briskly she pulls herself back to Bristol, where she now lives, and to the job in hand, which is talking to me about her writing. This stern self-discipline is a deep-rooted characteristic and stems from her childhood in the household of her father—a Presbyterian minister, a scholar, a great preacher, a saint to his parishioners—whom she adored; and her mother, a reserved, orderly, puritanical woman who could never quite come to terms with this daughter who wrote plays for the stage—'the equivalent of undressing in public'.

As a child in the manse Janet absorbed the emotions of the adult world—'bereavement, broken marriages, poverty, bewilderment came in by the front door'—and the embarrassment of class division was early brought home to her. For the Birkenhead church, where her father was minister for many years, had a dockland mission, and there Janet McNeill remembers all too painfully giving out prizes to the Band of Hope boys: 'I felt acutely aware that they'd rather punch my nose than shake hands.'

Writing began early—at school and as a Classics student at St Andrew's—but marriage to Robert Alexander, a civil engineer, cut short any dreams of a career in journalism or publishing and set her, unprepared, on the road to motherhood: 'I had never learned the domestic arts, but I plunged into them very deeply. I was living in the sort of small Irish town where white gloves, thin bread-and-butter and sponge cakes that' (here she made a light rising movement with her large capable fingers) 'were the thing—and I was damned if, with a good University degree, I couldn't do as well as my neighbour! I overdid the domestic act for a long, long time.' Until, in fact, a coincidence revived both the personal pride and the intellectual flame: the coincidence was her birthday for which her sister gave her a present of cosmetics ('"Jan, *dear*," I said to myself, "she must think you're really letting yourself *go*!"') and the announcement by the BBC of a play competition which she entered ('I'll show them!'), winning the second prize with *Gospel Truth*, a play about the dilemma of a young clergyman whose congregation believed every word he said, a little more readily than he expected. Seven years later came *A Child in the House*, Janet McNeill's best known radio play, which was the basis of her first novel (its theme is that one cannot make bargains with God) and was subsequently filmed, with Mandy Miller as juvenile lead ('locale transposed from Belfast to Park Lane, imagine!').

Scripting radio plays, watching them rehearsed, meeting actors and producers and other writers were both a satisfaction and a stimulus: this explains the sharpness of the characters in *The Battle of St George Without* (written years later) and her brilliant, natural, fast-flowing dialogue.

Once started in the Northern Ireland radio field Janet McNeill's rise to fame ('It's easy to be a big fish in a small pool,' she says disarmingly) was swift. But her writing has always taken second place ('I feel guilty about inconveniencing others') to her husband and family—three sons and a daughter, all of whom were embarrassed by their mother's public image when children—and to work for the community on many levels: she has been a Guider, an official of the Northern Ireland Juvenile Court known as a Child's Guardian—'I lost all my handkerchiefs that way; poor children, they'd done such silly things'—and a librarian to an old people's housing project where she met elderly ladies who had been 'scooped up from their little terrace houses where they could go to their front doors and get the whole chat of the street' and put into tower blocks 'where it was the convention that you didn't chum up even if you met in the lift. They were *so* lonely'. The old, the dotty, the middle-aged; courting couples, ten-year-olds and tots all appear in her books for young people.

Janet McNeill had been writing plays and stories for radio —the famous *Specs* series was originally written for 'Children's Hour'—and novels for adults for many years before she turned to novels for children. 'As I grow older childhood becomes more important to me.' For these books she draws on the deep well of her own experience both inside the home ('so much of what I write is family legend') and out ('the interplay of adults and children is enormously interesting. That adults are there and what they are like shapes the child's life').

The Battle of St George Without is set in one of Bristol's fine old squares which is fast crumbling. The terrace houses, each once the home of a single family, are now teeming with council tenants of all races, colours and creeds. In the centre of Dove Square, obscured by railings and dense trees and undergrowth, stands the disused Church of St George Without, formerly the focus of the social life of the community, now neglected, decaying and, as the children discover, in danger of mutilation.

Matt McGinley is the first of the group to find a way in to the church—and to find in the church a useful hideout for the stray animals which always seem to follow him home. He keeps his discovery to himself until one Saturday afternoon the parents of the children in Dove Square make a for-once-united effort to shoo their kids away from the steps, so that old Mr Harrison's funeral can take place in undisturbed solemnity. (Janet McNeill believes children resent adults tidying up tragedy for them.)

To solve the problem of where to go in their exile Matt leads his mates—snooty Madge, practical Gwen, smiling Jamaican Sidney and cocky Henry with his permanently attached little brother, 'the Trailer'—through the railings, into the tunnel and out into the old church. After a moment of awe they all begin to talk at the same time—Janet McNeill's glide into reported speech to create the feeling of hubbub and hot argument is tremendously effective:

> 'But it must have been beautiful once,' Gwen said, in her holy-holy voice.
>
> 'It's a right dump now,' Henry declared, 'not like a proper church at all.'
>
> Then Gwen fizzed up and said he should know, getting paid for going to the Cathedral, and that you didn't have to have stained glass and all sorts of fancy trimmings for a church to be a church, and Henry barked back that you had to have a bit more than four walls and a lot of spiders and a smell of damp, if you asked him, and Madge said nobody had, actually, and the Trailer, when it was his turn to come down off Sidney's back, landed on the cat's tail, and the cat let a screech out of him and frightened the Trailer who began to cry, and Sidney said, 'Please not to cry,' and when this didn't do any good Gwen told the Trailer you couldn't cry in church and Henry said why couldn't you, and Gwen said if he didn't know there was no sense in telling him, and Henry said people cried at funerals, didn't they, and they were reminded again of old Mr Harrison, and called a truce.

To their consternation they find not the deserted church which had fired their imagination with the romantic possibilities of hymnsinging, restoration and salvation, but an old building which is being gone over for saleable lead by Eddie, who is on probation, wanting to go straight but living in terror of Dannyboy, the real villain. Matt's lot gives chase to Eddie and the Flints through wilderness and storm, out into Dove Square. They all arrive in a horrified heap, just as the funeral party is 'crowded in the porch at the top of the steps, shaking hands with Miss Harrison'.

The scandalized parents insist that the children shall present themselves and their formal apology to Miss Harrison the following afternoon. Their embarrassment turns to delight and a dawning admiration when the blushing, lonely spinster invites them all in to finish up the overs of the funeral feast and regales them with stories of choir singing in the Church of St George Without in the old days when her father was caretaker.

> 'At Christmas,' she said, 'the church was full of the smell of frost on hay. And at Easter—'
>
> 'Tell us about Easter.'
>
> 'Lights everywhere! Full of light and crazy with daffodils. But the best service of all was on St George's Day . . . We had a special service and there were banks of flowers on all the window-sills and a flag flying outside on the flag-pole, and the trumpeters from the Barracks were up at the back of the gallery—'
>
> 'Trumpeters?'
>
> 'Six of them, in their uniform. Like six giants. You should have heard the noise when they joined in the special hymn that we sang at the end of the service . . . All the stops out of the organ and everyone singing their heads off and the trumpets . . . playing a tune of their own, like a ladder, high above the voices . . .'
>
> Sidney stood up unexpectedly and put his head back, and with his lips pushed forward sang 'Root-a-too-toot-TOOT!' like a bugle, and then sat down again, and though it didn't make any difference on him you knew he was blushing.
>
> 'Just like that,' Miss Harrison agreed. 'By the end of the last Amen I was floating about in the air with my head bobbing against the roof—we all were. They had to pull us down by our ankles.'
>
> They nodded, believing her.

Of such stuff is the storyteller made.

Janet McNeill is a spellbinder not only because she is a master of plot construction but because one feels as one reads her story that life itself is rushing by and that the children are catching hold of this or that and missing the other as we all do in reality.

They think, for instance, that they can save the Church of St George Without. They can't—for its day is over: a smaller, more modern church will probably be built on the new housing complex and anyway, as one of the grown-ups comments, 'It's machinery people listen to nowadays, not voices.' But, almost by accident, they do save something very important. They save the delinquent but reforming Eddie from slipping backwards into crime—by making an uneasy truce with him and supporting him in his struggle to free himself from the menacing Dannyboy.

Janet McNeill is a courageous, clear-sighted woman whose view of life is that it is open-ended and who reflects that view in the way she starts and finishes *The Battle of St George Without*—for every book is, in a sense, a life.

She plunges straight into her story like this: 'He didn't want a row over the cat. He hadn't even wanted the cat. It was the cat's idea.' And she is delighted to hear from a neighbour who read the book aloud to his family, that when he came to its final lines,

> 'I always wanted to ring a bell,' the Bishop said contemplatively.
>
> 'Every St George's Day they rang it,' Gwen said breathlessly casual. 'That's the proper day. Miss Harrison told us.'
>
> 'Ah!' said the Bishop. 'She did, did she?' and took off his coat.

the book was slammed shut to a chorus of 'Go on! Go ON!'

With such encouragement pealing, like the ancient bell of the Church of St George Without, in her ears Janet McNeill is propelled almost unwillingly away from washing the kitchen floor ('I'm confident I can make a good job of *that!*') up towards the tiny room, the typewriter and the blank sheet of paper which, even now, fills her with a paralysing fear.

Signal, 1971

BARBARA WILLARD
THE SPRINGS OF 'MANTLEMASS'

I don't think it ever entered my head that I could interview Barbara Willard in London, though I knew she often came there. She has deep roots in Sussex, and from those roots have sprung her succession of historical novels set in Ashdown Forest, now collectively known as the 'Mantlemass Series'. So to Ashdown Forest I went, and in it I experienced, with her, the power of the past.

'Up and over Ashdown Forest . . . down dreadful lane . . . through old Forest gate posts. Find "Forest Edge" on right.' It was a golden October day when, following Barbara Willard's careful instructions, I decided to escape from the A22 London-to-Nutley motorway and to drive, instead, along country roads, through the villages of West Kent and East Sussex, through beech woods still thick with leaf and pierced by blinding shafts of saffron sunlight, 'up and over Ashdown Forest', 'down dreadful lane' to her eighteenth-century squatters' cottage, part of the original tiny settlement of Nutley, a cottage aptly named 'Forest Edge'. As I drove to 'Forest Edge' I thought how lucky I was that the sunshine and age-old beech trees had put me in so foresty a mood when I was to meet Barbara Willard and talk to her about *The Grove of Green Holly*, which is set in Ashdown; but as I drove home I felt that it wasn't just luck, for Barbara had convinced me that in her life—and this meeting was part of her life—fate takes an uncannily big hand.

Barbara Willard is Sussex bred. She was born in Brighton, spent many holidays as a child with relations at Fittleworth, then lived at Kingston, near Lewes, 'right under the Downs' before the opportunity to buy 'Forest Edge' presented itself. Having bought it she would look out from its leaded windows over the uneven brick path with its giant pots of geranium and begonia, across the sloping lawn surrounded by flowers (she is a keen practical gardener) to the Forest—'and positively lust for the distant Downs'. But Barbara needed the Forest which was to bring out, like salt on steak, the best flavour from her writing; and, in a way, the Forest needed Barbara too, for it had secrets to reveal.

Barbara Willard comes from a theatre family: 'Sunday mornings huddled on Crewe station,' she recalls with a shiver. It might almost be said that she grew up trilingual. She spoke pure English; as a child she had soaked up the Sussex dialect, which she uses brilliantly in her Ashdown novels—colourful words like 'misheroon' and 'non-plush', which speak from the past but need no glossary; and she grew to understand Shakespeare through no conscious effort of her own. Her father was a Shakespearean actor ('an ac-*tor*' as she succinctly put it, encapsulating both the fantasy and the enormous vanity in one stressed syllable). Young Barbara, at Stratford pre-war, played the boys' parts—the son of Macduff, and so on—but when, in her teens, she became 'terribly tall, terribly thin and terribly shy' she gave up professional acting altogether. By then, having lived through her formative years at rehearsals, she had absorbed Shakespearean speech to the extent that no passage in the plays was 'difficult': it went straight into her soul, like the classical music she also loves and understands but whose message she cannot explain in words.

With her passionate interest in Sussex history—she is author of the *Sussex* volume in the series 'Batsford's Britain'—her experience of Shakespeare, and some years of writing both for adults and young children behind her, what more natural than that Barbara Willard, once tuned in to the Forest voices, should try her hand at a story for older children based on the trials of a Shakespearean actor's family, forced to hide from Cromwell's soldiers in Ashdown Forest during the Commonwealth? What would have happened, she asked herself, during those ten play-less years to the travelling players some of whom remembered Shakespeare and had his plays by heart? How would they have kept in contact with one another? Did they meet and perform privately to keep their art alive? For they must have believed that Charles Stuart would eventually return, and with him a new dawn for the theatre, a dawn which must not take them unawares. Ashdown Forest would have provided a perfect refuge.

On a hillside in Ashdown—we walked there along the horse-ride of John of Gaunt's great park with Barbara's dog Bliss bounding ecstatically ahead of us—there is a grove of green holly; the trees are old and tall and the branches meet together over a great open space which offers both protection from the weather and seclusion from prying eyes. Underfoot crackle the grey dry prickly leaves of centuries; one feels a *frisson* here. It is a place, as Barbara says, 'where people have been once but have gone. Sometimes I stamp with rage because it's frustrating to know you can't quite get through to them . . .'

In person, that is; but imaginatively, in *The Grove of Green Holly* Barbara Willard has got right through to the vainglorious old actor Gregory Trundle ('It was not much more than a minute's walk . . . but he made a march of it'), his daughter Margery and his grandchildren Rafe and Gilia Finch, who were hounded out of Shoreham by the rantings of gospeller Godsmark. Gregory and the Finch family, in their covered wagon, go into hiding in Ashdown ('Heigh ho, sing heigh ho, Unto the green holly,' quotes the ever-quoting Gregory) near that grove of green holly. And in the grove, Gregory ensures that his grandson Rafe is familiar with the plays, certain that Rafe will eventually follow him as a player; Margery and Gilia make a rough forest home for them all; and a Mr Lovet, a scholar who has a small dwelling in Ashdown, talks endlessly with the ageing actor about the text of Shakespeare as literature: for in the seventeenth century actors like Gregory Trundle were still taking many liberties with the parts.

But is Rafe Finch really going to be a player? He knows his Shakespeare well enough. When old Gregory goads him with '"Come what may, Time and the hour . . ." Rafe. "Time and the hour . . .?"' he can complete the quotation with '". . . run through the roughest day," *Macbeth*' but then he lies very still and pretends to be asleep.

For in Ashdown Forest young Rafe discovers another part of his being. He goes to work at the forge, for iron has been mined in the Forest since pre-Roman days. There the muscles in his arms grow prodigiously—somewhat unbecoming in a future Shakespearean heroine!—and he learns the joys of a glowing furnace, of clangouring hammers and of the art of fashioning decorative iron firebacks. 'He enjoyed acting with his grandfather in the grove but increasingly he loved his work at the forge. It was as though he wore on one hand an iron glove and on the other a glove of soft doeskin.' As the iron glove begins to take precedence Rafe is disturbed by feelings of disloyalty to the old man and to his own actor's blood.

But Kate, the smith's daughter, is claiming his heart. 'Her face was indeed shiny with sweat, as Prue had so needlessly told her. She smelt of herself and of straw, and of the hot sunshine of the declining year.' Then old Gregory, set upon by a witch-hunting Puritan mob, dies in Rafe's arms gabbling on about his wife and the Forest. This makes no sense to Rafe until another old player, come to seek out Gregory and Rafe and tell them that Charles Stuart is on his way back to Dover, explains that Rafe's grandmother was a smith's daughter—who ran away from Ashdown with Gregory, then a young travelling player. Rafe can finally choose iron with a clear conscience knowing that he is keeping up the tradition of one side of his family. Listen to him as he declares himself to Kate:

> 'I'll bide and niver go, no niver, Kate, till you send me.'
> She laughed then. 'What's come to you to talk so plain and foresty?'
> 'I met my grandmother first time ever,' he said. 'She learnt me.'

It is in the wealden iron of Ashdown that the Forest is, maybe, holding its secret for Barbara Willard too, leading her through the iron veins in the sandstone to discover her own origins. For whilst researching for her story in books, digging on local archaeological sites, considering the significance of Sussex place names—Boring Wheel Mill, Hammer Ponds—Barbara Willard discovered that at a forge near Robertsbridge working with the Sidneys (about whom she has also written) 'there was once . . . I don't know how to tell you this . . . there was once an iron master . . . called . . . David Willard'.

So it could be that Barbara Willard had found the mainstream for her creative writing. Ashdown Forest, which possibly bred her—she has yet to discover whether sixteenth-century David Willard is in fact an ancestor—may claim her talents and use them as a channel for revealing itself. Certainly Grant Uden's 'gift'—telling her that a Richard Plantagenet's death is recorded in the register of Eastwell in 1550—started her wondering whether, if this Richard was a grandson of Richard III as he claimed, he might have hidden in Ashdown after Bosworth Field, in 1485, as the Finch family hid after Cromwell took over in 1650. Barbara Willard's most recent book, *A Sprig of Broom* (sequel to

The Lark and the Laurel), covers the period from 1485 to the early part of the sixteenth century: in it Richard Plantagenet—'Dick Plashet'—is living as a forester.

There is now the possibility—she is excited to find that quite by chance she has laid the foundation for this—that she may fill in the hundred years or so between the end of *The Sprig of Broom* and the beginning of *The Grove of Green Holly* with a sequence of novels set in Elizabethan and early Stuart Ashdown. To her amazement the characters are there, at either end of the span, strategically poised and waiting to be joined together.

But will Barbara Willard be contented to be labelled an historical novelist in the teenage field? She hates labels of any kind and is delighted that novels for adolescents now find their way into adult libraries so that in fact her writing has come full circle.

Nevertheless, her work as a novelist and anthologist for teenagers (as well as author of short books for the very young) appears on publishers' children's lists and is reviewed on children's book pages. As a professional author who regards her development from author of adult fiction to children's fiction as a mark of progress—'I always wanted to write for children; it's a great challenge'—Barbara Willard has much to say both about the reviewing of children's books and about the relationship of the children's author to teachers and librarians.

She feels very strongly that practitioners in the craft should never be called upon to review one another. 'What's the point in my scratching ——'s back this week, knowing he'll have to scratch mine next?' Reviewers should be detached and professional; perhaps they would be, if more space were given to children's books as a branch of literature. 'Why is it,' she asks with the fires of old Gregory Trundle (who was fashioned on her father) blazing up within her, 'why is it that when we have a round-up of critics' choices at the end of the year, even the resident children's book critic seldom chooses a children's book?'

Meeting educationists at the BBC—when scripting a programme for 'Merry-Go-Round', for example—and at conferences, Barbara Willard feels uncomfortably that the way they look at historical writing and the way she views it are worlds apart. They want to hammer home the facts, slightly sugared. She wants to give modern child audiences the feeling of what it must have been like, for instance, at the age of seven to rise in the darkness and go to work in a Halifax mill for the first time, your childhood over for ever. 'But every time I make a *dramatic* point the director pulls it back to make a *teaching* one.' Teachers too are inclined, *en masse*, to make impossible demands of writers. '"What we want," they say, "and what you don't give us . . .",—as though we were a Civil Service department, or something.'

But Barbara Willard does not work to order. She is an artist and a craftsman. Inspiration comes as she gardens, walks, reads, sleeps. She writes one long novel a year, beginning in the late summer, working hard through the winter and enjoying garden, Forest, visitors and motoring in the summer months. There is always anxiety over the early chapters of a book, but when she dreams about a character in her novel and wakes in the night, her toes 'curled with pleasure', then she knows she is away.

She is engagingly frank about her writing. 'Yesterday,' she said, 'I re-read *The Grove of Green Holly* because I thought I'd better know what you were talking about! I thoroughly enjoyed it—what a dreadful admission!—and in places where I'd moved myself I even cried.' Because so much of Barbara Willard's warmth and humour and deep emotion goes into everything she writes, re-reading a book like *The Grove of Green Holly*, published five years ago, is for her like looking at an old photograph; moods and feelings come rushing forward from the past.

Walking out over Ashdown Forest with Barbara Willard, who points out there the old Roman road, here the site of sandstone brickworks and on the ground boulders veined with iron, one truly feels the past is speaking to her. Long may the conversation continue!

Signal, 1972

BARBARA SLEIGH
THE VOICE OF MAGIC

Anyone who had ever listened, as parent or child, to BBC 'Children's Hour' had a deep affection for Barbara Sleigh and her husband David Davis, two of its founts of wisdom and delight. Reading Barbara's autobiography, 'A Smell of Privet' made me want to meet her to discover more about that most cherished gift, the storyteller's magic.

'We remember, or misremember, what we do because of the people that we are,' says Barbara Sleigh in her enchanting autobiography of childhood, *A Smell of Privet*. It is no accident, therefore, that what she recalls and sets down in her honest, wry, no-nonsense-about-it manner are the humorous incidents of her young life: not the incidents which seemed to her funny at the time but those which, as an adult, now seem to be humorous simply because the child to whom they happened, the child whose persistence, logic and unknowing made them happen, was totally unaware of their overtones. *A Smell of Privet*, though written for adults, has 'the eye of the child at the centre', straight, unerring, all-seeing and often perplexed.

After reading it one is not at all surprised to discover that Barbara Sleigh became an original voice in the world of fantasy. Here she is at the Church of England College where her career, she says, was 'inky and undistinguished'.

> 'If I was two inches high,' I would say to myself, or sometimes one inch, or two and a half, to give variety, 'and the front of Mamselle's blouse was a mountain in Wales, I would hold on with my hands to *that* link of her chain, and put my left foot on the bottom button' (which had, of course, become a rock), 'and then I could just reach that sticking-out frill with my *right* foot, and with a great heave pull myself up on to that second button . . .'

This was the schoolgirl who had grown from a tot to whom her artist father told endless stories from myth and legend—sometimes to keep her still as she modelled for his stained-glass windows of biblical subjects, sometimes as they walked the countryside around Birmingham, elder brother Linwood being the focus for the stories, Barbara lagging on behind, trying to listen but catching only a lovely word here or a bright image there.

Once she learned to read she read omnivorously. But at first, like many children who are constantly read to, she 'read' by heart and was proud of it:

> My best friend below stairs was Mrs Steeds, who came twice a week to do the washing and scrub the floors and passages . . . What made her a figure of awed amazement to me was the fact that she could not read. She, a grown-up person! Brought up in a household to which reading was as necessary as eating, combined with the fact that I myself had achieved the dizzy heights of Cat-Mat-Sat, I found this almost impossible to believe. I would prepare little traps to make her explain that it really was so. She bore me no ill will; in fact, it developed into a kind of game. I would saunter up to her when she was drinking her mid-morning cup of tea, with one of my precious Beatrix Potter books, and point casually to some phrase I knew by heart from frequent readings aloud, and say:
>
> 'What does this say, Mrs Steeds?'
>
> She would plant a square, pink, water-crinkled finger on the page, purse her lips wisely for a minute, and say:
>
> 'Blessed if I know, dearie! You tell me.'
>
> 'It says "Lettuces are so soporific",' I would reply: or whatever I knew were the appropriate words opposite the picture.
>
> 'Lor!' Mrs Steeds would say in a tone of wonder. 'Fancy that! And you able to scan it off in a twinkle! Why, bless you! Old Mrs Steeds can't read nor write, not a word! Never could, dear!'
>
> And she would clap her large hands on her knees and go into gales of laughter, in which I would join as though it was the best joke in the world.
>
> It was Selina who took me to task.
>
> 'You didn't ought to make the poor old soul look so silly. She never had the chance to learn to read nor write. So don't you go on making a monkey of her no more.'
>
> I was contrite. It had never occurred to me that I was 'making a monkey' of my friend. Far from being a shortcoming, I had regarded the non-reading of Mrs Steeds as an achievement.

Soon Barbara discovered E. Nesbit, who was the spark that lit the trail that led to her development as an author of 'modern' fairy tales. 'I was enraptured,' she told me, 'with the idea of magic happening to my own contemporaries, children like the Bastables. I devoured all the Nesbits and absolutely loved them. David and I' (David is her husband, David Davis, former Head of BBC *Children's Hour*) 'went to see the film of *The Railway Children* twice recently and sat there quietly trickling. It was quite ridiculous . . .'—but very much in character.

For David and Barbara, whose three children are now adult and have left the comfortable house in Ealing with its light rooms, its bowls of simple flowers—daffodils and catkins when I was there—its well-cared-for garden with food for the birds hung away out of the reach of Barbara's cats, are the kind of adults for whom childhood is a living reality.

Barbara feels very strongly that 'the more mechanized we are, the more important it is that magic, wonder, whatever you like to call it, should be kept alive'. Of Ben, the village blacksmith of her youth she says, 'With his curly black hair and blue eyes I thought him worthy to have forged Excalibur itself. With the passage of time the inevitable happened. The forge had to be abandoned in favour of a garage. What had Excalibur to do with garages?'

And yet, to Barbara's astonishment and delight she still discovers magic in the most unlikely places—such as the North Circular Road, which she calls the Outer Circle of Hell. Quite suddenly, as she told me about this unexpected revelation, in her quiet voice with its considered phrases, I could grasp the qualities which endeared her to millions of *Children's Hour* listeners and impelled her to write ('It's like steam coming out of a kettle') *Jessamy*, her *Carbonel* fantasies, and her collections of legends and modern fairy tales. 'That night,' she began, 'it was freezing hard on the North Circular when we came to those two curved bridges. It was dark and they were festooned with icicles. The icicles were hanging down whilst the cars zoomed to and fro underneath, their headlights on so that some of the icicles were silver, some golden. It was pure magic. When we came back, there was a man with a long stick breaking the icicles off. My rational self thought "Well, of course it must be done; if they grow any longer they'll damage the cars." But my irrational self, my imaginative self, looks back on that man as becoming more and more evil and toad-like.'

Magic, as Barbara Sleigh points out in her introduction to *West of Widdershins*, 'like beauty, is in the eye of the beholder'. In all the best fairy tales ('I wish they weren't called "fairy" tales; "fairy" suggests spangles and silvery voices; there should be another name for them but I can't think what,') it is the simple everyday object—a cooking-pot, a carpet—which has magic powers. Why then the period costume? Mid-Victorian Alice embarked on her adventures through an overmantel looking-glass; Mary Norton's hero Paul, in *The Magic Bedknob*, a classic of the forties, used a brass bed-knob; today's children, Barbara Sleigh's heroes and heroines, find their magic in the supermarket, the primary school, the town garden.

Many of the *West of Widdershins* stories, magic notwithstanding, are set firmly in the 1970s. 'Bridget was running down the garden path when she got a fairy in her eye,' begins one; 'Simon was kneeling by the lake in the park when he saw the Unicorn,' starts another; and a third, one of the funniest in the book, opens with the plainest of plain statements: 'Once upon a time there was a teacher called Miss Peabody and a class called Lower 3a.'

Nothing fantastic about that, you would think. But when Miss Peabody went to a new doctor about her headaches and he prescribed two tiny bottles of medicine—one red, 'an egg shell full to be taken before breakfast; one green, labelled "The Antidote"'—Miss Peabody discovered to her alarm that her every wish, even the involuntary kind we all make from time to time, was to be granted.

'"Goodness, how late it is. And it's pouring with rain. I wish I was at school!"' she said one morning—and there she was, hair dishevelled wearing her scarlet slippers with the yellow pompoms in 3a classroom. 'Willy Brown and Nora Smith, who had come to school early to arrange some up-ended drawing pins, were staring at her with their mouths open.' But more surprises were in store.

When two members of her class were playing tiddly-winks with buttons, Miss Peabody absent-mindedly called out:

> 'I wish to have all the buttons in the room on my desk please.' She meant of course all the *loose* buttons in the room, but that was not what she had said. There was a pause, and then the air was filled with a number of little poppings, like the bursting of gorse buds on a hot June day, followed by the patter of small hard things falling like rain on the lid of Miss Peabody's desk.

775 buttons—and every boy clutching his trousers for dear life!

And so it goes on. Glorious entertainment for anyone who

lights on it, as all good stories in this genre should be. Like J. R. R. Tolkien, Barbara Sleigh believes wholeheartedly that folk tales are for everyone, and that their relegation to the nursery (or to the university for that matter) is a hideous example of twentieth-century pigeonholing. Whereas *West of Widdershins* is a collection of original stories, in *North of Nowhere* Barbara Sleigh retells, with her own magic, her favourite legends. 'Fairy tales and legends are oral material,' she stresses, 'tales told from generation to generation by people who loved them, by people who believed in magic and added to them as they went along, by people who wouldn't have listened to a dull tale. So the bad ones have dropped out and what has survived is the best of each nation's folklore, crossing and re-crossing the boundaries, the seas, the oceans—the same themes turning up again and again but each time in a distinctive local form. Although this may seem surprising, it isn't really, because all over the world people have the same sort of ambitions, the same wishes and dreams they'd like fulfilled.'

Before she married, Barbara Sleigh's career—having abandoned art teaching in Birmingham, which she didn't enjoy—was in sound radio at the BBC, for which she still does freelance work as writer of plays, stories, and adaptations. She describes delightfully how she submitted, when already working for *Children's Hour*, her first play, an adaptation of *Rumpelstiltskin*, under a pseudonym, and how 'Elizabeth' came bouncing out of her inner office shouting 'We've found a new writer for children, a new writer for children!' Barbara's blushes gave the game away.

Barbara Sleigh believes strongly in children being encouraged to form their own images—as they do when listening to stories on the radio or from their parents. She regards over-illustration of folk tales (as in the folk-tale picture books that flood the market at the present time) as a dubious development but concedes that period stories need a tactful illustration here and there to help the child set the scene in which his imagination can then work on its own.

Exceedingly house-proud ('I do housework only because I hate a messy-looking house') Barbara Sleigh, wife, mother, grandmother, always keeps some writing going. 'Even at the worst times during the war when the children were babies I did. It stops the washing-up water from seeping into your brains.' In what spare time she has she goes to the theatre and picture galleries and reads a great deal: Jane Austen (not surprisingly) over and over again, thrillers, biography, and of the modern novelists V. S. Naipaul, who gives her enormous pleasure, and Margaret Drabble; but seldom children's books.

Upright, firm, brisk with penetrating blue eyes, Barbara Sleigh is a little forbidding until she begins to speak: but the moment an anecdote begins, the first time she laughs, one knows at once that inside there is great warmth, a love of life, broad humour, vivid imagination and, yes, that kind of personal magic which is the hall-mark of a teller of tales.

Signal, 1972

RUMER GODDEN
PRINCE OF STORYTELLERS

I would never have dared on Signal's behalf to ask for an interview with Rumer Godden because I was aware of her intense professionalism and her determination not to waste valuable time on giving interviews. But Kaye Webb had persuaded her to give me an interview for young readers of 'Puffin Post', so I used that opportunity to the full, and two articles came from it. Having been handed a printed sheet with the facts of her life and the dates of publication of her books on it by her secretary before lunch—a very formal affair—I was surprised and delighted when, afterwards, she spoke so warmly and openly to me. I think it was because, unlike the normal run of journalists who are despatched by their editors today to write a quick piece for a gossip column tomorrow, I had read all her books and was prepared to spend time presenting her to 'real children and adults'—her own definition (see p.77) of her audience.

Rumer Godden, born in Sussex and now living in Rye, spent the formative years of her childhood in a remote part of Bengal where she drew into herself, through the roots she struck, the many-sidedness and the contradictions of Hindu philosophy as well as the mysterious power to reconcile them. This gives her and her work a peculiar richness whilst leaving the observer perhaps not utterly, but certainly partially, baffled. For the woman seems, in so many ways, at variance with the work.

And why not?

That an author is necessarily reflected in her novels or stories for children was the first of my preconceptions that Rumer Godden waved gently but firmly aside. 'Writing and painting are not self-expression as people think they are. They are nothing to do with self. Self probably gets in the way, I should say. When I was writing *The Kitchen Madonna* I was not expressing myself, I was expressing the boy, Gregory.'

But then we went on to talk at length about the central characters of her books for children, how Gregory in *The Kitchen Madonna*, Kizzy in *The Diddakoi*, Nona in *Miss Happiness and Miss Flower* are all lonely children caught between two cultures or two ways of life and forced by circumstances to make a bridge between, through the power of their imagination and their strength of will. It is not Miss Godden herself but her experience of two cultures, of being a hybrid, that is reflected in the strains and stresses and emotional growth of the children she creates, both in her stories for the young and in her adult novels. For many of her adult novels (notably *The River*, perhaps the most poignant and honest book about adolescence ever written) focus on children.

What is it that distinguishes writing for children from writing for adults? We are so often told that an author does not write for anyone, he writes for himself; that children's books and adult books are part of 'literature' and should be evaluated on the same critical principles. Rumer Godden has a great deal to say on this subject; most of it, running counter to fashionable pronouncements, embodies good sound sense—an assessment she will eschew because, as she said in another context (concerning Muhammedanism), 'It's very sensible, and I have never had much time for sense!'

Both *The Kitchen Madonna* and *The Diddakoi*, published here for children, were published in America for adults as well as for children. 'They became "twilight books",' says Miss Godden, 'and were reviewed as if inadequate adult literature. When you write for children you don't write in a childish vein, but you do write differently. It's a much stricter discipline. You have to have a story, and the only interest in a story is conflict. If you remove all the adult problems you can't make a story, and *it's the story that makes the young reader want to turn the page.*

'When you are writing an adult novel you can really do anything, anything you like; whereas writing for children you know perfectly well that the child is going to lose patience if, for instance, you have a lot of introspective thought or if you have a lot of description. You can't use the classic way of describing someone that you would use in an adult novel, slowly dropping in hints of character over a number of pages. Children want to know *at once* what somebody looks like.'

When Rumer Godden speaks of 'children' she really *means* children; the lack of innocence in so much entertainment that is ostensibly 'for children' appals her, which is why she describes the musical version of *Holly and Ivy*, on which she is working with David Henneker at the moment, as 'for little children and real adults,' adding, 'Nobody between the ages of ten and thirty should see it.' It is probably true that few young people between those ages would respond to Rumer Godden's books for children either, which is why, in her thinking, there is this sharp divide between two distinct techniques: writing for 'real adults' and writing for children.

She gave me a superb example, from *Holly and Ivy* since that was the book we had been discussing. Ivy, the six-year-old heroine with (note the direct description) 'straight hair cut in a fringe, blue-grey eyes and a turned-up nose', had had a very pathetic past—no father, no mother, no grandparents. 'In an adult novel you would have used flashbacks to Ivy's past—her father, her mother, her home—but for the very young reader flashback is too confusing and the description has to be pared right down.' So, to convey Ivy's past, Rumer Godden invented a short scene in which Ivy suddenly realizes that, unlike all the other boys and girls at St Agnes's, she is the one who has not been 'asked for by a kind lady or gentleman' for the Christmas holiday.

> 'I don't care,' said Ivy.
>
> Sometimes in Ivy there was an empty feeling, and the emptiness ached; it ached so much that she had to say something quickly in case she cried, and, 'I don't care at all,' said Ivy.

In that one tiny paragraph—in the two words 'at all', really—the whole feeling of Ivy's orphan past is instantly conveyed.

'Children apprehend where they don't comprehend,' says

Rumer Godden, who, like Beatrix Potter, uses the most exact words she can find, regardless of whether children will know their meaning: Mr Plantagenet, in *The Dolls' House*, for instance, had been 'hurt, *abused* and lost'. In that famous fictional correspondence between Mr V. Andal (editor of De Base Publishing Company, Inc.) and the ghost of Miss Beatrix Potter*—which is sharply witty as well as profoundly serious—Rumer Godden lays bare the appalling insensitivity and wrong-mindedness of editors who want to emasculate 'masterpieces' so that they exactly fit the 'mini-minds' that are waiting not to be fitted, but to be *stretched*. ('We can only tell you,' writes the exasperated Mr V. Andal, who has not succeeded in budging Miss Potter one inch, 'that it is our opinion, formed by expert advice, that in its present form, parents, teachers, and children will not buy, nor understand, nor like *Peter Rabbit*'; to which the ghost of Miss Potter confidently replies, 'Seven million have. I rest in peace'.) In the spirit of Miss Potter, Rumer Godden holds audiences of children as young as eight spellbound with her readings from Dylan Thomas and Gerard Manley Hopkins.

Rumer Godden clearly has a great regard for childhood, a period of growth, struggles, ferment, unfettered imagination and creativity. Dolls' houses, a miniature garden, the careful acquisition of materials for making a collage madonna and the intense concentration needed to assemble them into an icon, are each the catalyst in a Godden story for the young. So exact are the details the author gives of how the Japanese dolls' house or the miniature garden or the collage madonna are made, that any boy or girl reading the books can set about constructing them at once. Many do—and they write to tell the author of the pleasure this has given them. Surely Miss Godden is herself a craftsman, a creative artist in practical ways as well as in her writing? But, 'I'm hopeless,' she says—almost surprised that one should think anything else. 'I can't even arrange flowers; I fall into a panic if anyone gives them to me. A little while ago I tried to darn my granddaughter's grey school sock. She watched me, then heaved with laughter and said, "Grandmother, that looks like porridge. Give it to me." She took it, she's only eight, and darned it to perfection.'

*'An Imaginary Correspondence' (*Horn Book*, August 1963; reprinted in first edition only of Egoff, Stubbs and Ashley's *Only Connect*, OUP, 1969, p. 62).

But this porridge-darner is a worshipper of the immaculate and the minuscule; among her greatest treasures are the finest of fine Persian rugs, and a Pekinese sleeve-dog called Jade Button. Diminutive objects are as alive for Rumer Godden as they are for children, with whom she shares an obsession for dolls of character.

Of character?

Dolls set the imagination coursing with the possibility of their interaction, and Miss Godden's stories make a passionate appeal to children, to *consider* dolls' feelings and give them life—otherwise they are helpless and mute.

> 'There will be some little girl who is clever and kind,' [says Miss Happiness, one of the exiled Japanese dolls in *Miss Happiness and Miss Flower*].
>
> 'Will there be?' asked Miss Flower longingly.
>
> 'Yes.'
>
> 'Why will there be?'
>
> 'Because there always has been,' said Miss Happiness.
>
> All the same Miss Flower gave a doll shiver, which means she felt as though she shivered though it couldn't be seen. Miss Flower was always frightened; perhaps the child who made the chip in her ear had been rough. 'I wish we had not come,' said Miss Flower.
>
> Miss Happiness sighed and said, 'We were not asked.'

The story continues with the words 'Children are not asked either'; it is this feeling of being impotent—if adults are inconsiderate—that Rumer Godden transfers from the child to the dolls in their relationships with their 'mothers and fathers', the children who own them. Her books make a plea for communication, consideration and understanding but they make it magically in a way that the seven-, eight- or nine-year-old can perfectly 'apprehend'.

Because so much of a child's life is spent in interior dialogue Rumer Godden has adopted a unique and arresting way of using speech as merely the breakthrough point in thought, the short, intense switch-on of current between people that sets thought travelling again in, perhaps, a slightly different direction. In *The Kitchen Madonna* Gregory, trying to make an icon but lacking the money to buy what he believes he needs, is despondent; it was a foolish idea anyway, he says.

Then, 'It wasn't,' said Janet and Gregory lifted his head. He did not often let his younger sister contradict him.

'It was if I can't make it,' said Gregory.

'You can make it.'

'How can I make it without money?'

'You can make it with think,' said Janet.

It was not what she meant to say, yet oddly it said what she meant.

Gregory and Janet are the children of middle-class professional people. Kizzy, in *The Diddakoi*, is a gypsy child who finds herself 'ridin' in Rolls Royces' when the Admiral takes pity on her; the Plantagenets' behaviour in *The Dolls' House* mirrors the comfortable world in which the children who own the dolls' house live. Is Rumer Godden an anachronism, or is she relevant to today's child? How does she fare in a world where teachers search for reflections in books of the life of the inner-city child, and where critics use the words 'middle class' as though they were pejorative? Rumer Godden smiles. 'I am always told I have a Kensington voice,' she says, without a hint of embarrassment. 'If they mind, I am very sorry for them. I'm not going to try to be anything I am not. To me, if you are a writer or a painter you are lucky enough to be in a totally classless society. It doesn't matter who you are or what you do or how you talk, so long as you don't let it worry you. You are just a person doing your thing and whoever you encounter it's because of your work. You are free of all these pettinesses: I remember Katherine Mansfield saying "Artists are the cleanest people in the world: mentally clean."'

This philosophy is borne out in Rumer Godden's work. Whether she is writing a long, complex novel for adults like *In This House of Brede*, which has no less than eighty threads of women's lives woven into its intriguing pattern, or a short simple tale like *The Diddakoi* for children, Rumer Godden is 'clean' and sure and timeless in her appeal—for she is a prince among storytellers, combining rich imagination with minute attention to detail. Had she, I asked, lived with nuns in a house like Brede, or served on a juvenile bench such as the one that in the end decides on Kizzy's future in *The Diddakoi*? How else could she know so well the functioning of such disparate bodies? 'No, no. It's shop to me,' she said. Research she does, meticulously, humbly, carefully. But the story comes first, the checking and amendments afterwards. 'If you start with the research, the facts are so fascinating that you finish up with a documentary.'

So, which is she? The tidy Rumer Godden you meet with her three Pekinese in the immaculate old house in Rye, or the disorderly woman she says she is by nature; the brilliantly successful author for adults, or the much-loved children's story-teller; the practical woman or the 'porridge-darner'; the mother and grandmother who knows she must allow her writing to be interrupted by social claims—or the dedicated artist and researcher whose work is her life?

The mystery, the magic, the contradictions remain; for, like Harriet in *The River*, 'with all the glory she wished she could have kept herself a secret'.

Signal, 1975

* * *

Interviewing artists, I soon discovered, was less easy than interviewing authors. Authors are at ease with words; artists prefer the silent sweep of the pen or brush. For the *Children's Books of the Year* exhibitions in London we were fortunate to be able to borrow the artwork from which many of the picture books and illustrated books on display had been originated. This excited much interest from the public who visited the National Book League's gallery (then in Albemarle Street); and I, too, had the opportunity over the two to three weeks the exhibition lasted, to study at first hand the line drawings and paintings, page designs and jacket illustrations that make children's books such a rich feast for the eye.

KATHLEEN HALE
and 'ORLANDO THE MARMALADE CAT'

Kathleen Hale, whose first book about 'Orlando the Marmalade Cat' had been published in 1938, made a come-back in 1972 when Cape published 'Orlando and the Water Cats'. She lent us some of the original paintings for this when we were mounting the subsequent 'Children's Books of the Year' exhibition and came up herself as one of our guest artists to work with children in the National Book League gallery. Captivated by her, I asked if I could come to Oxfordshire to interview her for 'Signal'.

Although Kathleen Hale says that Noel Carrington at Country Life and Geoffrey Smith of Cowell's 'gave birth to Orlando' in the thirties, what she really means is that this far-sighted publisher and printer were the midwives. The Marmalade Cat was probably conceived early in the 1900s when Kathleen Hale, then a schoolgirl, wrote wildly imaginative essays, never on the subject set. Indeed, the Orlando tales might well have burst upon the world 'interleaved in a handy packet'—except that lavatory paper in those days only came in a continuous roll. For Kathleen Hale, the original drop-out whose success story should make heart-warming reading for parents of today's dissidents, was continually punished as a child by having her beloved drawing materials locked away: so she stole lavatory paper from people's houses and drew and drew and drew on that.

Now a cheerful, independent-minded, young-at-heart 74-year-old with close-cropped white hair, an inquisitive tilt of the head and a ready fund of anecdotes, she thinks nothing of shinning up a loft-ladder to her attic studio ('But can *you* manage it, dear? Mind your head!'). There her careful lithographic separation plates for the *Orlando* books were painstakingly made on a litho screen until quite recently. But now the automatic photo-litho process does this arduous work for her.

When Kathleen Hale made her first *Orlando* book—huge like the original *Babars*—before World War II, there was no alternative to hand separation. De Brunhoff was working that way in France; Ardizzone and Kathleen Hale began to make lithographic picture books in England. These three can be said to have pioneered the full-colour picture books we know today.

Why did Kathleen Hale start making picture books at all? She was already a mature artist, befriended by Augustus John and Dorelia, selling her metal collages at the Leicester Galleries, to shops like Fortnum & Mason, and to famous people such as Noel Coward. 'I started because I got bored with reading *Babar* and Beatrix Potter to my little boys every night; and that was all there was at that time, except for those nauseating books written by spinsters or young men who wanted to make some pocket-money, and published by people who should have stuck to printing postcards. They knew nothing about how to help children's imagination grow and had an entirely false sense of values. So I began making up my own stories about Orlando, *our* marmalade cat, who used to weave in and out of the supports of the playpen or sit contentedly whilst my son sucked his tail.'

Had she always had cats? 'Oh yes; we once had two who both had large families in the children's bath at the same time. One mother used to go shopping, as I always said, whilst the other baby-sat. When "Orlando I" died, the boys wouldn't let me call another cat Orlando, so we had Pyramus and Flute, Mild and Bitter and so on until the children were grown up when they said, "You can do what you like now, Ma!", so I had "Orlando II" who lived for nineteen and a half years.'

But the lovely little stone house in Oxfordshire, with its flowering rockeries and walls hung with drawings by John and sensitive portraits by Miss Hale herself, its graceful furniture ('You need a crinoline to sit on that day-bed but I always wear slacks'), its bowls full of shells and pebbles, has now no cat. Today Kathleen Hale lives—like *The Cat That Walked by Himself*—on her 'wild lone' because she does not want to be tied down.

'I've just been to Ipswich for a week to see my printers. There was a fantastic group of hippies at the bus station. I drew them in my sketch-book.' Does she still draw a lot? 'All the time; it's like a pianist practising scales.'

But to return to the *Orlando* books, whose success had hitherto been something of an enigma to me. A sophisticated text and those marvellous chalky pictures of cats, dogs and horses engaged in attractively unorthodox pursuits. Why did they fit together to make such a satisfying whole? For the pictures engross young children who don't give a fig for the actual text (though they love the *stories*) until they are seven or so. At least this had been my experience.

Kathleen Hale swept my enigma (what preconceived standards we all do apply these days!) straight out of the window. 'The *text* is for adults. Why make reading to the children at the end of a long, hard day a chore? Those sophisticated jokes are for the parents, but I make sure that the jokes never deprive the child of the sequence of the story; that and the pictures are for the children who look right into the illustrations and seize on the detail in a way adults don't bother to do.'

The characters are for children too. Paternal, competent, reliable Orlando (who does the mousework, you will remember), maternal, feminine, sprightly Grace (who does the housework), their kittenish daughters Pansy and Blanche and their mischievous son Tinkle ('He's not naughty, he just does things that upset people sometimes; as I say in one of the books—maybe he's artistic') are a model of family unity and affection. Deliberately so.

'I was writing about them during the war, you see, when children were evacuated—terrified and homesick in strange surroundings, fathers being killed, mothers running off . . . I thought, life will one day return to normal. I want these children to see what family love should be like, so that they will strive to get it for themselves when they are older.'

For Kathleen Hale, early in the century, there had been no secure family pattern. Her father died when she was five. Her mother, left with £500 and three children whom she didn't understand, 'bought a hideous house in the best suburb of Manchester' and took in lodgers to pay for her family's education.

'I'm very concerned about difficult children because I was very nearly delinquent when I was a child. The only sense of values in our house was "What will the neighbours think?" There was no word about loyalty or truthfulness. I started in on all that when I was seventeen.'

Just as Kathleen Hale was ahead of her time in the forties—understanding the need for stories which would help to compensate the lonely child for the loss of family life—so, in the first decade of this century, was the incredibly enlightened Sarah Burstall, her headmistress at Manchester High School.

'I spent nine years in the corridor of that school in disgrace,' says Kathleen. 'I loved disrupting the class and making people laugh. So I'm absolutely uneducated—couldn't tell you where Canada is in relation to South America, and I know no history so cannot relate today to the past. It's a terrible loss and makes me afraid of meeting intellectual people. Luckily my husband—he was a bacteriologist and died five years ago—had an encyclopaedic mind and loved teaching me. But I'm quite ineducable. I have no memory. I never had. And Miss Burstall didn't know what to do with me. She couldn't expel me because she admired my mother, so she let me drop everything but English, French and Art—and even managed to get Manchester Art School to allow me to do Life Classes at fifteen, which was unheard of in those days.'

It paid off. At seventeen Kathleen Hale, the rebel, the outsider, the ne'er-do-well, won an Open Scholarship to Reading University (College, as it then was) School of Art and stood upon the platform ('"Cor Blimey!" I thought, "What a lark! Me with all those prize-winners"') to receive a bit of paper that her extraordinarily perceptive and understanding Headmistress had rolled up (there was no such thing, physically, as a scholarship) and tied with red ribbon.

The first gleam of success. But many years were to pass—years of spasmodic triumphs in the art world interspersed with lean periods during which she shovelled manure as a Land Girl, delivered hand-bills or walked other people's babies on Hampstead Heath to help make ends meet before marriage and its stabilizing effect, motherhood and a growing awareness of the needs of children, brought Kathleen Hale to channel her talents into the picture book.

When she mentioned the idea of a picture book to C. K. Ogden, he was enthusiastic. 'It must be small, and in black and white,' he said. 'I'll have it turned into Basic English and published in Japan.' But the pages grew larger and larger; more and more colours crept in, until there were seven. Kathleen Hale—C. K. Ogden had disappeared from the scene by now—hawked the original *Orlando* for two years before sending it to Country Life. Noel Carrington, the pivotal figure of children's publishing in the thirties, fell in love with it but realized that in seven colours it was a totally uneconomic proposition. He showed it to Geoffrey Smith of Cowell's, who said the colours must be reduced to four. They were. *Orlando* broke into the limelight but was greeted with 'a resounding (the pun seems appropriate in Miss Hale's case) Tinkle'. So small were the sales that when Noel Carrington moved from Country Life to Puffin and asked Kathleen Hale to do some original *Orlando* picture books in paperback for him, Country Life, whose permission she had to ask, said 'We don't care *what* you do, Miss Hale.' They did care two years later when the Puffin *Orlando*s, advertising the Country Life hardbacks on the cover, had sent their own sales rocketing.

Orlando had caught on. He appeared in strip cartoon, as a ballet with music by Arthur Benjamin and choreography by Andrée Howard, and as a mural at the Festival of Britain. For Kathleen Hale, the unschooled genius, and Orlando, the father figure she created, fame—and fun. Imagine her, the madcap of Manchester High School, invited back years later to address the school and parents on Speech Day in the Free Trade Hall—'I was determined to break the rules just once more: I made them *laugh*.'

Sobering to reflect that in the early days, when Kathleen Hale and Enid Blyton once had tables for book-signing side by side at an Olympia book show, Miss Blyton's queue went round the hall and out into the street whilst Miss Hale had a mere half-dozen fans waiting. But on one occasion, at the Society of Authors, when Miss Blyton made a speech suggesting that all authors of children's books should be highly moral and see that good was rewarded and evil punished, Kathleen Hale stood up 'very tremblingly and said, "Please will the speaker define what she means by good and evil." It's a subtle problem, you see.'

But it is a problem this humbly great, ineducably wise, exuberantly serious, traditionally original, youthfully septuagenarian author-artist tackles in all her books with extraordinary aplomb.

Signal, 1972

PAULINE BAYNES
MISTRESS OF THE MARGIN

Pauline Baynes's line illustrations are well known to the thousands of admirers of C. S. Lewis's 'Narnia' stories yet few of these readers may recall her name. I tracked down this most retiring of artists to her studio in Surrey where, reluctantly at first, she talked with me about C. S. Lewis and J. R. R. Tolkien and about her detailed research for the mock-medieval margin illustrations for Grant Uden's 'Dictionary of Chivalry' for which she won the Kate Greenaway Medal.

On the borders of Surrey and Hampshire there is a road that winds through a pine forest, past a lonely inn towards a lane that twists and turns through steep hedgerows and green fields up hill, down dale, round corners. If you look very carefully next to the barn of a farm, you will find, behind well-kept hedges and a neat garden, a cottage. Inside the cottage a tidy kitchen opens on to a small passage. Go a little further, into the long, low living-room with its comfortable armchairs and dog-beds, its mantelshelf crammed with Victoriana, walls hung with pistols and knick-knacks, shelves and free-standing bookcases piled high with books, papers, dolls, puppets and models. These are the possessions of someone who has reverence for the artefacts of others, and a squirrel nature—possibly fostered by a childhood 'living in trunks'. It is the world of Pauline Baynes.

But where is Pauline? In the far corner of the room between two sets of leaded windows, from the ledges of which tumble the fronds of green flowering plants in happy profusion, there is a large flat-topped desk. On the left of it are neat piles of books giving the correct detail of cloak and clasp, arras and armour, sword and scythe, pot and pail that Pauline Baynes needs for her exquisite illustrations to books like Grant Uden's *Dictionary of Chivalry*, which took her two years to complete and won her the Kate Greenaway Medal in 1968. In the centre of the desk is her work space; to the right artist's materials (neatly stacked in pots and boxes) and four spectacle cases—an indication of the eye-strain involved in such fine work as hers. 'I do walk the dog without glasses,' said Pauline Baynes (she *was* there: warm, gay, charming yet self-effacing) 'but whereas other people might come in and say "I need a drink" I say "Where are my glasses?"'

It was after we had sat and talked that we wandered among the bookshelves and I pulled out a copy of E. H. Shepard's *Brock and Ben*. In it was a letter from 'Kip' Shepard, which Pauline allowed me to read. I quote from it because it excuses me for taking you step by patient step on the rewarding quest for this artist, the kind of quest she demands of the reader who looks deep into her illustrations of enchanted landscapes to find the tiny figures in the valley, the dragon on the hill, the volcano flames among the icy crags. Ernest Shepard wrote, 'I wish I could give you some of my optimism. You must have more confidence, darling, you must—you are much better than you think you are': the grand old man of English illustrating talking to the artist whose work is so much sought after that her routine extends even to the after-dinner hours, and late into the night. Sometimes her husband, Fritz (who served in Rommel's Afrika Korps and met Pauline after being freed from a local prisoner-of-war camp), will ask when she is going to enjoy herself, and the answer is that she enjoys working—'but it *is* work'.

The Pauline Baynes I met and know is a strictly disciplined person who has grown from a schoolgirl with a somewhat turbulent scholastic career. Sent as a boarder to a convent at the age of five—her father was in the Indian Civil Service, her mother an invalid who felt unable to make a home for her two daughters—Pauline says she was 'awful, wicked and fiendish' throughout her convent career, which ended abruptly at the age of eight, and in the small private school, only forty young ladies, to which she was subsequently sent. 'Every child but me had a position of authority and responsibility. All I was allowed to do was ring the chapel bell.' The only thing her education taught her, she says, was to feel guilty if she didn't do a planned amount of work each day. The guilt persists.

At fifteen Pauline went to Farnham Art School where she was taught none of the conventional disciplines because she chose to spend her time in the Design School, book illustration having been her passion from a very early age. At sixteen, in the early days of World War II, she spent two terms at the Slade—then in Oxford—drinking coffee and going to parties. Her sister Angela 'who is the clever one of the family' was there too. The moment Angela gained her Diploma, both girls left.

Always in Angela's shadow and very close to a protective mother, Pauline embarked on her own career almost by accident ('I've had a charmed life; it's been such fun'). Farnham Castle during the war was the Army Camouflage Centre. Angela and Pauline, fresh from the Slade and both good with their hands, were sent there by the W V S to help to make models. The Baynes sisters soon became part of the establishment of most unsoldierly soldiers—Victor Stiebel, the dress designer; Rowland Hilder, the landscape artist; and James Gardiner, later designer for the Festival of Britain, were all at the Castle. So was Powell Perry, who had his own printing firm; he was a corporal telephonist (orange shirt under the battledress tunic, feet on the table, a long cigar; should the officers salute him, they wondered?). It was

Powell Perry who gave seventeen-year-old Pauline Baynes her first commission in illustrating, a book called *Question Mark* for a children's paperback series he was planning. *Question Mark* has been eaten away by mice, but I saw some other books in the series, rather like the now almost extinct non-fiction Puffin Picture Books, all illustrated by the Farnham Castle alumni.

When the authorities began to weed out *dilettanti*, Pauline was hauled away from Farnham to the Admiralty in Bath where she worked enormously hard at the fine art of drawing charts all day—and went home at night to fulfil the small commissions for illustrating that at eighteen were already coming her way, largely as a result of her admiration for other people's efforts. She used to write fan letters to authors like Ernest Raymond and Horace Annesley Vachell. One day she wrote to Harry Price of 'Borley Rectory' ghost-story fame, and in the margin she drew a picture of a little Elizabethan ghost hanging up on a nail. Price, lunching at the Reform Club, showed the 'amusing picture' to Frank Whitaker of Country Life, who seized on it—and its creator: she was promptly asked to illustrate three children's books by Victoria Stephenson which he had just decided to publish. 'Nothing,' Pauline says of these illustrations, 'could be worse drawn. I'd never had a training and hadn't the faintest idea where one bone stopped and another started.'

Because Pauline Baynes is in no sense a *grande dame* I irreverently suggested here that maybe this was the reason she was so attracted to the medieval period; knightly armour, monkish habit and a maiden's flowing robe could cover a multitude of anatomical sins, could they not? But it was instantly clear that Pauline's love affair with the Middle Ages was nothing so frivolous. 'Do you believe in reincarnation?' she asked. 'I feel so at home in medieval times I really think I was pottering about in those days doing something or other. Perhaps I was a medieval dog, because I'm besotted with dogs.' She is also besotted with medieval painting, especially the work of Bosch and Memling; a fanciful thought, but could that wise little dog in the foreground of the Van Eyck *Arnolfini and his Wife* have been our artist in a pre-Pauline existence? Is that where she learned to paint miniatures like those of the early Renaissance painters? (Her only exhibit in the Royal Academy—'I like to do everything once, I never tried again'—was a miniature portrait of a man in a Tank Corps beret painted on plaster; because of some impurities in the material it began to erupt in spots after a time 'and the poor chap looked as though he had impetigo'.)

For all her light-hearted anecdotes and insistence that she is 'not a genius—just extremely hard-working, which is a bore', Pauline Baynes is a most gifted illustrator with a serious philosophy about her craft. In her view the illustrator is in the service of the author always, and she considers it to be bad manners for an artist to use a book as a vehicle for his own self-expression. The style must be dictated by the text, and the artist should approach each piece of illustration without any preconceived ideas.

In looking at her work one can see that she abides by her own rules. Much of it is in the medieval style: books like Grant Uden's *A Dictionary of Chivalry* and Jennifer Westwood's *Medieval Tales* are illustrated with fine marginal drawings and (in the former) paintings of jewel-like brilliance; the occasional thumb-nail landscapes, with their receding perspective, put one in mind of Bellini. It is not Pauline Baynes's fault that she has become recognized as supreme mistress of the margin, and is therefore sought after by publishers as illustrator for any relevant manuscript that comes along. But given a manuscript of an entirely different nature, she will immerse herself in it and produce a set of illustrations, a jacket or maps which match the author's work and become, for all time, an integral part of the text for young (or older) readers.

That she should be for ever associated with two mid-twentieth-century classics is no accident. When C. S. Lewis and J. R. R. Tolkien, both Oxford professors, wrote their famous fantasies—the 'Narnia' chronicles and *The Lord of the Rings* respectively—it was Pauline Baynes who was asked to illustrate *The Lion, the Witch and the Wardrobe* and its sequels, and provide box-cover and maps for the three-volume edition of *The Lord of the Rings*. She says that neither Lewis nor Tolkien was the slightest bit concerned about the physical look of his books. On one occasion C. S. Lewis met her for lunch at the Charing Cross Hotel, but was determined not to let a small matter like illustration make him miss his train. With the Tolkiens she and Fritz became very friendly (a rare triumph, lightly taken) but J. R. R. would wave away her jacket design or maps for *The Lord of the Rings*, pick up a bottle of Moselle and say 'Now Fritz, about this wine, what do you think?' So if Hobbitomanes find inaccuracies in some of the maps of Middle Earth, the fault is not entirely that of the painstaking artist.

Despite this apparent lack of interest in the 'whole book', both Tolkien and Lewis cared deeply about the literary aspect. Though based on stories told to his own children, Tolkien's *The Lord of the Rings* was not written for children; it is a major work of imaginative fiction which has been adopted by children in the way folklore also is. But C. S. Lewis was conscious of projecting his view of the world in a form children could assimilate and therefore thought the stories needed 'childlike' illustration. Looking at the pictures she drew for *The Lion, the Witch and the Wardrobe* nearly twenty-five years ago, Pauline Baynes sighs and says how much she would like to redraw them now. But could she better the drawing of Mr Tumnus in his armchair or the marvellous detail of Mr and Mrs Beaver's kitchen? For those of us to whom her vision and the Lewis text are one, she could not.

Pauline Baynes is a versatile and scholarly illustrator. Her illustrations for *Medieval Tales* could have come from one of those block books which were the precursors of Caxton's movable type; her head and tail pieces for Alison Uttley's *Recipes from an Old Farmhouse* might belong to the Bewick-Hassall tradition of wood-engraving (though they are, in fact, fine pen-and-ink drawings); her careful botanical and zoological paintings for Helen Piers's *The Snail and the Caterpillar* (Pauline's picture book, published last year) are those of an observant naturalist. But her most distinguished work descends directly from the monastic scriptorium where monks took immense care over the petals of a flower, the legs of an insect, a paved courtyard, a glove, a hawk—and planned the margins of their vellum manuscripts with the same infinite reverence and joy that readers detect as they marvel at the detail in *A Dictionary of Chivalry*.

Signal, 1973

RICHARD SCARRY
BOOKS ARE FUN

Richard Scarry's comic-style picture books with their thousands of little pictures of animals dressed as humans doing a day's work in town, in village, by the sea, are world-famous. Many critics think them too commonplace for serious consideration—but when Scarry, an American who lives in Switzerland, came to London I could not resist the invitation to meet the man who has made books fun for so many children.

'Books are fun!' These three words, stretched out along a pink streamer flying in the wind behind Wrong Way Roger's red aeroplane (on the back cover of Richard Scarry's *What Do People Do All Day?*) are Scarry's slogan.

Also on the back cover of *What Do People Do All Day?* there's a conventional sun and a red-brick school with a window through which you can see a rabbit teaching a cat and a goat to read, whilst another cat hurries in through the door and yet a third hovers round the side on his tricycle wondering whether he's just too late to go in. Next to the school you'll find a library with the lamp of learning emblazoned on it above the word VERITAS ('What's veritas, Mum?'); the public library sign is in the form of a book hung out on a wrought-iron frame over a street where a pig road-sweeper pushes his cart out of the way to make room for a red fire-engine, the hose of which has somehow extended itself vertically; clutching the nozzle of that hose for dear life in yellow mid-sky is a blue-suited fireman pig whose red hat is floating away over a half-timbered house at the other side of the street.

Covers of books, as Richard Scarry explained to me, have to be relatively simple.

And if you open the book—it's impossible not to—a glance at a page will show you at once that he wasn't joking.

Every page of a Scarry book is crammed to capacity with animals dressed like human beings busily engaged in human activities, with words (not just text, but labels too), with fun and with good sense. Yet every page is carefully planned, every drawing absolutely clear, every character consistent, every piece of advice—'FINISH YOUR MEALS', 'TRY TO BE GOOD'—the kind most parents would applaud.

Scarry is popular. Kids clamour for him because he gives them what they want: pictures, activity, words, humour—and information aplenty. How fortunate that an artist with the supreme ability to entertain is also a man who takes his work seriously: he cares about children, not in the sentimental way but, as he put it, 'You have to treat a two-year-old child with as much respect as the Queen of England.' His sincerity could never be in doubt, but proof of it is his resistance to the blandishments and dollars of American television companies who want to screen his stories. 'We'd only take an hour of your time to discuss it,' pleaded one network. 'We'd do all the adaptation ourselves.' But Scarry insists, 'I'll spend a lot of time doing my own adaptations when the right moment comes.'

Richard Scarry is a modest man with a proper sense of perspective. Large, bear-like, deep-voiced and in deadly earnest about fun, he has a gusty laugh which wells up from the hollows of his lungs and punctuates his philosophy at the most unexpected moments. Asked whether animal lovers complain about the way he dresses up animals in human clothing, for instance, this great big bear of a man draws up his large paws like bird claws in front of his mouth and takes on the personality of a prissy spinster. In his booming voice he declares, 'They're the same people who come home to their apartments and say to their pets (*high voice*) "Come here tootsie-wootsie, did you have a good day today?" (*booming voice again*) which is also treating animals as humans!' Gusty laugh.

Scarry can afford to laugh. He laughs gently, with a tinge of sadness, at those librarians in the States who are reluctant to stock his books because they are available in the supermarket. What kind of a policy is this? he asks. If kids want to read Scarry and Scarry is not only teaching them to read and to find out about house building, baking, farming, transport, hospitals and the postal service (just a few of the occupations covered in *What Do People Do All Day?*) but also helping them to discover that BOOKS ARE FUN, why *not* put them in libraries?

But being sold in supermarkets as well as bookstores is great. When the U S Treasury cut its grants to libraries a few years back, Scarry sat secure in the supermarkets selling by the score (those last ten words could come from the 'S' 's' page of a Scarry *A B C*) whilst Caldecott Medal winners and the trendy five-dollar picture books (twice the price of his with only thirty-two pages instead of over a hundred) stuck on the bookshop shelves or, worse still, in the publisher's warehouse.

Scarry genuinely believes that the *A B C* with a large beautifully painted apple opposite 'A' 'a' is cheating the child of a huge amount of stimulating entertainment. On the 'A' 'a' page of his own recent *Find Your A B C's*—(specially designed for the new Collins paperback Picture Lions series) there are *a*pples for sure, six of them. But if you're keen on the job of collecting *A*'s and *a*'s—which is what you are asked to do, 'then place them in Sam Cat's sack' so that he can make alphabet soup when you've gathered all the letters through to 'Z' 'z'—you'll find *A*lfred *A*llig*a*tor *a*nd *a*n *a*vi*a*tor in *a*n *a*irpl*a*ne *a*nd *a*n *a*ngry *a*nt with *a*n *a*rrow through his h*a*t, as well. Less elegant than many a beautiful A B C for sure, but Scarry's approach is a skilful adaptation of everyman's approach and therefore deserves, I would have thought, everyman's—and that includes every librarian's—support.

To me Scarry books have a connection with the tradition of the old comics; but Richard Scarry, brought up in the States without *Chick's Own* on Tuesdays or *Rainbow*, which made every Wednesday morning one to be looked forward to, resists attempts to tie him to the comic tradition. He sees comics as mainly for adolescents and adults—loves *Good ol' Charlie Brown*, admires the later *Tintin*, finds *Asterix* sophisticated but too crude for his taste—and thinks *Rupert Bear* the only acceptable strip character for kids.

Why does *he* use animals instead of people in his books? 'I use animals rather than humans firstly because they're more fun and it's easier to distinguish one character from another if one is a rabbit and the other a cat than if both are boys. Also children of all races will identify more easily with a bear or a goat doing this, that or the other, than they will with a child of a different colour. If a black child sees a Japanese child in a picture of a classroom he'll say to himself "That's not me". But if he sees a goat learning to read, the problem of colour and identity just doesn't arise.'

Because all Scarry's books have a joyful, simple atmosphere about them, one might imagine his use of accompanying words to be merely basic. Not at all. Richard Scarry is contemptuous of 'controlled vocabulary' schemes. 'Kids don't talk in controlled vocabulary,' he says. 'Can you think of anything more absurd than a scheme which has "airplane" as one of the words it uses but not "air"? Isn't that nonsense?' What Scarry does is to use the opportunity his pictures offer to introduce the child to as many new words as possible. He uses the right word for each object he draws, and because he draws the object next to the word—or rather puts the word under a drawing of the object—children read it all right. Take the 'Music Making' page in the inimitable *Best Word Book Ever* with the mouse playing the *piccolo*, a bear stretching the *accordion*, pig blowing the *tuba* and pussy plucking the strings of the *harp* whilst the rabbit *conductor* on the *podium* raises his *baton*. New words for some children, of course, but lovely varied words explained pictorially without fuss.

It was in connection with the alphabet page in the middle of the *Best Word Book Ever* that Richard Scarry received an angry letter from a mother complaining that for 'X' he had used the word *Xiphias* next to a picture of a xiphias —a kind of sword-fish— instead of harnessing the letter 'X' to the well-worn, over-played *Xylophone*. It had caused a great stir in her house, she said. No one knew what a xiphias was. They had had to go to a great deal of trouble to find out. Scarry's reaction was characteristic: 'Makes me really happy to think that that woman's kid will go through life till he lives to be ninety or a hundred never forgetting what a xiphias is!' (Again, the infectious laugh.)

The virtue of Scarry books is that children of almost any age look at them absorbed for hours. Very small children look at the pictures—hundreds of them, as many on one page as other artists use in a whole book. Children learning to read puzzle out the labels under the recognizable pictures of objects—'Sand', 'car', 'rake', 'drum', 'socks'. Older children read the text and follow the marvellous diagrams which show how paper is made, the parts of a ship, what happens when you post a letter—or they read the hilarious *Funniest Story Book Ever* to their younger brothers and sisters, enjoying every word of it themselves.

Totally unpretentious, bubbling with humour, alive with activity, peppered with words of wisdom and corny jokes ('All kids go through a corny joke stage,' says Richard, 'so I put in a few here and there'), Scarry books are a marvellous combination of entertainment, always on a child's level, and incidental instruction. They occupy a unique place in the learning-to-read process. Their bulky, ebullient presence in supermarket, bookshop, library and sitting-room (every floor should have one) indicate that for children Scarry is supreme and that he is getting his message across good and strong. BOOKS ARE FUN!

Signal, 1974

QUENTIN BLAKE
HUMOUR IS A SERIOUS BUSINESS

Quentin Blake, Professor of Illustration at the Royal College of Art, is quite prepared to go down on his knees among children and, on a roll of wall-lining paper stretched across the floor, draw a black outline of a long, long monster carrying assorted passengers on its back. His wide-eyed audience then colours it in. He had nobly supported the 'Children's Books of the Year' exhibition many times in this fashion. In 1975 he designed our poster for us—and agreed to talk to me about his view of his work.

When I suggested to Quentin Blake that the purpose of my visiting him in his large, rambling, book-filled flat off the Old Brompton Road in London was to discuss the serious contribution of the humorist to children's illustration, he laughed, kindly: and the glint in his eye told me that a cartoon was bubbling up inside him. For the absurdity of sitting down to discuss such a topic with straight faces instead of feasting merrily on Quentin's books and drawings which were playing hide-and-seek with one another on the shelves and stacked against the walls, was instantly apparent to us both.

But Quentin Blake is gentle, unassuming and accommodating. So he sat and talked politely and seriously about humour, his brown eyes alight with intelligence, his small white hands—deprived of pencil and paper for once—constantly moving to help him express his ideas in words instead of, as is more natural to him, in line.

Ever since he was a schoolboy in suburban Sidcup (he grew up with the suburb in the thirties, the school being for him a cultural oasis in a philistine desert) he had wanted to draw. His career as a cartoonist began, indeed, on the backs of exercise books. But the cartoons soon took a balletic leap straight into the pages of *Punch*, which was paying Quentin seven pounds each for illustrated jokes before he was out of the sixth form. Didn't this make him something of a hero? He shrugs off the idea. Did it bring his parents round to support his leanings towards a career in humorous art? No, because, quite understandably, they wanted security for him, 'something like banking or teaching'.

For Quentin shone in other ways, though he is rather careful not to say this. He suggests, modestly, that it was the good teaching of his English master, J. H. Walsh (of *Roundabout by the Sea* fame) that 'got him in' to Downing College, Cambridge, where he took an English degree, going on to the Institute of Education in London for a year's teacher training. Then, fully fledged as a graduate English teacher, he decided *not* to teach. 'If I start doing it I might like it, I thought'—so at last he turned his attention, seriously, to humorous art.

If you think making cartoons for *Punch* is a light-hearted, easy occupation for an artist, Quentin will quickly disabuse you of the notion. He discovered, when he began to indulge in his passion full-time, that 'you spend hours thinking up jokes with great labour; so many ideas are funny but not visual. It's a gruelling business and most of the while you are not drawing, which was what I really wanted to be doing.'

So, still maintaining the *Punch* contact, he decided he 'should get a bit of art training'. He sought out Brian Robb, painter, illustrator, cartoonist and lecturer at Chelsea, who advised him on what part-time courses to take. 'Don't come to mine on illustration!' he said. Thus began a lifelong friendship and professional association, for Quentin now teaches in Brian Robb's illustration department at the Royal College of Art.

Strangely enough, it was Quentin Blake's covers for the *Spectator*—'it was like being in repertory, playing a different role each week'—that finally brought him into the children's book field. John Ryder, collecting material about children's book illustrators for *Artists of a Certain Line* in the early sixties, asked Quentin for a contribution, having seen his cover illustration for a *Spectator* children's book number. Quentin, with characteristic honesty, said he 'wasn't a children's book illustrator but would very much like to be'. And quickly he set about becoming one by providing a set of line illustrations to a book of stories called *A Drink of Water* by his friend John Yeoman.

Although keen on becoming an illustrator for children, Quentin was determined not to allow a new market to compromise his established style of drawing. 'If they like it, I'll do it. If they don't, I'll give up.' 'They' (meaning, I suppose, publishers, reviewers and above all children) did like it; and, crowned as he now is by the Whitbread Award (1974) for his illustrations to Russell Hoban's *How Tom Beat Captain Najork and his Hired Sportsmen*, he is unlikely to be allowed to give up.

Quentin Blake is sometimes author as well as artist, producing the texts for his own picture books, but he insists that he is not essentially a writer and that *Patrick, Jack and Nancy, Angelo* and *Snuff* were thought of first in terms of pictures 'with bits written in underneath afterwards'. He starts with a notion of the kind of pictures he'd like to make—music's visual kaleidoscope (*Patrick*), a tightrope and some *commedia dell' arte* characters (*Angelo*)—and then extends them gradually to make a story. He is delighted that Weston Woods has produced an animated film of *Patrick* with no words—just a violin accompaniment.

Quentin Blake enjoys making picture books on his own, but he also finds it stimulating to collaborate with an author, whose text must be matched, in its humour, by his illustrations. Almost always the text comes first, presenting to Quentin the problems he enjoys solving. For he believes that these invoke his ingenuity and stretch his powers so that the resulting piece of illustration is altogether better than it would have been, had the problems inherent in the text not existed.

When John Yeoman showed him the text for *Sixes and Sevens*, for instance, Quentin recognized it at once as an ingenious counting book, potentially full of interest. But how could he turn a deliberately repetitive text—about a boy poling a raft up river 'from here to Limber Lea' and picking up 1 kitten, 2 mice, 3 school-mistresses, etc., at successive landing stages—into a picture book in which each opening challenged the eye and mind? Anyone who knows the book will remember with joy Quentin's triumph. The scene changes, the weather changes, and each new addition to the raft's steadily increasing load causes its own special chaos. Although Quentin Blake speaks with mild affront at an author's temerity in writing about 'hundreds' of mice—John Yeoman's *Mouse Trouble*—one feels that he was secretly delighted at the prospect of having to draw them. Indeed, one of his most inspired illustrations is a double page showing 'hundreds of mice' in the old mill having a marvellous time 'using the great millstone as a roundabout . . . balancing on the turning beams . . . and sliding down the grain chutes'.

These books are pure fun. *Captain Najork* is an altogether more sophisticated collaboration between an established fantasist, Russell Hoban, and perhaps the only illustrator who could have given visual form to his text without underplaying or overplaying the absurdity. When Cape sent Quentin the manuscript of this story, along with two others, he instantly chose *Captain Najork* and couldn't wait to get his hands on it. Instead of the sample drawing the publisher asked for, he supplied quick, rough sketches for the whole book, developing the characters as he went along. 'Russell Hoban apparently said "OK, let him do it" and I did it in a way I've never worked before: I didn't show the book to anyone till it was finished. The story is so positive and complete and structured that a meeting with Russell Hoban would have been irrelevant. The vibrations were so strong that I needed nothing more. So I worked and worked and then turned up at Cape saying, "Here it is!"'

The text of *Captain Najork* is comparatively long for a picture book, and it was Quentin's admiration for it as a distinguished piece of humorous literature, his sensitivity as a reader, that enabled him to match it with his illustrations. In discussing the problems it threw in his path his whole philosophy of illustration became manifest. The story is about a 'fooling-around' boy, Tom, whose aunt, Aunt Fidget Wonkham-Strong, sends for the disciplinarian Captain Najork and his four hired red-striped sportsmen to beat the 'sportive infant' at what turn out to be merely complicated variations of Tom's personal 'fooling-around' games. So Tom, of course, manages to out-womble, out-muck and out-sneedball the lot of them. 'The games had to look plausible,' says Quentin, 'without me trying to show exactly how they worked. Sneedball sounds terribly convincing—a marvellous word. So you mustn't ruin the author's joke by making the illustration too specific. You leave a bit to the reader's imagination, the least you can do that enables them to see the joke the better. Then there was the weight and balance of every sentence and paragraph of Hoban's: you could only break the text at certain points without damaging this, but accepting the challenge, which meant rearranging the design of the pages very often, is an example of how overcoming difficulties can actually improve illustration.'

Quentin Blake is not only a picture-book artist. His line drawings enliven the text of many a novel for children, notably the *Agaton Sax* detective stories and the *Uncle* saga. 'Illustrating someone else's novel is like acting in a play—or producing it,' he says. 'You give visual form to a host of characters.' Certainly the huge cast of the *Uncle* books owes an enormous debt to his illustrator; so does many an author whose novel has been given the humorous trade-mark of a Blake jacket.

Just occasionally, as with *Mind Your Own Business*, Michael Rosen's profile of a boy in a series of poems, one feels that Quentin Blake is more than an illustrator: he is the genius who turns a difficult manuscript into a thoroughly acceptable and beckoning book. 'Some of the poems were light and amusing, some more serious, some quite complicated. Where pictures would have interfered with the effect of the poems, I kept off illustrating altogether. *Illustrating, as an activity distinct from drawing, demands a sense of what you simply mustn't do.*'

Quentin Blake was by now being very serious indeed about humorous drawing, about the way he solves layout problems and shape problems before doing the finished black-and-white sketches of the people who skip and prance and almost fly sometimes across the pages of, say, *The Armada Lion Book of Verse* or *The Puffin Joke Book*—just two of the many anthologies he has enlivened. It is this implied sense of movement in his drawings (he admires inordinately the serial drawings of Caran d'Ache, who could imply a train passing a field by making four consecutive drawings of a cow with her head and eyes moving to follow its imaginary passage) that makes him wary of embarking on cartoon film. For in cartoon film you make movement *actually* happen; so movement by *implication* loses its power. Blake's stills (if one can call anything he draws a 'still') for Jackanory's presentation of Rosemary Manning's *Dragon in Danger* and Joan Aiken's *Tales of Arabel's Raven* seemed to me far more effective than any cartoon film could have been.

But Quentin is interested in film, particularly in the work of Jacques Tati, whose humour depends so often on a way of looking at otherwise quite ordinary things in special juxtaposition. 'Many people who in Renaissance times would have been painters are today working in theatre or films.'

Illustration pulls influences in from the general art world—from drama as well as from painting. Quentin Blake admires those painters of the past (it's going out of fashion now) whose pictures were almost one-act plays. He speaks with warmth about Tintoretto and Goya and with passion about Daumier who, through his sense of form and the strength of his line, can emphasize the relationships between the people he draws. 'The captions were often written by other people. The jokes in themselves might be feeble, but the humour and drama were there in the pictures.'

It is the abundant humour and light drama in Quentin Blake's pictures that children instantly respond to. Though professing to know very little about children ('I haven't got any, you know,' he says cheerfully) one has only to see him submerged by the clamouring young when he agrees to draw for them at a book exhibition to know that his rapport with them is natural. 'I never think of myself as an adult and ask "what do *they* want?" It's more a feeling of being a child with them.'

Signal, 1975

RAYMOND BRIGGS
BRITISH ATTITUDES TO STRIP CARTOON

Picture books for children do not usually produce uproar and outrage. Raymond Briggs's 'Fungus the Bogeyman', an alternative view of human behaviour and aspirations, did just that. Could this really be a picture book for young children? some asked. Others, like me, began to ask a different question. Why should picture books be thought to be only for the very young? If adults were entitled to enjoy political or social comment in strip cartoon, why should older children be denied the pleasure?

'Gosh, boy! Is that all you want to do?' These were the words with which the Principal of Wimbledon College of Art greeted the fifteen-year-old Raymond Briggs when he said that his ambition, indeed his reason for applying for a place at the college, was that he wished to tell stories in strip cartoon. 'Thirty years later,' says Raymond, 'I'm doing just that. Golly' (he talks like his own Father Christmas sometimes), 'it's funny when you think of it.'

Raymond Briggs is a gentle, considerate man, who says quite candidly that he knows hardly anything about children; he was an only child and is now a childless widower. If his cartoon stories give pleasure to readers of any age, he's happy: 'Ten-year-olds at your school like *Fungus*, do they? Gosh. Yes. Good.' That he has pierced a rich vein of storytelling that spans young and old is, he would have us believe, more luck than good judgement.

Success in his chosen art form was a long time coming. Four years at Wimbledon studying Renaissance painting: 'Fifteen-year-olds trying to be Piero della Francesca. We thought we were revolutionary liking the Impressionists, but we were out of date.' Then two years in the army followed by two at the Slade. The Slade is the home of pure painting, and it was here that Raymond Briggs's talent for painting scenes from the imagination and making them realistic was recognized for what it was. 'You are,' they said, 'illustrator's "colour"'—and that, Raymond explains, was a term of abuse.

After a few commissions for newspapers, book jackets and advertising Raymond Briggs found himself getting work for children's book publishers, mostly line drawing for series like the early 'Gazelles' and 'Antelopes'. He thought the texts fairly mundane so wrote two himself—*Strange House* and *Midnight Adventure*—both of which, to his utter amazement, were accepted.

People are important to Raymond Briggs in his working life. One big factor in his decision to abandon advertising for children's books was that Richard Hough, and later Julia MacRae, at Hamish Hamilton, together with Alice Torrey of Coward McCann in New York (who had a huge influence on Briggs's development as a young illustrator), were so much more receptive to an artist's thinking. They were also less overtly commercial and more patient than the ad agencies. 'None of this Omo performance: "Draw a housewife at the sink. Don't make her too old/young, too middle class/too working class and bring it in tomorrow . . ." And the day after it appears, it's thrown away.'

Durability and a large public both appeal to Raymond. As a pure painter he would have reached only a few *cognoscenti*; he has no urge to paint the stretch of Sussex countryside outside his studio window, but it undoubtedly inspires him as he works. He is a passionate conservationist and remarked bitterly, when talking of Brighton where he now teaches young students, that local councils have destroyed more fine buildings since 1945 than the Nazis destroyed in this country during World War II. ('Bloomin' shame!')

When he speaks of his students he is rather gloomy. Colour and photo-realism are all the rage now, and few of them want to work in line. 'If you ask them to do more than three pieces of work for the illustration of a story, they have a fit. If you asked for forty-five drawings, they'd think you were mad.' So where will the narrative illustrators in the tradition of Shepard and Ardizzone come from?

Maybe the tradition is dying, or is being translated, by artists like Raymond Briggs, into storytelling through pictures rather than illustrated word narrative. It is too early yet to see the developments of our own time in perspective, but one day the succession in the genre may be traced from the Ardizzone picture books with their thread of bubble talk as counterpoint to the narrative, through the Briggs strip-cartoon storybooks, to the Ahlbergs' *Brick Street Boys*, Mark Kahn's *It's a Dog's Life* and beyond.

Raymond Briggs himself was, he would now agree, prepared

for his pioneer work in strip-cartoon picture books in England, by the demands for bumper-sized books with hundreds of pictures for the American market. Alice Torrey spotted his unusual talent but rejected his plan to use a single nursery rhyme and turn it into what he calls the 'Caldecott kind of thing', illustrating almost every line of the verse on a different page. She persuaded him, with Hamish Hamilton in support, to embark on the huge *Mother Goose Treasury*, for which he used the same technique of copious illustration for each rhyme, and painted no less than 897 pictures —a fact he probably keeps hidden from his students, who might otherwise apply to him the verdict he passes on that Principal at Wimbledon who dismissed cartoon as worthless: 'a dear old bloke, but crackers'.

Raymond Briggs began illustrating nursery rhymes not because they were for children but because they were 'quite rude, quite tough, adult gutsy material about money and marriage and work and laziness and theft—not sweet innocent pink and blue baby stuff'. In this reaction he confirms all the Opies' research into nursery rhymes; it was, in fact, their texts of the rhymes that were used in *The Mother Goose Treasury*. Certainly the Briggs illustrations are mostly of adults behaving childishly (as adults often do). Children therefore love them. 'Do they? That's good,' is Raymond's comment.

It sounds detached, and is, in a way. But he does care that his *Mother Goose Treasury* and *Fairy Tale Treasury* (fairy tales selected and retold by Virginia Haviland) have brought pleasure to so many families around the world. He cares, but regards it as a happy accident.

What he is very serious about is strip cartoon as narrative and the snobbery of the English in refusing to recognize it as an art form—a minor art form—worthy of considered criticism. With the *Father Christmas* books, *Fungus the Bogeyman* and *The Snowman* to his credit (and to his publisher's, for the books were not easy to launch in a market where one head teacher spoke for the multitude when he wrote, 'These are not books at all, *merely* strip cartoons'), Raymond Briggs is in a position to attack the prevailing critical silence, which his sales figures challenge.

'If anything becomes part of the folk culture of an age, you can't just pretend it's a lot of rubbish,' says Raymond Briggs, referring not to *Father Christmas* or *Fungus* (he is too modest for that) but to Rupert, Peanuts, Tintin, Asterix. He is an inordinate admirer of the early Rupert—'fantastic drawing and marvellous composition'—loves Peanuts, finds Tintin frames remarkably well organized but the text a bit banal, whereas the Asterix texts are full of verbal wit but the frames 'so tortuous that I can hardly bear to "read" them'.

The word 'read' applied to pictures is interesting, for children do read pictures in the way Raymond's remarks suggest that he does (and in the way illiterate peasants 'read' the frescoes of the Italian Renaissance so beloved by that Wimbledon Principal). In the latest Briggs picture book, *The Snowman*, there are no words at all, but the poignancy of the story—silent like snow—is none the less sharp.

Raymond Briggs really combines in *Father Christmas* and in *Fungus the Bogeyman* two art forms that the British see as separate. *Father Christmas* won the Kate Greenaway Medal but, says Raymond with feeling, it was given to him for the artwork alone, since no one seems to see people like himself and John Burningham as storymakers in the way novelists are, but storymakers spanning two media. Of course the Kate Greenaway is an illustrator's award, but Raymond Briggs found it significant of the prevailing attitude towards art that, as he put it, 'Even when I was getting the blessed Medal, the lady giving it said [passing on to the Carnegie winner, Penelope Lively] "We now come to the *senior* of the two Awards".'

In this Raymond sees a hangover from medieval cultural snobbery, which regarded the painter as a craftsman because he got his hands dirty, and the writer as a superior being, an intellectual, a scholar who kept himself clean. 'Fungus, and the Snowman?' I asked. 'Perhaps . . . mm . . . Perhaps,' said Raymond.

Certainly Fungus represents the dirt in everyone's daily life, something we all have to cope with but don't talk about. Why not bring dandruff into the open (shampoo advertisements on TV do just this)? Why not celebrate our victory over toenails that grow, sweat that we can't control (remember those TV ads for antiperspirants) and the other petty nastinesses that most of us (including Raymond, whose studio is like a new pin) confine to the bathroom or the dustbin?

Raymond thought *Fungus the Bogeyman* would really appeal to dropouts—'rather grubby, rather lazy anti-establishment intellectuals, messing about hitch-hiking round the world with their guitars.' It does. But it has also caught the imagination of the latent adolescent, of all ages, because it dares to challenge the standards not of decent behaviour (Fungus is a model citizen) but of subjects that can be decently discussed. Eleven-year-old sniggers are now open laughs. A healthy 'surface' development? Or an invasion by an adult of the bogeyworld that properly belongs to the eleven-year-old?

The dictionary was a happy hunting-ground for Bogey words and ideas, and Briggs found himself reading one from end to end; then, not fully satisfied, he went out and bought the two-volume *Shorter Oxford*. Bogeyology became an obsession and it now fills a whole drawer in his filing cabinet. About a third of it was used in *Fungus*, the rest is stored away for future use.

'But the point about Fungus,' says his creator, 'is that, like all of us, he wonders what he's alive for. *Fungus the Bogeyman* is about his search for a role.'

At this point I asked, 'Do you think of Fungus as a sad character?'

RB: Yes. Very sad, yes.

EM: Is he real? Does he represent something in all of us?

RB: I'm noticing all my characters now are sad old men or, rather, sad middle-aged men, which is what I am probably. [Laughter] Life is sad really but there's always love, which makes life worth living. Fungus has a loving relationship with his wife, which makes it bearable.

EM: Do you think failure is sadder than success?

RB: I've been terribly lucky.

EM: Has it made you happier?

RB: No, I don't think so. But I don't know what I'd have been like without it. I might have been miserable and embittered like I was at the Slade when I recognized that I was a rotten painter . . . Only about a handful of my students will make a real success of anything . . . We are educating people beyond their own capacity for fulfilment, which I think is very sad . . .

Of course Raymond Briggs is not a 'rotten painter' as anyone who looks at the frames in *Father Christmas*, for example, will discover. The problem is that, critically, very little attention is focused on 'mere' cartoons in England.

Sadly Raymond goes to his studio and brings back into the living room huge tomes of criticism from France, Italy or Germany—where magazines like *Phenix, Linus, Alter Alter* flourish—to demonstrate that in other countries cartoon strips are taken as seriously as films, radio plays or light novels; here they are thought of 'as a low form of life equivalent to the daily tabloids'. A pity.

SHIRLEY HUGHES
'WHERE'S THA COLOURS?'

I was already fired with the idea of picture books for older readers and had begun using them in Fleet Primary School (see p. 124) when Shirley Hughes produced 'Up and Up', a wordless two-colour cartoon story. That prompted me to go and talk to her about the changing face of children's book illustration and her view of the importance of picture books in the lives of children of all ages.

Shirley Hughes, whose warm, untidy line drawings of babies in push-chairs, toddlers in steamy kitchens, children in park playgrounds complement her own and other people's stories, is an anachronism as an illustrator in the 1980s. But, paradoxically, she is a woman of our time, deeply conscious of the needs of young children in a world that does too much for them in the area of televisual presentation, too little in parental companionship.

She is an anachronism as an illustrator because, since the Post Impressionists, there has been (in Shirley Hughes's own words) 'a flight from the study of the human form' which has affected illustrators as well as painters. Industrial data have become the mainspring of art; but narrative illustration demands line drawing —and line drawing of people. For in Shirley Hughes's view the story is the vital element in a picture book and stories are about people, about things that happen to them and how they behave. If you have an eye to the international market you anthropomorphize animal characters (Shirley Hughes doesn't) and use as your setting a never-never land (Shirley Hughes uses her own back garden). You also splash colour around. ('Lead me away from oil paints,' says Shirley Hughes, though she does, in most of her more recent picture books, use tempera.)

It was in Rochdale, during one of the many sessions she generously gives to children's book fairs, that, having drawn with her thick black felt pen for hours to entertain the crowds that watch her at work, she stopped for a moment and said, 'Now, any questions?'

'Yes, miss,' came the prompt reply. 'Where's tha colours?'

Shirley Hughes tells this story knowing that, accidentally, that boy had hit on the key to her work as an illustrator. But she firmly rejects the equations in children's book production that theorists would like to live by:

little children = colour picture books;
slightly older children = line drawings at the rate of a full page and two half-pages per chapter;
older children = no pictures at all.

'This,' says Shirley Hughes, 'is total nonsense. What they all need is a good nourishing mix.' She cites Joan Hassall's tiny wood engravings (black and white, of course) for the *Oxford Book of Nursery Rhymes*, to which one of her own children, as a toddler, became addicted.

Which comes first, the story or the pictures? If you are illustrating other people's texts, as Shirley Hughes has illustrated Dorothy Edwards's, the Corrins' collections of stories, and countless others, then the words are already there and you, the illustrator, stand in relation to them as a producer does to the script of a play. 'You must give the story visual form, a style of its own; you must point up jokes, accentuate drama, set the scene. You must make empathy with the text.'

Does Shirley Hughes think that, ideally, author and artist should be the same person? Yes, on the whole she does because the work will have greater unity. 'But Quentin Blake and Russell Hoban, Edward Ardizzone and James Reeves are outstanding examples of fortuitous combination brought about by perspicacious publishers.'

'If you think in pictures as I do,' she says, 'all your stories are like silent movies. You fill in your own background and conceive the thing as a whole from the first idea you have. It [the picture-book story] is bound to be easier for the artist.' When I suggested tentatively that in her picture books her text was, perhaps, the illustration of her artwork, she readily agreed. 'Yes, they are two totally different mental processes.'

As with Raymond Briggs*, it became obvious that Shirley Hughes considered it a challenge to work as an illustrator in a society that treats the author with more respect than the artist. She spoke of the superiority in design of technical and adult educational publications in some countries, like Italy, where literacy among workers cannot be taken for granted. In Britain it cannot be taken for granted either, but because we consider ourselves to be a literate society we make very little effort when it comes to designing functional material. This is what the study of graphics is all about. This is where students will find work. This is where the emphasis now is in art school courses. Rightly, says Shirley Hughes (who teaches illustration but knows there will be little work for many of her students in pure narrative art).

Although Shirley Hughes is the absolute antithesis of the calculating researcher who will supply on demand a product to fill a need, she is an acute and sympathetic observer of modern social conditions and of the young child's place within them. 'You have only to look at a child, and designs for picture books suggest themselves. Once one might have thought automatically in terms of a lap, a book, an infant. Now you know that all too often the lap isn't there. Instead the child looking at a picture book will be part of a group, with the adult sitting on the floor showing large pictures. The pictures must be clear, in this kind of book—which doesn't mean you can't have lots of detail for the time when children can look closely at the pages on their own. This stimulus of the visual sense is tremendously important, and if it cannot be on a one-to-one basis, then we must make sure it is possible in groups.'

Although Shirley Hughes had plenty to say about picture books for all, about librarians' recognition of the more sophisticated

* See aforegoing article.

picture book and the problems of shelving it in the relevant places, about the tolerance one should extend to publicists who alert people to picture books that have an adult appeal, she did sound a word of warning. Children can and do, on occasions, read adult literature that is potentially harmful to the immature; but that problem is as nothing compared to the possibility of young children seeing disturbing pictures that instantly impress themselves deeply on the mind: she spoke of a picture book, from Pierrot, based on the SF stories of Brian Aldiss, which shows horrific pictures of mutants. Fantasy always attracts artists because the imagination is freed from the confines of reality.

While Shirley Hughes herself enjoys illustrating fairy tales and legends, she is passionately concerned with little children and the 'famine' of books for them. *Lucy and Tom's Day, Moving Molly, Dogger, Helpers* are about the simple everyday things that make up toddlers' lives—but that artists today don't want to tackle. Even humour, which bubbles over in Shirley Hughes's conversation, can only be implicit in the situations she illustrates because a young child's view of the world has to be solid before it can be safely put on a banana skin.

Everyday life, of course, need not be the everyday life of the 1980s. Many artists try to re-create the child's daily round in days gone by; but in doing so many of them slip into what Shirley Hughes calls 'romantic archaism'. She talks of John Goodall, Kate Greenaway, Satomi Ichikawa, all of whom withdraw from their particular 'present' into an idealized past, 'which wasn't at all like that for the child who actually lived in it'.

But now, with *Up and Up*, Shirley Hughes has allowed herself a flight away from realism, away from the eighties and into humour and fantasy, in boxes. *Up and Up* is told in cartoon strip without words and without (except for a background tone to the boxes which 'warms the page') colour. It didn't just happen. Shirley Hughes 'took ages discovering the limitations and experimenting with the possibilities' of this, for her, new storytelling medium. And when, months later, she had her story 'boxed', its metamorphosis into the picture book that is selling 'like hot cakes' all over the world (no translation involved, of course) was the result of long deliberation and 'a meticulous exercise in combination of thought' between Shirley Hughes, Judy Taylor (her editor at The

Bodley Head) and the eminent designer, John Ryder.

Up and Up is a fantasy about a little girl who longed to fly, decided that the reason birds could fly was that they came out of eggs, ate her way out of a huge chocolate Easter egg conveniently delivered by the postman—and became airborne. Parents, a motley queue at a bus stop, her school friends and an inventor with his own gas balloon all join in what they consider to be a rescue operation. But the little girl sails and loops over town and countryside, deflating (literally—or, rather, visually) every attempt to bring her down to earth, until *she* is ready.

'Putting the story into boxes was absolutely mind-blowing,' says Shirley Hughes. 'It has such an enormous effect on your design because you are presenting things in a completely different, almost filmic, way and you have to manage without so much of the detail and text that you would put into a double-page spread in a conventional picture book. Having to simplify is exciting, but having to do without words (I was identifying with the child to whom printed words on a page mean nothing) was a tremendous challenge. It made me realize how important words are, particularly dialogue. In an ordinary picture book, even if the text is slight it carries the storyline. But in wordless cartoon the line drawings must not only do this, but also show clearly each character's reaction, by his or her facial expression, to what is happening. I learnt a lot about the combination of words and pictures by not having words.'

Up and Up is like a silent movie. The 'reader'—and Shirley Hughes uses that word, conscious of its print association, advisedly—must work hard visually to extract from it the full sensation of flight, and the mounting humour of the story. Children, she says, read cartoons (even those like Tintin and Asterix, with their complicated dialogue balloons) very fast and very accurately. She is glad they respond to *Up and Up* verbally—by telling the story and even putting into it their own personal variants—but what she is most concerned to stimulate is the eye of the beholder.

'In animated film everything is done for the viewer; but in cartoon-strip it is the eye of the beholder that itself provides the animation. The images are still, but if you are sufficiently cunning you can make people see movement. You are using imagery in a way that stimulates visual imagination and that is crucially important, because other media tend to make children passive about images.'

Far from decrying television Shirley Hughes commends it as a medium for helping people look at nature in close-up and at architecture. Could photographs have achieved the vertiginous perspectives she has drawn so meticulously in *Up and Up*?

'No,' says Shirley Hughes, 'because my perspectives are rigged—rigged to give the reader a dizzying sense of height, or of flying right into the book.' There is one page, for instance, on which two tall frames stand side by side. In the left-hand frame the balloonist and the little flying girl are just above the roof tops, and the pursuing crowd gesticulates below. In the right-hand frame the two main characters have soared skywards, the scene below therefore extending to the countryside around the town; but the crowd, now seen from a great height, is still composed of identifiable, if tiny, people. (We have, earlier on, had a good look at them as they queued at the bus stop, sat at the breakfast table or did sums at school.) So the eye is constantly busy seeing. And the artist helps, not just by choosing points of view, but by exaggerating the perspectives to increase the sensation.

The doublespread at the beginning of *Up and Up* is a bird's-eye view (birds larger than houses) of the town. In it the careful looker will see not only the school, the inventor's house, the balloon and the TV aerial which play such a large part in the story to come but also a little girl (size approximately 3 mm) sitting, rather bored, in a back garden near some cabbages gazing upwards: at the birds. Turn the page—and zoom into frame one: same girl, size 33 mm, in same location.

Not everyone will spend so long on the first double spread, of course. Time, particularly for adults at the pace their world moves, is a scarce commodity. *Up and Up*, however, is primarily for children. They will look, and learn and grow from looking, if the adults around them give them the opportunity and the encouragement. Shirley Hughes has provided a first-rate tool. It is for the rest of us to get on with the job.

Looking back, I can see that once the *Children's Books of the Year* exhibition became a national summer event there was no hope that I could have remained, even had I wanted to, a critic only. In the mid 1970s media people, enticed by the National Book League's publicity girls, first Marilyn Edwards, then Marianna Googan, flocked to the press day with their notebooks and Uher recording machines at the ready. (On one such day I gave no fewer than fourteen mini-interviews!) Being media people they asked the kind of questions about children and reading that most of us would rather not have to answer in thirty seconds flat. Their favourite topics were: sex and violence in teenage reading, why children 'read less nowadays', the influence of television, the so-called high price of children's books, sexism and racism in children's books and so on.

The time had come when I should try to become a commentator on the whole scene; and in order to do that I needed both to stand back from it and take a detached look at certain publishing trends, and also to plunge right in and become active in using books in school, selling them in street market or playground, getting first-hand knowledge of what children's publishing is all about.

The pieces that follow reflect this period of dual experience.

THE ADULT-ERATION OF CHILDREN'S BOOKS

In November 1973 the Children's Book Circle (then a society of people editorially involved in publishing children's books, now an association open to anyone interested in any aspect of children and books) and the London and Home Counties Branch of the Youth Libraries Group held a joint meeting. Four speakers, of whom I was one, were invited to open a discussion on the subject 'Are children's books becoming too sophisticated?' This was part of the running battle between the books-as-a-branch of literature critics and those who saw child readers as part of the pattern that demanded consideration. By 1973 a sizeable body of teenage fiction of a literary (Jane Gardam, Alan Garner) and less demanding (Topliner) nature was on the market. Why was the former given the lion's share of children's *book review space, the latter almost none? I let my cat out among the fluttering literary pigeons, knowingly.*

Are children's books becoming too sophisticated? In attempting to answer this question in the ten minutes allotted to me, I shall try to look at the children's book scene as it is today with all its virtues of high standards of writing and production, together with the sales figures that publishers have achieved, and ask whether the moment hasn't now come, not for destroying what we have built up, but for a shift of emphasis.

By holding this meeting on this subject all of us who are concerned with children and books—all children and all their books—are demonstrating our healthy awareness that we stand on the edge of a precipice, the precipice of over-sophistication in an area where approachableness is, for the majority of children, the most important aspect of the product we have to sell. To sell, mark you! For we must face the fact that today the idea of reading for pleasure has to be sold to most children.

But let us be clear about terms. Sophistication really means the adulteration of something by the introduction of elements foreign to the original substance. I find the use of *adulteration* in the Oxford Dictionary definition very helpful, and I propose for this discussion to use the word in a hyphenated form—ADULT-ERATION: for that I think, is what we are really here to discuss—the ADULT-eration of children's books.

Looking at children's books over the years, the trend towards adult-eration is indeed alarming. Could the root cause be specialization, I wonder? Children's books—for better and for worse—are no longer published for fun by editors who spend four-fifths of their time in other fields and devote, perhaps, a relaxing Friday to the odd junior manuscript that may have come into the office—as Ursula Moray Williams's *Adventures of the Little Wooden Horse* came in to George Harrap's office, or Tolkien's *The Hobbit* into Allen & Unwin's in the thirties. You—the children's book editors—are professionally involved with children's books from Monday to Friday and sometimes on Saturdays and Sundays as well, and you are adults with the literary and artistic standards of adults. You—the children's librarians—are also professional, also fully involved and also fully committed; you meet children, but in the main book-orientated children. Similarly we reviewers tend to be specialist and—here we all are once again, specialists on children's books *talking to each other*. This is necessary; but it can be dangerous, because when we go out into the world—a world in which the illiteracy rate is disturbing—when we go out into the world, which is where we belong, we find that we have developed a deadly in-jargon and that we fling around ourselves a veil of quite unnecessary sophistication. The first step back from the precipice is to discard this veil. Our specialist task is to know more—much more—than the public, but to wear our knowledge so lightly, and present books to people—the right books to the right people at the right time—in so easy a manner, that no one would guess we were specialists.

Now to the adult-eration of children's books themselves. The long preamble is relevant; for, being adult, being so involved, wanting high quality in children's books, wishing (some of us) even to have children's books regarded as adult reading and reviewed on the same general critical principles as adult literature, we are all of us responsible for the adulteration—or sophistication if you like—of children's books.

The high quality of some of today's children's books and teenage books is, then, a direct result of the total involvement of dedicated publishers, librarians and reviewers who have made the path of excellence shine golden for literary authors and painterly artists. Respectable libraries stock their work (though some report that it sticks on the shelves), concerned parents know their names, furniture designers have discovered that their books look wonderfully warm on nursery bookshelves. (Look at the colour supplements on Sunday and you'll see what I mean.)

We need these authors and artists; we respect their publishers; but we must be aware that in detecting only *their* merits, in praising only *them* publicly, in writing learned papers about just *these* books, we are merely skimming cream and pretending that the milk is of no importance—whereas there are few children who can digest undiluted cream and the mass of young readers will only look at milk, and would indeed like it better if it came in Coke tins. In short, *we* are becoming élitist. But this meeting proves that we are, at least, not complacently so. We seem to have discovered that the moment for a shift of emphasis towards anti-adulteration is here and now.

Those of us who are middle-aged remember a childhood when we gratefully read whatever was available—from *Rainbow*, through the densely packed columns of *Schoolboys'* or *Schoolgirls' Own*, to pony stories, school stories or whatever. Opening these appallingly produced books was like taking the first step into a mysterious forest: who knew what was lurking behind those trees? Certainly our parents didn't—which made the expedition more private and exciting. Do today's handsomely produced books, which I confess I enjoy handling and recommending as much as anybody, exert the same magnet-ized (forgive the pun) tug into the unknown? I wonder.

Certainly paperback publishing is teaching us some interesting lessons. Take *Agaton Sax*, for example (he is the Swedish private eye whose wit and verve make him the criminal's most dreaded detective on both sides of the North Sea). There is nothing wrong with the handsome Deutsch hardcover editions of Agaton Sax books—except that they are handsome (or we reviewers might have condemned them as worthless) and hardcovered (otherwise, the libraries would not have bought them). But in the Target paper-covered editions—bright, accessible looking, pocket-worthy and easy to read under the bedclothes—thousands of children are going to become Sax fans. And Sax books are wonderful reading.

Presentation *is* important, in non-fiction as well as in fiction. We may admire and praise in our reviews the lovely publications of the high-class publishers; and some of our children certainly fall on them and are enthralled, so far be it from me to condemn them. Now look at the *Hamlyn Children's History of the World*, and you will surely see at once that it is a book to be considered seriously. But how many reviews of it did you read last year? Hamlyn are serving—to Hamlyn children (which is most children)—attractive, digestible, nourishing fare: an iced cake, maybe, but one made with eggs. Children are great dippers, and brightness encourages dipping.

If we mute colours, if we insist that the only worthwhile book is the one which deals with a subject in depth, we shall turn potential readers into non-readers. First steps must be sure—but easy.

Trendy picture books in which sensitive artists explore the psychological problems of childhood are beautiful to look at, fascinating for *us* to think about, and useful with special children who have particular problems; but reviews of these books tend to focus on the beautiful artwork with never a mention of the potential audience. The books we *should* devote most of our attention to are the picture books that are on a child level throughout, like the immortal (I hope) *Rosie's Walk*—and the sadly mortal (it is now out of print) *Clever Bill*: we have moved far away from William Nicholson's unadulterated, utterly simple concept of a small child and his picture book. The emphasis is now on the picture book: it must return to the child.

There isn't time to examine books for the middle years in any depth; which doesn't matter particularly, since in this area adulteration is least marked—and, of course, review space given, less generous. I would like to say in passing, though, that children could do with more new straight undemanding adventure stories properly written—books that would oust for ever the Blyton series now being reissued, which Margery Fisher, in a recent number of *Growing Point*, condemns as 'slow poison'. Enid Blyton demonstrated that children are so hungry for *stories* that they will read the same story over and over, slightly disguised. If adulteration has taught us anything—and surely it has—it has taught us that children also respond to good writing. Perhaps the moment has *now* come for better stories, well written? The success at all levels of Ted Hughes's *The Iron Man* is just one proof that we are not crying for the moon.

And so, to teenage fiction. This is the area on which there will, I am sure, be most discussion. It is the area which attracts a disproportionate amount of children's book review space—since the books reviewed are often acclaimed, rightly, as superb *adult* reading. Writers of good stories (and stories are as important in teenage reading as they are at every other stage of child development)—authors like K. M. Peyton, Barbara Willard and Leon Garfield—sit happily on children's lists and are read avidly by young and old alike. Fair enough. But when novelists who have sharpened their pens in the children's field assume—as they have every right to assume—the present-day adult novelist's techniques and obscurities, his psychoanalytical approaches, his obsession with the person rather than the story, I suggest that *there* the children's editor should draw the line and let the book sink or swim as adult fiction. Such books belong on the adult shelf, to be borrowed, read and revered by the exceptional teenager for whom it is not, I think, our business (since the world is already his oyster) to publish at all.

But publishing for the ordinary younger teenager and for the reluctant teenage reader *is* our business, and here I would like merely to remind those who criticize the content of some teenage fiction that its readers watch television and have probably seen the film of *Clockwork Orange*. Today's teenagers know it all—superficially. Are we not therefore right to explore in some depth, in the course of a *story* for them, the topics glibly glossed over in celluloid or on the box? Is this not a specific area in which the adulteration of children's books is not merely justified but vital? Better surely an S. E. Hinton story than an Ian Fleming: the serious, as opposed to the glamorous treatment, in literature, of sex and violence is of paramount importance.

So, by adult-eration, we gain and we lose. That's life. Quite certainly the 'Golden Age' has been worth while: it has pushed back the frontiers, shown us what can be done. We must now concentrate on using our experience to provide more approachable-looking books and better written *stories* for the broader mass of young readers.

Our job, having painfully climbed up the ivory tower, is to come down again, if we dare, and test our values in the market place. It will not be easy to maintain proven standards whilst adapting them to wider horizons. But it is a challenge we face. And it is a challenge we must meet. If we do not, we shall very soon be serving only ourselves. And that would be the ultimate in adult-eration.

Signal, 1974

A MIRROR IN THE MARKET PLACE

Being co-opted into a group of social workers who had decided to run an open-air children's bookstall on Saturdays in Whitechapel market in the East End of London was a lucky break for me. An outsider, I had been invited in. I made the most of this unique opportunity to stand around informally chatting with people of all races and ages about the books they might enjoy.

'Our job, having climbed up into the ivory tower, is to come down again if we dare and test our values in the market place.' Who issued that challenge to librarians, publishers and critics? I did. Where? In a ten-minute discussion-opener at the Library Association*. I had no idea, then, that fate, in one of its jocular moods, had pre-ordained that I should be the one to pick up the gauntlet I had so rashly thrown down. But that is what has happened.

A group of young social workers and teachers in the East End of London who believe that the problem of bookless areas is not that people 'down there' don't read, but that people 'up here' fail to supply them with the right goods in the right place in the right way, decided to start a bookstall in a street market *every* Saturday (point one). They knew all about the street markets; how to become a 'casual' stallholder, how to reserve your pitch, at what unearthly hour you have to present yourself to the market inspector, wet weather and fine, in order to hold on to it (point two). They knew a great deal about East End people and their interests (point three), about community politics, about housing, about education, about local talent in writing and poster making.

But (point four) what they weren't so sure about was how to spend the £100 in the kitty (ten idealists had contributed £10, hard-earned, towards the realization of their dream) on a basic stock of, mainly, children's paperbacks with some locally written material, sociological literature and adult novels thrown in. Would I help them buy the stock for Stepney Books?

What an opportunity! And how grateful I am to them for counting an outsider in on an experiment that is both stimulating and educative. For, needless to say, having helped them to

* See aforegoing article.

become booksellers' agents and to choose the stock, I could not resist being in on the selling. And they seem to be happy to let me come and go, talk and test, suggest and supply whenever I can get there (which I have to admit is never at eight o'clock on a wet Saturday morning).

I can honestly say that the most satisfying hours of the children's book part of my life are spent on that kerbside. Facing us is a pub. Behind us is the gents. (Being midway on the route between one and the other may prevent us from having the storytelling sessions we plan.) On our left is a fruit stall which we guard when the owner nips off for a minute. On our right a clothing stall run by a Pakistani family with whom contact is difficult because they form a self-contained excluding unit. Some day the little four-year-old girl who crouches under their stall will be given a picture book—but I'm waiting till I find one with a Pakistani child in it. How old will she be by the time I do?

I know now why Leila Berg talks so often about the need for books to be a mirror of the child's own experience. But I know also that the *parents* of the children for whom she designed Nippers reject them time and again in favour of the colourful and competitively priced Breakthrough books, or of 'escapist' stories such as those about *Gumdrop* or *The Very Hungry Caterpillar*. But at the initial stage, the stage of introducing the children *themselves* to books and reading (and with immigrants the initial stage as regards books in English can be any age between two and fourteen), she is right: identifying lights the vital spark.

The desperate need for picture books with black or Asian children in them is evident every minute of the day. Britain has been very slow off the mark in this respect, and we are lucky indeed to have available in paperback the 'Peter' books by Ezra Jack Keats, a white American artist and writer who has broken new ground with his brown-skinned hero and who faces squarely the limits of achievement open to him. He recently spoke eloquently to me about the philosophy behind the 'Peter' books (*Whistle for Willie, Peter's Chair*, etc.). 'One cannot actually teach people to tolerate each other, to be accepting, to have good manners, to be kind. I don't dream that anyone could do that through a book or in any other way. What I want to do in the "Peter" series is to help children to look at one another and to see one another as human beings. I don't attempt to portray the black experience. The most I can ever do is to open children's eyes. You can't preach. You can't make children make friends. All you can do is to reveal people to one another and hope.'

Certainly paperback copies of Keats's *Hi, Cat!*, *Goggles!* and all the others are seized upon by Jamaican families in the market with evident delight. But they are also, happily, popular generally because they reflect, in Ezra Jack Keats's words, 'the life we all carry with us. I wanted,' he said, '*The Snowy Day* to be a chunk of life, the sensory experience in word and picture of what it feels like to hear your own body making sounds in the snow. Crunch . . . crunch . . . And the joy of being alive. Awareness . . . awareness. The modern state operates on a *lack* of awareness of ourselves and others. It reduces people to cyphers that may function beautifully. But one might as well be dead.'

Petronella Breinburg, a black woman who was born in multiracial Suriname, and Errol Lloyd, a Jamaican, have recently collaborated on two British picture books centring on a black child, Sean. The books, *My Brother Sean* and *Doctor Sean*, are not yet available in paperback; when they are they will surely attract the Jamaican community in the market the way the Keats books now do. But Petronella Breinburg and Errol Lloyd strongly and rightly resented the suggestion (made by a minion of the BBC who was attempting to charm them on to a programme) that the two of them were 'interesting because they are the first author and artist in Britain to make books *about* black children *for* black children'. They stress that their books are for *all* children: by publishing them as front-ranking picture books The Bodley Head has not only flown in the face of other publishers' rejection of the stories (on the absurd grounds that 'Jamaicans don't buy books'—as though the books weren't for a white readership as well as for an avid black one) but has demonstrated the belief that a flood of second-rate material to fill the gap that at last is seen to exist would be a disaster. The political and social consequences of an apartheid approach to children's books is very apparent to Petronella; she put forward her views on books for *all* children at a Women's Lib meeting recently and reports, sadly, that she was howled down by those who fail to think their tailor-made philosophies through. Errol Lloyd, who has just taken his bar finals and will soon have to decide between a pin-striped suit and his present relaxed appearance as an artist, says mildly that publishers are in business and by and large feel under no obligation to venture into series which fill a sociological need.

How important it is for white children that the gap should be filled was then demonstrated by Petronella, who is a teacher in a secondary school in Sidcup. She told of a fourteen-year-old boy who was resistant to being taught English by a Negro. 'What do you expect, Miss?' he said. 'Negroes are not teachers. They're bus conductors and they work in hospitals.' Far from being appalled by this, Petronella sympathized with her pupil. 'On TV and in books that is what he sees. Naturally the child says, "What is going on?"' What, indeed.

But whilst pressing for what we haven't yet got, we must make the most of what we have. We need a mirror in the market place, but the experience by children of all races and creeds of so many books that provide common ground is also enormously important. Alphabets, nursery rhymes, folk tales, adventure stories, SF, animals, dinosaurs and football are universally popular; so is anything, from *The Magic Roundabout* to *Star Trek*, that originates on TV. *Books* are the novelty now! Will people whose budgets are small buy them? They will.

But in the initial stages, despite the fact that many of the helpers on the stall were known to local families and we often had child volunteers (drop-outs from the schools who go readily to a centre set up by two of the teachers involved in the bookstall), a fear of the unknown surrounded us like an invisible but impenetrable veil. Clusters of kids, family groups, stood and surveyed us from outside the pub as though we or the books might spring at them with nasty consequences. New books. Closed books. Books whose prices were discreetly hidden on their back cover. No wonder some of our potential customers—who are now actual and regular customers—felt suspicious.

We learned many things. To sell from the sides of the stall instead of the front or the back. To open up enticing books like *Where the Wild Things Are*, and intriguing ones like *The Very Hungry Caterpillar*, and specially attractive ones like *Whistle for Willie*. To put prices in prominent positions. Some of our stock has become a little worn-looking now, so that soon—next week, I hope—we can legitimately have a bargain box, and that will help enormously. Help to attract customers, I mean. Financially, selling only paperbacks and operating on a ten per cent margin, we shall not break even if too many books begin to look tired. If we sell £30 worth of books on a Saturday—and that's about average—our profit is £3, of which £2.50 goes on rent for the stall.

But we do not count our success in pence, let alone pounds. What we have done, so far, is make a very small beginning. Hundreds of paperbacks have been sold to teachers, to hospital workers (from the London Hospital across the road), to dockers, to other street traders, but above all to East End children out doing the family shopping—books that otherwise would not have been sold to people who would, whether they knew it or not, have been hungrier than they are now.

All kinds of books have been brought within reach of all kinds of people—most of whom might never, we feel, have opened a glass door and ventured into the forbidding atmosphere of a bookshop, even if there had been a bookshop within miles, which of course there isn't. In the whole area of Tower Hamlets, one of London's larger boroughs, new books are only sold on one day a week from a wooden trestle table, size six feet by two. But that table now has a life of its own and a much longer story to tell than there is room for here.

Signal, 1974

THEM'S FOR THE INFANTS, MISS
PICTURE BOOKS AND THE OLDER READER

I had often said airily, during my years as a freelance critic, that what I ought to do was go back to working with children and books; but I never thought I would get the opportunity to do so because library posts are normally full-time. In 1976, however, Edith Kahn, the Head of Fleet Primary School in Hampstead, told me she was trying to persuade the Inner London Education Authority to let her employ a qualified children's librarian for one day a week. If she succeeded, would I be interested in the job? It was exactly what I needed (or so I thought because

I had not foreseen some of the pitfalls). One of the many experiments the staff of Fleet and I set in motion was the use of picture books with children of all ages.*

Because of the unusual job I'm now doing for just one day a week as primary school librarian in Inner London (no longer unique, for happily I now have *a* colleague in another school) I meet many heads, many teachers. What has hit me most forcefully is the emphasis so many visitors to our school place on information books at the expense of the far more important—educationally speaking—fairy tales, stories, novels, poetry; and how few of these *concerned* teachers know that today there are picture books that not only can be used but ask to be used with children from eight to eleven.

True, picture books were, once, for the very young and their parents. True, booksellers regard picture books as being for toddlers and would not dream of displaying them with books for older children. Public libraries also place together all picture books for whatever age because picture books do not fit, physically, on to the fiction shelves. So by what magic should we expect the hard-pressed teacher suddenly to become aware that among today's picture books there are not only books with long texts (like V. H. Drummond's *Mrs Easter and the Storks* and Philippa Pearce's *Mrs Cockle's Cat*, both classic stories) but books that neatly, if subconsciously on the part of the authors and artists, fill the older child's need for humour, sophisticated word play, social comment and fantasy in the stories he reads?

It is this group that is largely misjudged (condemned because the books are indeed 'unsuitable for five-year-olds'); and it is these children, bright eight- to eleven-year-olds, who are being deprived of the delights that they could be sharing with us reviewers (!) because we are not managing to say to the teachers clearly enough when we meet them, strongly enough when we write for them, that the work of Michael Foreman, Raymond Briggs, Graham Oakley, Anthony Browne, Quentin Blake—to name but a few—should be widely available at the top of the junior school and indeed in all comprehensives.

*See 'The Dream and the Reality; a Children's Book Critic goes back to School,' p. 176.

We are so busy being professional literary critics who forbear to suggest the readership reflected in the book under consideration that the book misses its market—and, more important, the market (the child) misses some great books altogether.

When I took my own copies of these artists' books to the school where I work, there was no problem at all in persuading the staff that we should allocate a fair-sized proportion of our slender book fund to buying copies for the school library. That Michael Foreman's *Panda's Puzzle* was not only mesmerically beautiful but had a great deal to offer to the child of about ten who was beginning to think in terms of his own identity (black, white, brown, yellow or, like Panda, a mixture) was obvious *once the book was in the staff room.* It was quickly realized too that Anthony Browne, in *A Walk in the Park*, was offering not only an introduction to surrealist art to children who would 'read' the sophisticated jokes in his pictures, but that the text, by using simple words deftly chosen, was a supreme example of sharp satire.

But children are more hidebound, more conscious of status symbols because we have made them so. Those of about ten who were already reading Penelope Lively and Betsy Byars, Joan Aiken and E. Nesbit, Noel Streatfeild, Scott O'Dell, Nicholas Fisk and John Christopher, happily and silently practised one-upmanship over others in their group who still struggled with Dr Seuss and 'Gazelles'. But they were vociferously crushing when what appeared to them at first glance to be 'baby' picture books were first brought into the classroom. 'Them's for the infants, miss.'

The book that did most to change their attitude was John Burningham's *Come Away from the Water, Shirley*, a challenging, experimental picture book. Had Burningham, I wondered, succeeded in using the picture book to convey to children a double experience—a restful windy day on the beach for parents, and, simultaneously, a fantasy adventure for their daughter Shirley, with pirates and buried treasure? I took the book in to school and used it with children from five years old right up to eleven to find out.

There were some *at every age* who did not manage to make the jump across the 'gutter' from left-hand pages where the parents sit, occasionally addressing the unseen Shirley, to the right-hand pages on which Shirley is seen synthesizing a real rowing boat and stray dog on the shore into the fabric of her vivid daydream. These children concentrated entirely on the textless daydream pages because here, told visually, was an exciting treasure-cum-pirate story. 'Like *Peter Pan*, miss'; 'No, like *Captain Pugwash*.' Oh, the opportunities!

But far more children, again at all ages, did make the jump and were intrigued by the clues John Burningham laid for them. Although Shirley is not seen on the left-hand pages, 'She must have been there or her mum and dad wouldn't have kept talkin' to her, would they'; 'Her body was there for them to tell not to do things, like "Don't play with that dog, you don't know where he's been", but her think was with the pirates'; 'She probably made a boat out of sand like I do and sailed away on it to the island'. These few comments, taken at random from a long tape, show the child reader, or listener, making his own contribution, which is the complement to the artist's picture book. Cape's poster for this book is up in the library, and even now, a year afterwards, it excites comment, nostalgic memory, renewed demand for another look at the book (which is hardly ever there because it is on the my-turn-next circuit among the older children).

Along with the children, the teachers leapt across the divide. If *Come Away from the Water, Shirley* was so successful, what else was there like it? Nothing like it—which is why it is so good; but plenty of other author-artists whose picture books deserve honoured places in the book corners of junior classrooms.

There are Graham Oakley's *Church Mouse* books, for instance, with their immensely detailed pictures of thousands of mice in vestry, graveyard and organ loft and their witty texts, which bear comparison with Margery Sharp's *Miss Bianca* (mice again!). In *The Church Mice and the Moon* it is the scientists who are 'sent up', not the capsule containing Arthur and Henry mouse.

> The scientists' eyes were fixed on the TV screen. The next thing they saw would have made most people give up science for ever. But when they had got over the shock, the two scientists agreed they hadn't seen what they'd seen because, if they had, it would prove that certain things exist which every good scientist knew jolly well didn't.

Sport, no less than science, can be a laughing matter, for some of the disciplines and rules, seen as training for life, are absurd —exquisitely so when explored by Russell Hoban and Quentin Blake in *How Tom Beat Captain Najork and his Hired Sportsmen*. Hoban's story is a perfect short tale with wildly exaggerated characters that we nevertheless instantly recognize as full of human frailty. Its plot (to stop Tom mucking about and fooling around by training him to play, and be beaten at, Womble and Sneedball) is doomed from the start. Reading this book and absorbing Quentin Blake's intricately lunatic illustrations is no pastime for infants who, after all, should be encouraged to muck about and fool around, as Tom-aged boys, the natural audience for this witty book, are not. Colin McNaughton's *The Rat Race* can be seen both as a humorous gloss on athletics and as a look, from beneath a quizzical, raised eyebrow, at the rewards life offers to those of us who have a good track record: 'First Prize—King for a Day; Second Prize—Marriage to One of the King's Daughters; Third Prize—Marriage to Two of the King's Daughters.'

The cartoon has long been a vehicle for social and political satire, so it is not surprising to find artists like Papas (erstwhile *Guardian* cartoonist) and Michael Foreman using picture books not necessarily to carry messages but to open up among older children issues that need to be discussed. Papas, in *Tasso* and *The Story of Mr Nero*, looks at the human sadness that mechanization and modernization leave in their wake; because he is a humorist he makes sure that the Greek villagers triumph over the soulless pieces of equipment. The same theme inspired Virginia Lee Burton's tender, gentle *Mike Mulligan and His Steam Shovel* but the Papas treatment of it is sharp and sophisticated and therefore better suited to the older reader. Michael Foreman's picture books, direct descendants of the pre-war comics like *Rainbow*, have a limitless visual appeal, but young children are obviously put out by the lack of concrete answers (in their terms) to the questions Foreman poses. To them it is most unsatisfactory that, in *Panda's Puzzle*, they follow the bear on his long quest to find out whether he is a black bear with white patches or a white bear with black patches, only to discover that it doesn't really matter. Older readers understand the deeper philosophical content of this book. They read *Moose* as a political commentary on the sabre-rattling that goes on between Russia (Bear in the story) and the United

States (a fierce Eagle); and they are intrigued by the idea of dinosaurs finding modern Earth too disgusting to live on—an idea Michael Foreman explores in *Dinosaurs and All that Rubbish*. His *All the King's Horses* is the only funny book I know about woman power and therefore wields more clout (it is about an Amazonian princess who wrestles all her suitors out of the ring) than all the deadly serious tomes on Women's Lib put together.

Charles Keeping is an artist whose work can be seen either as a barrier breaker or as having come before its time. Often, as I listen to conversations in bookshops or libraries, I have heard this major artist condemned because his exploration of the emotions is outside the comprehension of a five-year-old. His work—from straightforward *Richard*, which portrays the life of a police horse, to *Inter-City* and *The River*, textless picture books that perplex even the experienced adult—could fuel a doctoral thesis. Indeed, it probably already has.

My purpose here is merely to point out that the books whose interest level lies between these two extremes have texts and pictures that thrust deep into the growing emotional consciousness of the prepubescent youngster. *Through the Window*, *Joseph's Yard*, *Wasteground Circus*—to take three of many—are personal and demanding books that use the medium of colour printing to convey messages about human weakness, violence, fear, love. *Through the Window* is the most heart-rending and terrifying, the story of little Jacob 'alone in his front room . . . He moved across to the window and looked out. The street was all Jacob knew of the world, so it was the whole world to him.' Death comes into his net-curtained world when the brewery horses run amok, killing the skeleton-thin dog who is life itself to an old woman. The book ends with Jacob finger-drawing the crone and her pet (smiling, content in each other's company) on the breath-steamed window pane. How else should we remember the dead? What is the meaning of resurrection? Jacob knew.

Joseph's Yard is a lesson in love. Joseph exchanges the rusty old iron in his yard—'A brick wall, a wooden fence, stone paving and a rusty old iron; that's all there was in this yard'—for a plant. The plant is a living thing. Joseph is responsible for it, and he smothers it with love, protects it from birds, insects, cats, and even from the sun and rain. The plant withers. And Joseph is bitterly ashamed that he has betrayed 'the beautiful thing in his yard'. But spring comes, and with it new life—for the rose tree, for insects, for cats, for birds, but above all for Joseph. In *Wasteground Circus* Keeping uses colour, grey or bright, to show how a circus on a piece of waste land affects two boys after it has gone. For one the wasteground is suffused with the afterglow of excitement, a place for ever bright; for the other it becomes grey again as though the circus had never been.

It is a paradox that arguably the greatest picture-book artist of our time should be exploring the world of the under-privileged child so brilliantly, yet should go unrecognized by those who search for art and literature that reflect other than the middle-class experience.

Mother Goose Comes to Cable Street is more overt. This book of nursery rhymes was selected by Rosemary Stones and Andrew Mann because the words could be interpreted by Dan Jones, already a well-known naïf painter, to highlight modern socio-logical changes, developments, messages. Purists probably all agree that, although the nursery rhyme has evolved from tavern songs and was originally a reflection of, or commentary on, life both seemly and seamy, Mother Goose collections intended for the nursery are best illustrated by artists like *Harold* Jones, who leaves the young child free to dream. No illustrations could be more tied to reality than those of *Dan* Jones: the setting is London's East End; the people are East Enders in the seventies —'one was yellow and one was black and one had eyes of blue'; the situations—a funeral, street market, urban school, fairground at night ('Girls and boys come out to play')—comment wittily on the old rhymes. Older children looking at this book see it not as a Mother Goose but as a lively picture book celebrating themselves.

In many schools *Asterix* books are frowned upon. Yet I have found them invaluable. Non-readers pounce on them to read the pictures. Beginning readers attempt the text: using the pictures as complement, but still of course not properly understanding the sophisticated jokes. One little seven-year-old, intelligent and shy, was in the library burbling away, deep in *Asterix*. I thought the monotone buzz was in imitation of others reading. But when I listened carefully, I heard, 'Come, oh Kah-eezer . . .' (Caesar). The phonics had sunk in; and the story was certainly making as much sense to him as 'Come, Dick, come. Run, run, Fluff'. Later I gave him a book in the Antelope series, and to his astonishment he discovered he could read a story without a comic strip. The *words* spoke to him now, and he was enthralled.

I am not joking when I say you can teach with Asterix. The opportunity arose when a class teacher was suddenly taken ill. Her thiry-five nine-year-olds arrived in the library like a visitation of locusts—expecting to eat me, not devour the books. Asterix, brave Gaul, to the rescue.

'Stop this cacophony!' I shouted.

'What's a cocker-what-you-said, miss?'

'Who has heard of Cacofonix?'

'Oh, miss, miss . . . Asterix!'

And we're away on names, on how names give clues to character ('What's an obelisk made of?' 'Dunno.' 'Who has seen Cleopatra's Needle?'). Then history, Druidry, and music follow. Music? Perhaps you haven't yet seen *Asterix and the Normans*, in which the Rolling Menhirs ('Surely Obelix is entitled to a bit of Rock') feature heavily, 'By Thor', 'By Odin', 'By gum . . .'

Comic-strip books of the class of Asterix and Tintin bring picture books in the large picture-book format into the junior school. Even if I did not personally admire *Asterix* for its brilliant text in Anthea Bell and Derek Hockridge's outstanding translation, and Tintin for Hergé's amazing artwork, correct in every technical detail, I would applaud them for opening up virgin territory. For in the wake of these two adventurers can follow a battalion of books in the same format: picture books for the older reader.

(Abridged from two articles)

INFORMATION BOOKS
HOME THOUGHTS ABOUT THE TES AWARDS AND THE EFFECT OF TELEVISION ON PUBLISHING

In 1972 Margery Fisher had published 'Matters of Fact', an eye-opening treatise on the approach to and purposes of information books for children. In the previous decade Margaret Spencer (Margaret Meek) at the University of London Institute of Education had masterminded and participated in projects concerning the use of reference materials in schools. Cecilia Gordon, librarian of Haverstock Comprehensive School in London, spoke vehemently at several meetings about the slipshod standards of some of the most popular series—such as Macdonald's Starters. Rosemary Stones, Robert Leeson and others on the Left were busy scurrying through out-dated school textbooks whose colonial, class-ridden and sexist attitudes were offensive to a Britain moving into an egalitarian and multicultural future.

The Times Educational Supplement's Information Book Awards had been established in 1972 to highlight excellence in this field (if it could be found) and to stimulate thought, discussion and action among publishers and others concerned.

By 1978 I had been 'back at school' for two years observing the potential of information books and the problems children come up against when trying to use them. The TES Information Book Award in the senior section for that year really alarmed me.

It's odd the way ideas float into the consciousness at moments when notebooks and pens are ungrabbable. When I'm in the bath or peeling potatoes or out walking, I suddenly want to write, and what's more I know exactly what I'd say, if only . . . The other morning I was doing a stack of ironing and thinking about the 1977 *TES* Information Book Awards in a constructive sort of way. Awards are funny things; usually there is little point in making any comment on the winners, who are vehicles (among many who could be chosen) for conveying to the public at large the qualities that specialists look for in a particular field. In this way awards serve a double purpose, I mused to myself, because the winning books also focus the attention of publishers on desirable standards and on welcome new directions. Welcome new directions? The Joy of Knowledge Library?

It was at this point in my thinking that I decided to replace the tape I was listening to on my cassette player with a blank one—and talk my thoughts into it. Since this was a Sunday morning, no one came into the kitchen to ask what on earth I was doing. The tape ran on. *Signal*'s editor thought it was worth transcribing. So here, complete, informal and unexpurgated except for the place where I scorched a handkerchief, is my conversation with myself about the *TES* Information Book Awards and the effects of television on certain kinds of publishing.

The prize for the 1976–7 *Times Educational Supplement* Junior Information Book went to a superb book, *Street Flowers* by Richard Mabey; there could be no qualms on anybody's part about that except to wonder whether perhaps the book was only for juniors since it should certainly also find a place in the library of every comprehensive school. Its great virtues are that it is vividly written by an enthusiast and that it has beautiful and accurate illustrations; so that once you have read it, when next you walk along the street or across a piece of scrub land, you keep your eyes open and suddenly do begin to notice the plants that are growing around that stone or sprouting from the top of the roof or out of a drainpipe. This is really what non-fiction books are about: opening your eyes to the world so that you see things you would otherwise have missed. Because of *one* enthusiast's ('one' is rather important) enthusiasm you begin to be an enthusiast yourself. You begin to understand what you are looking at, to have what is commonly known as a *revelation* about the world. (This is what Freya Stark means when she talks about travelling in depth instead of travelling distances. What matters, she says, is that what you see shall reveal something new to you.) *Street Flowers* is a revealing book in this sense, and I had no hesitation in saying this to Michael Church of the *TES* when he asked me what I thought of the Award books.

I had more hesitation when he asked 'What do you think about the Senior Book Award?' I hedged a little because this was the presentation party and I had no wish to act thirteenth godmother. But he pressed me, so I said, 'Well, I'm not too sure that it's a *book*; to me the Joy of Knowledge Library in general [*Man and*

Machines, the *TES* winner, £12.50, is one of its ten volumes] is more like a TV series transferred on to pages.'

And I want to expand on that a little, on what I think a real book is. There is a great deal of discussion nowadays about books and/or the other media, but too little about the influence television has had, not on the child directly but on information books that are given to him. Now this influence can be good and it can be bad. Television transmits information in a very digestible form if it presents it slowly in series like *The World About Us*, which do a marvellous job in showing children, and indeed adults, what life is like in other places. And the best nature films must be unsurpassed as whetters of appetite, often because they are presented by scientists or naturalists who are willing, are anxious, to share their love of their subject, their joy in it with the viewer person-to-person. So there is no carping at the way television at its best presents material. Such books as *Window into a Nest* by Geraldine Lux Flanagan and Sean Morris, an earlier *TES* Award winner, were directly and beneficially influenced by these programmes.

But we also have gobbet presentation by the magazine programmes. You may, for instance, be invited by *Blue Peter* or *Magpie* to visit a farm for five minutes. How much you will understand about mechanical milking—how much you will *want* to understand—is anybody's guess. (TV producers are terrified of boring child audiences by length so they often fail to engage interest because their programmes are so superficial.) It's this kind of bitty presentation that really does bother me. I would say, having been in on the research end of television programmes, that producers try to see that the research is pretty thoroughly done before it is given to the presenter to present, but the trouble is that there *is* a presenter standing between the person who has the knowledge and the child or adult viewer who is going to receive the facts but perhaps not the message, and certainly not the passion.

Now we have the same problem when we come to composite publishing. And this is my quarrel with the *TES* Information Book Award, in the Senior Section, to *Man and Machines*, a perfectly acceptable volume in a glossy encyclopaedia enterprise. When James Mitchell was receiving the award on behalf of Mitchell Beazley—and it is interesting that in this case the publisher received the award because there was no author (what is a book if it has no author?)—he made the audience laugh when he said that, as the award was £100, if all the authors who had written pieces of *Man and Machines* were to receive a fair proportion of the prize money, each author would get ten pence because there were one thousand authors concerned in the making of this book. So now we come to the big question: What is a book; and should an Information Book Award be given to one unit in a ten-volume library, a book that has been the work of one thousand writers, and has artwork credited to four columns full of Art Editors, Visualizers, Artists, Studios and Agents?

I might write myself off as an old-fashioned fuddy-duddy who hasn't come to terms with the demands of modern publishing in world co-editions and who cannot accept that, regardless of these demands, the highest standards can be maintained. I might, except that I was on the receiving end of the enquiries of one of the researchers for another Mitchell Beazley volume. The young lady who approached me and asked if I had five minutes to spare to talk to her on the subject of picture books was in no sense at all an expert in the area she was researching. Neither was I—for the subject turned out to be nothing less than the development of visual perception in children between the ages of two and five. What really appalled me was that she had no background for writing the short piece allotted to her; she had no idea what would come before it or after it; she had written down some vague guidelines for parents (which seemed suspect, to say the least) and had not realized that the uninformed parent would take her words as gospel. Furthermore, the speed at which she was expected to deliver her copy made even the scantiest reading on her part out of the question.

This is journalism—and though journalism is an inescapable ingredient in most kinds of non-fiction, it should be entirely absent from the encyclopaedia. It is present in inspired information books about, say, conservation because the author is probably passionate about the need to alert the reader to the dangers of using up resources too fast. Parents, teachers, librarians and critics should not, and on the whole do not, demand naked truth. What is important, therefore, is that older readers develop judgement, indulge in mistrust of the printed word and realize that authors are fallible, that true knowledge comes only from the broad pursuit of it in many directions. Margery Fisher sums up her thesis, explored in depth in *Matters of Fact*, with the words 'an information book is a teacher, and the role of a teacher is to lead his pupils towards a considered independence of thought and action. Instruction is important, but freedom of thought is more important still.'

Is *Man and Machines* a 'teacher' in Margery Fisher's sense? Does it, any more than the Macdonald Starters or Macdonald's endless stream of topic books for the junior school, ask intelligent questions and lead the reader on; or does it compress knowledge and give answers that may satisfy an examiner even if the reader has only partially understood the import of his in-put and out-put? (That hideous sentence was directly inspired by the award winner!) Giving the *TES* Information Book Award to a project like The Joy of Knowledge gives the stamp of academic approval to a kind of publishing in which teamwork, technical expertise in production, the formula approach (one doublespread to each subject regardless of its relative importance to the whole) replace the inspired enthusiast who can make personal contact with the reader.

The comments of the judges* show that all of them had reservations. Charles Stuart-Jervis noted some jarring features —the photograph of Lord Butler knocking portentously on the great door of Trinity College, for instance, and the popularizing use of words like 'fun' and 'treasure hunt'. Valerie Alderson was clearly unhappy, most justifiably, about the compressed nature of the individual articles. (To write a compressed article the author must be not only a great expert on his subject but also a brilliant teacher; James Mitchell had to look for one thousand of these rare birds for this single volume in his Joy of Knowledge Library.) Edward Blishen, while in common with the other judges ostensibly supporting the Award, revealed a longing to discover 'fresh approaches to manageable subsections of that whirly chaos which is the world of information'.

That hits the nail on the head. Why were the judges unable to find a book in the Senior Section with the individual flavour of *Street Flowers*, the winner in the Junior Section? I do not know.

* *TES*, 21 October 1977.

But I have a suspicion, from looking at what they say and from reading the list of submissions recommended, that there is something wrong with the whole conception of the *TES* Award for the senior reader. James Mitchell published *Man and Machines* for adults but nevertheless cleverly submitted it to the *TES*. Is there such a thing as an information book 'for teenagers'? Any reading child over thirteen who is interested in a subject can absorb a whole range of books or articles written for the general public on that subject. If other publishers had had the wit to submit books on astronomy, conservation, glass-making, philately, religions—books from their *adult* lists—to the *TES*, would Mitchell Beazley's *Man and Machines* have stood a chance? I cannot believe that these judges, given one book of personal commitment to an important subject, would have been dazzled by the technical expertise and allured by the cut-away illustrations into giving the award to *Man and Machines*.

James Mitchell has opened our eyes to the need for new thinking about one part of a major children's book award.

Signal, 1978

The Seventies in British Children's Books

For Signal's tenth anniversary (a momentous occasion for any small magazine) Kestrel published a celebration volume, 'The Signal Approach to Children's Books' (1980) edited by Nancy Chambers. It was to consist in the main of reprints of articles that had appeared in Signal over the years; but three new essays were commissioned, one of which was 'The Seventies in British Children's Books'. Throughout the 1970s my introductions to the 'Children's Books of the Year' catalogue had sought to identify trends and developments in children's book publishing and promotion. The record was there, in those ten volumes. For 'The Seventies in British Children's Books' I attempted a synthesis and some conclusions.

My morning post (19 June 1979) has just arrived. I find in it a letter asking me to address a meeting of the Educational Publishers Council and the Children's Book Group of the

Publishers Association, a sign that school books and leisure reading are drawing closer together; there are copies of two new children's book magazines: *Children's Book Bulletin* 'for news of progressive moves in children's literature', and *Dragon's Teeth*, Bulletin of the National Committee on Racism; and a parcel full of Oxford University Press novels reprinted on paper that this publisher would not have used as stuffing for packages a decade ago.

My mail on any particular day cannot justifiably be said to reflect anything. Nevertheless, ten years ago, when I was embarking on the *Children's Books of the Year* venture, I am fairly sure that none of the social or economic interests mirrored in the random mail I received this morning would have been manifest.

Looking back on a decade of children's book publishing when the decade isn't over is like asking oneself whether yesterday was well spent. Only tomorrow will tell; which is good in a way because one has the opportunity to hazard guesses, to put forward hopes, to give early warnings—and to be proved wrong.

Before I began to consider the children's books of the 1970s objectively—as a development from the 1960s and as a precursor to the 1980s—I had not realized how distinctive decades, which one thinks of as arbitrary notches on the calendar, can be.

To write about children's books and authors in the sixties it would have been sufficient to be a responsive literary person, with an eye capable of seeing picture books as works of art: the decade that brought us Brian Wildsmith's *ABC* and Raymond Briggs's *Mother Goose Treasury* (two landmarks in the history of illustration) brought us also Alan Garner's development from *The Weirdstone of Brisingamen* (1960) to *The Owl Service* (1967), Philippa Pearce's *A Dog So Small*, Helen Cresswell's *The Piemakers*. It was a quality decade in children's books in which the only consumer considered by reviewers was the child who could absorb the literary story, the painterly picture book: these were published in profusion.

But in Morna Stuart's *Marassa and Midnight* (a story about Negro twin slaves, one in San Domingo and one in Revolutionary France), Nina Bawden's *On the Run* (a multicultural inner-city adventure), Goscinny and Uderzo's *Asterix the Gaul* cartoon stories, Wezel's *The Good Bird Nepomuk* (a wordless picture book from Czechoslovakia), K. M. Peyton's *Flambards* trilogy for teenagers who enjoyed reading and Pan/Macmillan's Topliners for the uncommitted reader we had (but did we realize this in 1969?) the seeds of the many developments that were to become conscious issues in the seventies.

The broadening of the scene in the 1970s has scattered the viewpoints from which commentators analyse it. The literary reviewer of children's novels, the art critic as picture-book buff, survive. Like dinosaurs in a noisy modern zoo they are respected as the prototypes from which trendier animals, in response to a changed climate, have evolved.

Sociological Concerns of the Seventies

By the beginning of 1970 the atmosphere surrounding children's books was altering perceptibly. The blossoming of the genre in the sixties had earned children's books a respectability never before contemplated, let alone demanded. Space in national newspapers was given to them, and specialist journals were devoted to them. The best of both worlds was thought to be worth striving for: children's books were different (requiring separate treatment and specialist reviewers) but the same (in the mainstream of national literature and entitled to serious critical study on that level). The assumption that only the literary book was worth consideration, the neglect of the needs of the learning, perhaps non-literary, child, sowed the seeds of the polarity—pure criticism versus child-oriented comment—that has been a mark of the seventies.

The 1970s were child-centred in the realms of education; they were years in which Britain was coming to terms with its post-Imperial role as a multicultural nation; they were feminist (rather different from non-sexist) years. All these factors had their bearing on the content of the books children were offered.

In education the decade began with the setting up of the Bullock Committee (1972) to examine language across the curriculum. In 1975 *A Language for Life*, its report, was published. Thorough in its examination of the status quo and far-reaching in its recommendations for increasing children's awareness of books through changing attitudes and approaches in teaching, the

Report has had some impact. Though most of its recommendations have not been implemented, it has significantly strengthened the hands of those who believe in books as being part of the life of all children all the time.

As satellites to the Bullock Report, though unconnected with it in any direct sense, Penguin Education published many books on language in education, notably Patrick Creber's *Lost for Words* and Connie Rosen's *The Language of Primary Schoolchildren*. Longman's Breakthroughs, a series pioneered by David Mackay and based on speech patterns of young children, were one of the first results of the concentration of educationists on language as a key to learning, to reach the five-year-old direct. With their unstilted prose and their illustrations by artists who looked at urban life and interpreted it in a lively manner, Breakthroughs, along with Leila Berg's Nippers for Macmillan, brought the real book closer to the classroom. The erosion of the barrier between books children read for pleasure and school textbooks, between 'net' and 'non-net' books as the trade calls them, had begun.

The Exeter Conference, initiated in 1969 by the late Sidney Robbins as a way to bring teachers into direct contact with the authors of children's books, was a good seventies-type idea which had some positive spin-off (such as the journal *Children's Literature in Education*) but was in part counter-productive. There were authors who felt quite properly that it was no concern of theirs how teachers and children responded to their books: a novel for children is, or can be, a work of art with a right to live regardless of its potential consumer. And there were teachers who, while interested to listen to and meet the children's book establishment, recognized that their own experience, of large mixed-ability classes and little time, was so far away from the solitary life of the author (particularly the author who claimed he was 'writing for himself') that debate could only end in acrimony. The bridge across this divide has begun to be built. The Arts Council Writers in Schools project has forged links among authors, teachers and school students, releasing and channelling creative energy, often with dramatic results.

The Schools Council Project *Children's Reading Interests* reported in mid-decade, with few surprises but some interesting individual studies of child readers' preferences. Aidan

Chambers's *Introducing Books to Children* was published in 1973 to support teachers in their difficult task of mediating books (output of publishers up, up, up in the seventies) to the young. For *The Cool Web* Margaret Meek and her colleagues at the University of London Institute of Education collected academic papers and journalistic pieces that, in unison and well organized, make a strong thrust from both banks—the educationist's and the author's. And it is not without significance that among the new authors for children in the seventies there are, as we shall see later, several teachers.

But the architects of the bridge must take care. There is dynamite around, in the shape of activists who are less concerned with standards of literacy and bookless homes and schools than they are with what they consider to be inaccurate reflections of our society in the children's books most young people will never read. We do not live in a society with equal opportunities for the sexes: if our children's novels and picture books uniformly represented such a society, the image would be false. But we do live in a multi-ethnic nation, and children's books have been tardy in their adjustment to the post-war changes. Among the media, children's books are a soft option for attack, and attackers have tended to concentrate on surface blemishes while ignoring the literary quality, emotional content (so often the ingredient that children identify with) and philosophical messages *as a whole*. At the beginning of the decade anyone deeply concerned with children's books and desperately trying to reach children with all that was available was apt to find his/her path strewn with red herrings.

Rosie's Walk, Pat Hutchins's wryly humorous picture book about a hen who walks calmly through the farmyard oblivious (or *was* she?) of the fox's constantly hampered efforts to catch her, was described as anti-feminist by commentators who had missed the whole point of the story because they had stood too close to it. About *Little Black Sambo* there was much real cause for concern; a stereotyped black hero called Sambo would have died the natural death that Janet Hill, in a wise article in the *Times Literary Supplement*, said was his due in the 1970s, had it not been for the fact that Helen Bannerman (in 1899) had hit on a classic picture-book formula. *Little Black Sambo* was not banned in Britain; he was allowed to live on under a heavy, much-publicized cloud.

Banning is censorship. Censorship deprives people of the experience of making their own judgements and leads towards the imposed standards of a totalitarian society. In Britain, where even a core curriculum in schools is viewed with deep mistrust, healthy scepticism may do battle with and defeat the attempt that appears, as 1984 looms, to be threatening the source material of children's publishing. The first issue of the 'progressive' *Children's Book Bulletin* (which, as you may remember, arrived the morning I started writing this survey) has in it a code of practice called 'Guidelines to be used in the Production of Anti-Racist Non-Sexist Books'. One need scarcely pause to consider the effect on fiction (information books and reading schemes are altogether different) of using 'guidelines', since all of us have seen series which, for one purpose or another, have been written within prescribed limits. Rosemary Stones and Andrew Mann, the editors of the new magazine, have done a great deal through the Children's Rights Workshop and the Other Award to show how relevant existing material can be brought to more children who need it but whose teachers or parents may not know about it. So far, so good. But the first number of their *Children's Book Bulletin*, while carrying some thought-provoking reviews, goes a great way further along the road American activists have taken towards censorship at source. If we do not want to follow this road in Britain in the 1980s we must quickly awaken to the significance of its direction.

Certainly the foundations of this highway to pre-fab politikidlit have been laid, eccentrically sometimes and without much sense of history or perspective, in the seventies. Bob Dixon's *Catching them Young*, for instance, or the Writers and Readers Co-operative's *Sexism in Children's Books: Facts, Figures and Guidelines* (guidelines again!) can only make their mark with those who are interested in the sociological content of literature but unmindful of its peculiar essence, part of which is the beauty of a language they seek to put in splints. More far-reaching and much more entertaining in the sex-equality stakes is Cadogan and Craig's study of stories for girls, *You're a Brick, Angela!*, which is subtle and persuasive instead of strident and hectoring.

The publication in 1979 of Robert Jeffcoate's *Positive Image* is the most encouraging sign that a central path through the minefield of race relations can be trod if the British of all colours are made aware that there is indeed a way forward in the 1980s. Mr Jeffcoate's wide experience in schools in Kenya and Britain, his passion for books, his willingness to describe experiments that backfired as well as those that worked, make his book a beacon of hope for the future.

Economics of Publishing

Educational thinking and political thrusts were not alone in exerting influence on children's books in the 1970s. The economic state of Britain affected every business enterprise in the country, and publishing for children reflected the strains and constraints, the initiatives and the curtailments that survival in this climate was to demand.

The Introductions to the nine volumes of *Children's Books of the Year* (the tenth is still in the making) record, amongst gloomy forebodings, many significant changes dictated by economic pressure. 'We shall be witnessing the far-reaching effect of the industrial and economic situation on children's books' (1970). 1973 might go down 'as a year in which publishers made the most of the boom conditions that still prevailed' (a 25% rise in production that was to prove an unhealthy trend later in the decade) 'feeling in their bones that an enforced restructuring of the whole children's book scene was round the corner'. The Introduction to the 1974 volume is prefaced by Mel Calman's cartoon 'Spare a penny to help publish a book' and is spattered with economic references; 2,618 new children's books published despite the many pushed forward into 1975 by the knock-on effect of the Heath three-day week; an acute paper shortage; the beginning of publishers' headaches over keeping backlist books in print, because of warehouse costs and printing costs rising simultaneously. How would a declining backlist (in children's publishing the profit on backlist books had, up till now, been the wealth that could be invested in new ventures) affect the children's book editor's view of the future? Would safety become the only method of survival? And was safety to be found in international editions of picture books printed abroad, in international packages of glossy non-fiction, in hardback publishers starting their own paperback lists, in smaller books (at a relatively high price) or in larger books that looked worth £3 or more?

Children's book publishing depends heavily on the institutional market of libraries and schools; 1976 was the Local Authority crisis year, with headlines in newspapers such as *Bookless in Bucks* indicating the slashing of library services. To the layman it would have seemed sensible for publishers, faced with a contracting home market, to have reduced their numbers of new titles; but economics is a discipline with its own mystique, of which butter mountains in Europe are a symbol. Economics dictated that more and more new titles should be published to meet the reduced demand for books generally; the reason for this was the shortage of cash and the desperate need for quick return on investment. New titles sell faster than backlist books. Cash can be re-invested in more new titles. But the new titles had to be published in short print runs to avoid the cost of warehousing. So, in 1976, 25% more children's titles were published than in 1971 but in very short print runs, a dangerous and sad practice which meant that new books could go out of print for ever after perhaps two years of life. 'Buy now!' one said to anyone lucky enough to have a book fund. And to editors, between the devil (the computer printout supplied by the sales director) and the deep blue sea (a contracting institutional market and rising costs): 'Back your own judgement.' For, one could fairly ask, which sales director, what computer, would have predicted the phenomenal success in market terms of an immensely long novel (with Greek quotations at the head of each chapter) about displaced rabbits on Watership Down?

Libraries and schools, as the decade advanced, were faced with the choice of buying multiple copies of a book in paperback or a single hard-covered edition. Libraries that had never bought paperbacks began to do so. Publishers of hardbacks started to experiment with simultaneous hard and paperbound editions of the same book: Kestrel/Puffin, Collins/Fontana Lions, Abelard Schuman/Grasshoppers, and the Usborne books faced both ways at once. Faber sold off some of its paperback rights to Puffin, but is currently investing in a stiff paperbound hybrid in an attempt to keep libraries supplied with backlist titles. Oxford University Press began a paperback list early in the decade, then axed it; but in order to keep some of its better-known titles in print it has resorted to the practice of using excessively cheap paper and illustrated board bindings—the princes disguised as paupers that were part of my morning mail on June 19th. A splendidly produced series of information books from Pan Piccolo (the Explorers series) is also available in hard covers from Ward Lock, whereas certain paperback Dinosaurs appear in hardback, now, on the Evans list. So to some extent the pattern of original hardback publishing followed by a paperback edition of the book perhaps two years later (the norm in 1970) has been reversed, hardback publishers now occasionally buying rights from originating paperback houses. This profusion of practices mirrors the economic complexity of the decade.

1979 is still with us. During the decade we have seen a 50% increase in the number of new children's titles published annually (from just under 2,000 to just over 3,000); we have seen the price of a hardback children's novel rise from about £1 to an average of £3.50; we have seen the paperback price go up from 20 pence, or thereabouts, to 60 pence, and there are murmurs about very steep increases in price to come—if the market will bear it.

Looking back, one can see that children's book publishing has become the victim of its own success. Booming into a profitability that in several instances spawned separate children's book companies within general publishing firms, it suddenly had to face up to the strains recession and inflation were imposing on industry as a whole. Companies that have been bought as part of large business empires' diversification plans are under severe pressure of a kind that is foreign to and inimical to good children's publishing. In the past the popular, and predictably fast-selling, title was considered to be the foundation from which a promising new author could be launched at an initial loss. In the brave new world of decisions led by sales forecasts, however, every book is supposed to pay its way, and editors who lack crusading zeal can find their wings not just clipped but pinned firmly to their sides. As we enter the eighties, the battle between the editor-with-flair and the sales-department-with-figures appears to be shaking some of the edifices of good children's book publishing, both hardback and paperback. It seems doubtful, in this economic climate, that we shall see many publishers embarking on small select lists with an individual flavour such as Julia MacRae Books (1979), as a division of Franklin Watts Ltd, hopes to establish.

Fiction in the Seventies

But what of the books themselves, and of the authors and artists whose work for children was so prolifically published in the turbulent seventies? It is impossible to look back on the decade in its final year and predict which of its books, if any, will become 'classics', for children's classics must have that enduring child appeal which cannot be judged by adults standing up close to books not written for them anyway. All one can usefully do is try to identify those that are examples of trends we have seen developing.

So, Alan Garner's *Stone Book* quartet? Richard Adams's *Watership Down*? The *Stone Book* quartet seems likely to survive as a literary peak; one can imagine observers of the future remarking that Alan Garner's work was a symphony rousing the intellectual young reader of the seventies to an awareness of the dying crafts that once gave man his dignity, and the local dialects that used to distinguish him from his fellow countrymen. In the year 2001 the historical researcher may handle the first editions of the Garner quartet printed (well, photo-lithographed) on fine cream paper and illustrated with etchings by Michael Foreman, and marvel at the skill with which author, artist, publisher and printer could interweave their crafts and make the medium—a finely produced book—reflect the author's message.

Watership Down, on the other hand, must surely be the supreme example of a freak success that resulted in self-perpetuating sales stimulated partly by the non-book media, so much a feature of the scene in the latter half of the twentieth century. An ugly, expensive, unillustrated hard-cover book with a cheap black-line jacket design printed on buff-coloured paper (probably soon to be worth a fortune on the antiquarian market, for it was a small first edition) then became a children's paperback, a deluxe hard-cover book illustrated (in matching slipcase) by John Lawrence, a paperback for adults, an animated cartoon film (with a book of the film); and, from the film's musical score, came a hit single in the 'Top Twenty'.

But was either of these phenomena really a children's book?

What *is* a children's book was the question being asked throughout the seventies when adults were gradually discovering that the genre so described could be the repository of fine writing as well as of the coarser bran that is part of the stuff of children's reading. Is there a line to be drawn between children's novels and adults'? If so, where does it come?

The needs of the reading adolescent became a preoccupation of the seventies—as a counterbalance, perhaps, to the alarmist press reports on illiteracy among school-leavers (which led to the Adult Literacy campaign). But could the teenage reader who had read literary children's books avidly, jump into modern adult fiction with its avant garde themes and experimental techniques? A century ago the progress from *Alice's Adventures in Wonderland* to Dickens, the Brontës and Thackeray was natural and gentle. But nowadays the jump from the best in children's fiction—*Tom's Midnight Garden*, say—to a Booker Award winner such as John Berger's *G* was a veritable moonshot into uncharted territory. Some kind of bridge literature was thought to be necessary.

It is commonly said, and wrongly, that the narrative art is dead in adult fiction. The thrillers of Frederick Forsyth, the fantasies of Ian Fleming, the romances of Barbara Cartland (to name but a few British bestsellers) to be found on every station and airport bookstall are visible proof that the narrative art is alive in popular adult fiction and is big business. Teenagers read adult bestsellers, of course; they also read magazines and the various series that are published by educational departments of publishing houses for direct sale to schools. What is missing in their leisure reading is, it has been felt, the literary novel with an adolescent hero or heroine seen coming to terms with the world and self. Both Salinger's *Catcher in the Rye* and Golding's *Lord of the Flies*, published on adult lists, had attracted a huge following among adolescents because each was a literary masterpiece born out of the author's personal obsession with the flowering of personality, with youth in dilemma. Such books stood out. Was there not therefore a place within the widening area of so-called children's publishing for literary books, perhaps technically unconventional, with a strong adolescent theme?

William Mayne's *A Game of Dark*, John Gordon's *The House on the Brink*, Jane Gardam's *Bilgewater*, Ivan Southall's *Josh* and

William Corlett's *Gate of Eden* were published, with jackets carefully designed to invite the intended readership, on children's lists. So were Alan Garner's complex and challenging *Red Shift* and Jan Mark's haunting fantasy of the future, *The Ennead*. Even Gollancz, with its outstanding list of American teenage novels (including Hinton's *That Was Then, This Is Now* and Cormier's *I Am the Cheese*—good examples of, respectively, realism and new fictional techniques used with startling brilliance), does not have a separate series for its adolescent fiction. Only The Bodley Head, with its New Adult label, has chosen to identify those books whose form and content remove them from the sphere of interest of under-twelves.* Launched with Paul Zindel's seminal book in the field, *The Pigman* (first published in America), it has gone on to publish novels from Scandinavia by Gunnel Beckman, from Australia by J. M. Couper, and home-grown—by Emma Smith, Peggy Woodford, Aidan Chambers. The teenage novel, given impetus by the New Adult label of The Bodley Head, now finds its way into adult libraries and on to special shelves in youth libraries, whereas before, because it fell between two spheres of interest, it had tended to be ignored.

In bookshops, however, where to put these hybrid creatures (too advanced in literary construction or subject matter for children yet not sufficiently fully explored to give satisfaction to the mature adult reader) has been a major headache. Because the problem has not been resolved, paperback teenage fiction has not had the outlet it deserves through bookshops, which cater for children and for adults but generally speaking do not recognize the bridge. This was defined for me by Jill Paton Walsh when she said that, had *Goldengrove* and *Unleaving* been intended for adults, she would have approached the writing quite differently; yet no one could describe them as children's books.

Is the teenage novel towards which many children's authors have gravitated because of the good critical reception accorded to it on children's book pages (where it does not properly belong) and the recognition that follows, a real art form? In the sixties the novels of Rosemary Sutcliff, Barbara Willard, Henry Treece and

*The 'Oxford Novels' with their fine printing and line illustrations are an entirely sixties concept.

K. M. Peyton could mingle pleasantly with children's books or with adult historical novels. But the teenage novel set in the seventies has the aggression and the character of its intended readership, and is therefore an awkward phenomenon uneasily accommodated. Is it a bridge to adult fiction—if such a bridge is necessary? Or is it, as some authors who have written well-received novels in the genre tend to fear, a literary cul-de-sac? Finite answers to these questions will not be forthcoming until the current wave of concentration on the adolescent recedes.

Our researcher in the year 2001 (who took a look at the *Stone Book* quartet, you will remember) might decide to study the change in the background to and characters in children's fiction in the process of examining what was happening in the world around him when he, in his thirties in 2001, was a child in the 1970s. The popularity of science fiction in the period when the Man *on* the Moon joined hands with the Man *in* the Moon as a fantasy figure (there is no boundary between the real and the imaginary when the real experience is vicarious) will be evident. Teenagers were offered hundreds of SF titles, often by authors for adults, while the younger child's heroes tended to be by-products of American or British TV series, the *Star Trek* books or *Dr Who* stories.

The researcher would discover that the children's novel was only slowly beginning to reflect the multicultural nation that he remembered from his own schooldays. He would observe that, though the British tradition in fantasy literature was being maintained by authors like Penelope Lively and Diana Wynne Jones, children's fiction was being stretched to envelop contemporary situations that cut across class and colour. And if he is sharp, he will notice the efforts that were being made to retain literary standards while accommodating valid fresh demands from those who recognized the importance, at a certain stage of development in a person's life, of identification with fictional situations in practical as well as emotional terms.

The authors most likely to interest him will be Jean MacGibbon and Alison Prince, Bernard Ashley, Jan Mark and Gene Kemp, who between them resuscitated the defunct school story (three of them are teachers), and wrote not about *The Fifth Form at St Dominic's* or *The School at the Chalet*, but about the local comprehensive (in *Hal* and *The Doubting Kind*) or primary (in *Terry on the Fence, Thunder and Lightnings* and *The Turbulent Term of Tyke Tiler*). Jan Needle tackled the problems faced by an immigrant Pakistani family in Bradford in a novel called *My Mate Shofiq*, a book that offended some white liberal guidelines-addicts because abusive epithets were not edited out of the dialogue: we were being asked, it seems, to present a realistic picture of Pakistani experience in Bradford without showing the hero's subjection to the unsavoury nicknames that were part of the reality. Farrukh Dhondy, an Indian teacher and a gifted author, described the book as 'funny, violent and authentic. Its positive strength,' he added, 'is that it doesn't see Asians as victims. *Shofiq* is probably the first book written in Britain which tackles race and refuses to fall into community relations bathos' (*Children's Book Bulletin* No. 1, June 1979). Farrukh Dhondy himself won the Collins prize for a group of multi-ethnic short stories with *Come to Mecca*, a compassionate, sad, funny, even-handed collection (for teenagers) of great power and persuasion; this book more than any other may emerge as the reliable barometer of seventies' aspiration.

Collins' initiative in launching this prize was a sign of the dearth of multi-ethnic material, as well as an earnest of the good-will awaiting it when time was ripe for it to emerge. But during the 1970s the need for novels of good quality centring on non-white heroes or heroines was filled to a large extent by the publication in Britain of novels that originated in the United States—by authors such as Rosa Guy, Virginia Hamilton and Louise Fitzhugh.

Race relations, though far and away the most important sociological concern to emerge in children's fiction, was not the only contender for a place in front of the mirror. The politics of Ulster found their reflection in the series of non-sectarian novels by Joan Lingard (beginning with *The Twelfth Day of July*), in Sam McBratney's *Mark Time*, in Peter Carter's *Under Goliath*. Life at the bottom (of a pile of cans in the supermarket when shelf-filling, for instance) was illuminated by the work of Susan Price in *Sticks and Stones* and other novels; Winifred Cawley and Gwen Grant wrote with cheerful gusto about their own working-class child-hoods, and Stanley Watts was acclaimed as a young person's D. H. Lawrence when *The Breaking of Arnold* was published in 1971.

Anti-sexism took many forms; Marjorie Darke in *A Question of Courage* looked back to suffragette struggles; Gene Kemp in *The Turbulent Term of Tyke Tiler* painted an unforgettable picture of a unisex eleven-year-old immersed in the everyday politics of home and primary school (the surprise ending of this book causes an uproar when it is read aloud to mixed groups of Tyke's age); Michael Foreman in *All the King's Horses*, a tongue-in-cheek picture book about an Amazonian princess who wrestles her suitors out of the ring, succeeded in getting across the message that girls can be other than blue-eyed fair creatures whose fathers pick husbands for them, far better than the so-called 'non-sexist' picture books imported from Italy by the Writers and Readers Publishing Co-operative: these were aggressively anti-male.

Picture Books and Verse

Michael Foreman emerges as just one of the many picture-book artists in the seventies who began to use the medium to express ideas beyond the comprehension of the under-sevens, the traditional picture-book age. Although under-sevens look at and enjoy picture books by Charles Keeping, Quentin Blake, Graham Oakley, Anthony Browne, Colin McNaughton and Michael Foreman himself, the social and political satire is appreciated only by the more mature reader, from the age of nine upwards. As 1979 draws to a close, many of those who use books with children are a long way from recognizing the readership for this new art form, despite the glare of publicity for it attracted by the publication of Raymond Briggs's *Fungus the Bogeyman*, an evocation of a murky sub-world (the Alternative Society?) spun in gloom-green watercolour and a vocabulary of punning virtuosity.

Along with this upward trend in interest in picture books there developed a compensatory swing towards simplicity. John Burningham's *Mr Gumpy's Outing* and his Little Books series, Helen Oxenbury's *A B C of Things*, Ray and Catriona Smith's *The Long Slide*, Allan and Janet Ahlberg's *Each Peach Pear Plum*, Robert Crowther's *Most Amazing Hide-and-Seek Alphabet Book*, Mary Rayner's *Mr and Mrs Pig's Evening Out* and Pascale Allamand's *The Camel Who Left the Zoo* were among the outstanding picture books for the very young to emerge in the decade; while Nicola Bayley, launched by Jonathan Cape with her minutely detailed, jewel-like illustrations for *Nicola Bayley's Book of Nursery Rhymes*, had a double appeal to patient child and perceptive adult.

Dan Jones, an East London painter of the Lowry school, provided an inner-city, 1970s, political gloss on many an old nursery rhyme in *Mother Goose Comes to Cable Street*, one of the few effortlessly multicultural picture books to emerge in the decade. (Other artists in this field were Errol Lloyd and Ossie Murray, who illustrated Petronella Breinburg's *Sean* and *Sally-Ann* books.) *Mother Goose Comes to Cable Street* has a vogue among older children who enjoy the fun of the fresh interpretation of rhymes they already know. The verse of poets like Mike Rosen in *Mind Your Own Business* and Roger McGough in *In the Glassroom* is in the same catch-life-and-look-at-it spirit. Colloquial and sharply humorous, their work (they are joint authors of *You Tell Me*) has direct appeal in an age when creative writing by school-children, encouraged by the Arts Council's Writers in Schools project, has been flourishing.

Perhaps this is the place to record the mushroom growth of community publishing which, sparked off by Centerprise in Hackney, encourages embryonic talent by giving it local exposure in booklet, or indeed book, form. As technology develops and word processors descend from the realm of wishful possession into common practical use, outlets will increase. Maybe in the year 2001 a child (paraphrasing the title of a popular seventies picture book) may ask 'Why are there more writers than readers, Grand-dad?' But that is a question we do not have to answer in 1979. What we do know is that, here and now, the writing of authors published by community publishers is reaching a readership that was non-existent at the beginning of the decade. Whether there will develop from this a new readership for the books published by mainstream publishers, whether the work of authors for community projects will cross-fertilize with that of authors published nationally, it is too early to tell. But it would be sad if the two rivers did not find their way into a common sea.

Information Books

The technological revolution has already had an immense influence on the information books of the seventies. The possibility of packaging series for the international market seized upon by

Octopus, Hamlyn, Macdonald, Usborne and many others brought into being the corporate authorship of many flavourless books by committees of experts. The glossy bland colour photography (dug up by a researcher from a photo library), the two-page spread devoted to each aspect (whether important or minor) of the subject, the captions, the potted, often meaningless, text became unbearably familiar—though Usborne's Know How series struck sparks from their readers by inviting them to share in the fun of experimenting with science, conjuring, detection.

Spurned as dehydrated food by the critics, these 'packages' were welcomed and bought by teachers for many reasons, of which total accuracy could not have been one. (Margery Fisher's *Matters of Fact*, published in 1972, had interesting things to say on the subject of accuracy and the dangers of blind belief in the printed word.) Where else, teachers asked with some reason, could you find pictures and basic information that might be offered to a child of perhaps thirteen with a reading age of seven or eight? And for children *of* seven or eight, with an average to high reading age, the Macdonald type book was a first step to discovering for themselves how fishes live, what games Romans played, how their own grandparents travelled about. With so much project-based learning in primary schools, resulting in the decline in the use of the history or geography textbooks that had been sold in sets by non-net publishers, the rise of Macdonald style information books was inevitable. This does not mean that there is not plenty of scope for improvement in these series which, though designed for school use, are individually sold as 'net' books. Their success highlights the need for the committed zoologist, archaeologist, botanist, sportsman, historian to write stimulating personal books about their own fields of interest for the young disciple.

Canute-like, and in this spirit, the *Times Educational Supplement* set up its Information Book Awards to encourage publishers to improve their standards in this area, giving its prize in the second year to David Hay's *Human Populations*, part of Penguin Education's ill-fated schools project, a brilliantly conceived, far-sighted series that, despite being ahead of its time, should somehow have survived. As the years went by, two publishers became conspicuously successful in winning *TES* awards:

Kestrel with books on single subjects (*Window into a Nest, Street Flowers, Tournaments*) and The Bodley Head, with books that are part of their Archaeology and New Biology series. Each book was a shining example of what can be done by specialists working for children, and richly deserved the limelight thrown on it by the *TES*. Odd, therefore, that the winner in the senior section in 1977 should have been the volume called *Man and Machines* in Mitchell Beazley's Joy of Knowledge encyclopaedia, for this is an advanced example of the authorship-by-committee, design-by-convenience, multinational-edition publication that has been such a widespread feature of information book publishing in the decade.

Television is one medium that is often made the scapegoat for 'falling standards' in education; yet, looking at the seventies, one can see that in the field of information it has made an enormous contribution, even leaving aside the programmes specially tailored for school use. As one example, David Attenborough's *Life on Earth* was watched by children of all ages who then clamoured for the BBC book based on the series. Its complex text is enlivened by captioned colour photographs of the highest quality that illustrate Mr Attenborough's quest (children love quests) to discover the roots and growth of life on this planet. In response to pressure from some less literate children (in the nine- to ten-year-old group) I decided to buy this single volume, which cost around £8 and was published for the adult market, for the primary school library in which I work. It has received greater attention, attracted deeper and more far-reaching discussion than Macdonald's *The Life of Fishes*, *The Life of Birds*, *The Life of Plants*, which together cost more, cover less and lack the personal touch, that magic spark which sets light to creative thinking.

Nature photography of a high calibre such as the Oxford Scientific Film Unit has produced (for Flanagan and Morris's *Window into a Nest*, for example, and the Whizzard/Deutsch Nature's Way series) invites the child in to observe nature's secrets, slowly unfolding. For other documentary-type books, too, the camera, which is generally believed to be a truthful recorder, has proved useful. A. & C. Black's series called Strands, showing the daily life, religious practices, eating habits, occupations of the many ethnic groups that make up modern British society, is one outstanding example; Kestrel's monotone-photograph series on people at work (*Newspaperworker, Railwayworker*, etc.) is another.

Books and other media are mutually supportive on the whole, but it is also true that the provision of books in schools has been threatened to some extent in the 1970s by audio-visual equipment. I cannot regard books as a 'medium for information retrieval' (though they are one, of course); but I have no difficulty whatsoever in applying that awkward term to 'hardware' and its accompanying 'software'. The place of audio-visual aids as part of education is only my concern in so far as it affects the provision of books. The relatively high cost of other media equipment must in some measure be responsible for the state of affairs described by the Books for Schools working party in the National Book League pamphlet *Books in Schools*. The purchase of 'software' (film, slides, tapes) for 'hardware' (cameras, projectors, cassette players) that is not fully operational cannot make financial sense in a period of economic crisis. Books may fall apart from use but they do not go out of order.

Reviewing and Promotion

So what has been the dominant theme of the seventies in children's books? We have seen social forces at work: educational thinking, sex-politics and race relations have entered the field strongly, not in opposition to the literary book but as centrifugal forces which will spread the pattern of content and the points of physical identification across sex, class and colour.

Centrifugalism was evident too in the business of publishing, where international editions of picture books and series of information books 'packaged' for sale throughout the world have become the lynchpins of many a list. With this emphasis on diffusion, it is not surprising to discover that in reviewing, promotion and bookselling, decentralization has also become the keyword.

In criticism, the growth of a strong literary establishment view of children's books early in the decade gave rise to factional opposition later. *The Times*, *The Sunday Times*, the *TLS*, *The Guardian*, the two *Telegraphs*, *The Observer*, and Margery Fisher's

Growing Point became the bastions of general children's book reviewing; while the *TES*, Woodfield and Stanley's *Junior Bookshelf* and the School Library Association's *School Librarian* catered for librarians and teachers. Many 1970s projects swept through the breach that Anne Wood's *Books for Your Children* (and the activities of the Federation of Children's Book Groups) had, in the sixties, made in the establishment wall, and thrust out in all directions.

Looking back, in the summer of '79 when *The Sunday Times*, *The Times* and all its supplements have been off the streets for seven months due to an industrial dispute over new technology (another force that influenced the course of publishing in the seventies was trade union activity, one result of which was a decision by the Society of Authors to affiliate with the Trades Union Congress), these thrusts seem to have been fortuitous. Everywhere the voices of teachers, librarians, parents (combined with those of children in Hertfordshire's carefully blended *Material Matters*) are being heard on the subject of children's books. The proliferation of book review sheets and small journals published by various schools library services, local education authorities, and colleges of education is heartening: these in no way replace the need for national press coverage but they are evidence of a welcome upsurge in do-it-yourself comment, a parallel to the community publishing already mentioned. Indeed those two new magazines that arrived in my mail on 19 June 1979 were both offshoots of community groups.

But let us return to the year 1970, which saw the birth of two journals: *Signal*, whose decade of life, independent of publisher support by way of advertising and untied by its open-door policy to any particular aspect of children's books, is celebrated this year; and *Children's Literature in Education*, originally intended to be the vehicle for carrying the words of wisdom spoken at the Exeter Conference to the world outside (but now a rather less happy American/British mix of classroom-oriented articles, published in the USA). Neither of these journals is a medium for straight reviewing: *Children's Book Review*, which began publication in 1971, was just that, but its life proved short.

The decade saw a flood of books on children's literature, however; some originated in America, others here. By and large the contributions worth noting were original works rather than the compilation of reprints of articles by a variety of authors roughly sewn together by editors and pushed through presses. The shining exception to this generalization is *The Cool Web* which, because of Margaret Meek's gift for editing, shaping and writing fresh linking commentary, for bringing articles together in order to throw questions into the arena, involves the reader in her argument.

Among the original books on children's literature published during the decade there was *The Thorny Paradise*, for which compilation Edward Blishen invited well-known children's authors to write articles on why and how they write for children; and there was John Rowe Townsend's *A Sense of Story*, which concentrated on the narrative art of major writers, both British and American.

Though not strictly within my terms of reference, since it is American in origin, Bruno Bettelheim's *The Uses of Enchantment* made such a vital contribution to the thinking of the decade that to omit it would be absurd. Subtitled 'The Meaning and Importance of Fairy Tales', it is a most significant statement on the life-enriching force of story in childhood. Since folk and fairy tale are universal and for all time, this book, born of disciplines related to but other than our own, reinforces from outside our conviction that the *emotional* content of traditional tales speaks more directly to all children (from single-parent families, immigrant communities, residential homes) than the surface *physical* similarities that agitators for pre-fab politikidlit urge publishers to produce.

Gillian Avery helped us to see modern movements in perspective with *Childhood's Pattern*, in which she demonstrated clearly that society has always sought its own reflection and the reflection of its moral standards in the heroes and heroines it offers young readers. Margery Fisher in *Who's Who in Children's Books* puts all those characters into their own settings, a mammoth task which, incidentally, has proved popular with children as well as invaluable to workers in the field. Dorothy Butler's *Cushla and Her Books* is an exploration of the part picture books can play in infancy, based (1970s style) on the experience of using them with one severely handicapped child. That book, along with Brian Alderson's academic and idiosyncratic catalogue for the National Book

League's *Looking at Picture Books* exhibition, may point towards more critical interest in this expanding field in the 1980s.

For *After 'Alice'*, an exhibition of 'children's reading' to celebrate the centenary of the Library Association in 1977, Christine Kloet selected books and comics that children, left to themselves, have chosen as favourites (Biggles, Blyton, Borrowers, Beano, Basil Brush) as well as the literary landmarks of the century. The catalogue for this exhibition was notable for its superb production as well as for its author's sense of perspective.

Exhibitions were just one of the promotional channels that typified the centrifugal forces at work in the seventies. The National Book League Touring Exhibitions—of which my own *Children's Books of the Year*, which began its life in 1970, is one—spread and developed into a network that covered the British Isles, while the catalogues to the exhibitions found their way all over the world. Other organizations such as the Youth Libraries Group and the School Library Association were making booklists too, to help teachers and parents cope with the huge number of children's books in print. *Signal* entered the field with Alan Tucker's *Poetry Books for Children*, Lance Salway's *Humorous Books for Children* and Jill Bennett's *Learning to Read with Picture Books*, all of which were used as bases for NBL Touring Exhibitions, as indeed were the four *Reading for Enjoyment* booklists originally published in 1970 by Children's Booknews Ltd, a subsidiary of the Children's Book Centre.

The Children's Book Centre itself, the biggest children's bookshop in Britain (the world?), which sold children's books far and wide, moved into grand new premises in the latter part of the decade—and into a financial situation that resulted in control of the enterprise being taken over by Jim Slater (of Slater Walker repute) from Eric Baker, a committed children's bookman. That this was a sign of the (bad) times one glance at the windows of Children's Book Centre today (crammed with adult bestsellers and mammoth stuffed toys) will demonstrate.

But all was by no means gloomy on the bookselling front in the 1970s. Several new children's bookshops appeared; Heffers of Cambridge in 1979 transformed its children's bookshop into a model of what children's bookselling can be; the Book Boat was launched on the Thames (next to the *Cutty Sark*); Centerprise of

Hackney became the first of a long line of community booksellers, most of which have support either from the local authority or from an Arts Association, to open a children's department. By far the most exciting and imaginative development, however, was the foundation of the School Bookshop Association (in 1976) as the centre for information about the setting up of bookshops in schools. There were already bookshops in some schools, due to the initiative of Penguin. But until the Bullock Report declared that it 'becomes increasingly the responsibility of the school to make it possible for children and parents together to see and select books which can be bought and taken home', a full-scale open thrust into schools was impossible. Peter Kennerley was the initiator of the movement and edited its magazine, *School Bookshop News* [later to become *Books for Keeps*].

School bookshops enabled parents and children to 'see and select'; there were also, in the 1970s, several mail order book clubs (Scholastic, Bookworm, Puffin School Book Club) in operation. These paperback ventures appear to be highly successful, but there is some evidence that the selling of hard-cover children's books by mail order through book clubs is less so.

Taking all these developments into account and adding to them the nationwide activities of the Federation of Children's Book Groups (which celebrated its tenth anniversary in mid decade) one can see that the sale of books directly to the children who will be tomorrow's adult readers increased substantially in an era when the economic trends threatened the supplies of books available for borrowing through school and public libraries.

But publishers must still promote their books if anyone with funds to spend is to buy them. Giant promotion schemes like the Publishers' Association Children's Book Show, a prominent feature of the London children's book calendar in the sixties, also went through a stage of decentralization (Leeds 1971, London and Bristol 1972, Manchester 1973, Glasgow 1974) as a preliminary to giving way to a much less ambitious and costly two-day event, the Bloomsbury Conference and Trade Fair in 1975. In 1976 the Conference subject was, significantly, 'Are we publishing the right children's books?' and the voice of every sphere of interest covered in this survey was heard. In 1977 the Book Fair itself was dropped, which means that there is now no major children's book show or fair in Britain, though many small shows take place with publisher support. National Children's Book Week, which has now come to rest in October, has the advantage of attracting publicity from the media; but cramming hundreds of events into a single week means that publishers, authors and artists are in impossibly heavy demand over a short seven-day stretch, whereas many would prefer to spread their support for events throughout the year.

A number of prizes for children's books are announced in or around National Children's Book Week, including the Library Association's medals. In 1970 there were only three established prizes for children's books: the Library Association's Carnegie and Kate Greenaway Medals, and the *Guardian* Award. In 1979 there are eight, with others pending. Again the centrifugal force is in operation, for there is now the Other Award (which concentrates on content of a multicultural, anti-sexist or working-class nature), the occasional inclusion of a children's book award among the Whitbread Prizes, the Mother Goose Award for new illustrators, the *TES* Awards (see above) and the Signal Poetry Award; and there is talk of two fresh awards, from the Arts Council and the Society of Authors, coming in the eighties. If the spread of awards comes to mean the highlighting of different kinds of books (according to the terms of reference for each prize), that must be healthy; but the tendency for award givers to reflect one another's leanings, manifest at the present moment, is rather disturbing.

The only award given annually in the children's book field for work that is not authorship or illustration is the Eleanor Farjeon Award 'for distinguished services to children's books'. If any quick pointer were to be sought to dominant trends of children's book activity in the 1970s, the list of winners of this award would provide it. By and large the recipients have been people actively engaged, through teacher training, storytelling in parks, book clubs, exhibitions and the establishment of a study centre outside Melbourne in Australia, in the spread of knowledge about children's books to the people who are in a position to reach out with those books to children. Television has helped all of us to reach the child at home: by the serialization of children's novels, with programmes like *Playschool* and *Jackanory*, and Yorkshire TV's new series of programmes about children's books called *Book Tower*. That the last Eleanor Farjeon Award announced in the seventies (in 1979 for the year 1978) was to Joy Whitby, who was responsible for the initiation of all these programmes, was symbolic of a decade in which it was recognized that if books were to be published for children, the children who were the potential readers were an important consideration. This may sound like a truism, but in some quarters it is still anathema.

In the 1970s the emphasis shifted from the adults who wrote, illustrated, published and criticized children's books to the channels through which these books could be brought into the hands of the child. For whatever the child's race, sex, circumstance, stories are the medium through which he can come to terms with his existence and become that supreme being, his own person. Because the seventies were the period during which these movements gained impetus, years in which the needs of children were recognized and considered, years in which the child was seen as an integral part of the book he read, this survey of the decade was entitled not *British Children's Books in the Seventies* but, a subtle difference, *The Seventies in British Children's Books*. For the spirit of the age has deeply affected our view of what we are doing. For better or worse? We do not know.

The Signal Approach to Children's Books, 1980

PART 3
RECORDED DELIVERIES
1979–1985

Illustration from *Father Christmas*, © Raymond Briggs

In 1979, after ten years, I gave up selecting *Children's Books of the Year* and Barbara Sherrard-Smith, who had co-operated with me on the tenth volume, took over.

Children's Books of the Year had addressed itself mainly to the librarians and teachers whose book funds, though increasingly threatened, had not yet reached the nadir of the mid-eighties. Already in the late seventies publishers, raising their eyes from the crystal ball, had begun to focus them on the bookshop and to produce the toy-books and puzzle books (*Masquerade* was published in 1979) that attract a non-reading public into the market. The big challenge that faced the children's book trade in the late seventies, and still faces it today, is not how to sell gimmickry to the non-reader (though that is what the marketing men are interested in) but how to build on that sale and develop from it readers of real books.

When *The Good Book Guide*, which had come into being in 1977, again asked me to become its Children's Books Adviser in 1980 (I had refused in 1977 because of my commitment to *Children's Books of the Year*) I was delighted. I sensed that this lively enterprise, of which the ebullient Bing Taylor is the literary heart, would come to make its mark in children's as well as adult bookselling. A new concept, the Guide combines a bi-monthly magazine, in which books selected by the editors and their specialist advisers are reviewed, with a mail order bookselling service for readers wishing to avail themselves of it. Every book selected is stocked ready for mail order. Unlike subscribers to book clubs, however, readers of *The Good Book Guide* are under no obligation ever to purchase a single book. But they do buy books by mail order through the Guide's 'Bookpost' service because book distribution through bookshops to the public is the weakest link in the British book trade. Thousands of potential book-buyers are lost each year because, appetite whetted by a review in a newspaper, they then cannot find a bookshop that stocks, or can obtain in a few days, the book they want.

As a reviewer of children's books over the preceding twenty years I was by 1980 acutely aware of parents' and teachers' problems in tracking down copies of books recommended. Here at last was an opportunity to recommend *and sell* children's books to subscribers all over Britain and, indeed, overseas. This was the real world in which reviewer and consumer would meet eyeball to eyeball, the world in which parents were loath to spend money on children's books but were buying videos and computer software without, it would seem, a second's thought. Through the Guide's publications—which in 1983 came to include *The Good Book Guide to Children's Books*—we could give space to the cream of picture books, folk tale collections, novels in paperback and information books, with a passing reference to the money spinners of the moment such as pop-ups or fighting fantasy game books, the Coke and crisps of the trade. Wc could then watch the sales patterns. These showed that whilst the gimmicky products sell themselves (yet are perpetually promoted by huge publisher investment into even bigger bestsellers) one can also sell real children's books to parents by reviewing them and having them stocked for immediate sale by mail order. Over forty copies of the hardback edition of Philippa Pearce's *The Way to Sattin Shore* flew out of the Guide's warehouse as the result of a rave review in the magazine.

That there is a market for the best in children's books if one can reach it, is a point worth making in the mid-eighties because the children's book world is in danger of being taken over by media and marketing people to the extent that one sometimes wonders whether they understand, or care about, the threat they are posing to the goose who still labours to produce the truly golden, in intrinsic terms, egg. Yes, they can make a certain part of the children's book business look trendier and more profitable by banging the seductive hollow drum. The book business *is* a business and must survive in economic terms. But if the main purpose of children's publishing—creating books for the adventurous and contented reading child—is not to be lost sight of, we should take an occasional look in the rear mirror to see what we might now be in danger of edging permanently on to the hard shoulder.

If ever there was a time to speak out about children's books and *reading*, it is the 1980s.

It is comfortably assumed by most of us that anyone who has an interesting life in a particular field can talk about it in public. Throughout the 1970s I had ducked many invitations to talk about children and books to teachers, librarians and parents. Radio I could manage, since I always felt I was talking to myself or having a private chat with the interviewer. As a guest on a television programme you sink into comfortable obscurity since the legions of technicians with their lights, cameras, sound recording equipment are far too busy attending the technical quality to take any notice of what you are actually saying. But the idea of standing up before a live audience had always terrified me.

Then, out of the blue and on to my doormat, fell a handsome cream-laid envelope from The Center for the Book at the Library of Congress in Washington. Inside was a courteous letter from Mr John Y. Cole inviting me to speak as the British half of a 'program' designed to celebrate the International Year of the Child in 1979. Barbara Rollock of the New York Public Library would address herself to the chosen subject—The Audience for Children's Books—from the standpoint of the United States. Would I do the same for Britain?

Here was an invitation that was the equivalent of a royal command. Unless I was due to be orbiting the Earth on an Apollo space mission there was no way I could refuse. Surely I would wake up from this nightmare with a sigh of relief? But I did not. I wrote back to Mr Cole thanking him for the invitation, and six months later, speech written and rehearsed (and rehearsed), new evening attire bought and carefully packed, I was on my way—not just to Washington but to an awareness that even I, who had muffed my lines as Brutus in a scene from *Julius Caesar* at the age of eight and dreamed about it spasmodically ever since, could speak in public.

Between 1979 and 1985 I found myself speaking to teachers, librarians and parents at PTA meetings, seminars, in-service training sessions up and down the country. Most of these were informal sessions designed to energize and encourage a wide variety of audiences to read, read, read to children; and to read children's literature of all kinds to themselves so that they could advise children and respond to children's comments on books. Enthusiasm and a willingness to carry with me loads of books that would make my point for me seemed to compensate for my hesitant performance as an extempore speaker.

But it was during this time too that I was invited on four

occasions to deliver formal lectures: the International Year of the Child address at the Library of Congress; the Sidney Robbins Memorial Lecture at the University of London Institute of Education; the Woodfield Lecture at Loughborough University; and a lecture at the 16th Loughborough International Seminar on Children's Literature at the University of Wales School of Librarianship in Aberystwyth.

Each of these gave me the opportunity to pull together different strands of the pattern of which I am part.

THE AUDIENCE FOR CHILDREN'S BOOKS

The topic chosen by the Library of Congress for its International Year of the Child 'program' in 1979 threw the ball right into my court. The 'audience for children's books' never to be lost sight of is the child—not the critic, the sociologist, the psychiatrist, the teacher of children's literature in a university or any other adult whose interest in his own discipline leads him to comment on a field that rightfully belongs to someone else. Here was an opportunity to bring the broad range of children back into the centre of the stage. I took it with some trepidation because my American audience was likely to be composed largely of those I wished to dismiss to the perimeter.

When the invitation to take part in this symposium on *The Audience for Children's Books* arrived in London, I was filled with conflicting emotions. One of them was an overwhelming sense of the honour the Library of Congress and the Center for the Book were conferring upon me by asking me to be the British voice at this meeting, their contribution to the events that mark the International Year of the Child.

This Library is not, as I understand it, an élitist institution reserved for senators, congressmen, and scholars, but a library for ordinary citizens too. So I need not, I think, apologize for bringing children in among you tonight. Indeed, we all belong together, the adult, the child, and his book.

And where better to begin than with Robert Louis Stevenson, a British author who drew our two nations together when he dedicated his best known work, *Treasure Island*, to Lloyd Osborne, his stepson—'an American gentleman'. This American gentleman was, I once read, aged between ten and twelve when he and his stepfather were at work creating Long John Silver, Israel Hands, and the rest of the colourful crew of the *Hispaniola*. Between ten and twelve. As this talk turns full circle, I shall suggest that the proper audience for all real children's books is aged about eleven.

But let us stay with Stevenson for a moment and listen to the verses he wrote for English children in Victorian times, years before jet travel forced the layman to come to terms physically with the movement of the planets.

> When at eve I rise from tea,
> Day dawns beyond the Atlantic Sea,
> And all the children in the West
> Are getting up and being dressed.

Stevenson's poem, with its cosy vision of 'each little Indian sleepy-head . . . being kissed and put to bed' is a far cry from the United Nations' concern with the practical realities of childhood as seen by today's sun 'as round the World his way he makes.' The purpose of the International Year of the Child is to focus on deprivation among the world's children. This trans-Atlantic seminar concentrates on food not for the child's body but for his mind, and in particular on books for children in the English language.

In its title 'The *Audience* for Children's Books,' this symposium invites, if I am not mistaken, comment on the scope of, and readership for, the vast number of books that make up the profitable children's book market in the United States and in Great Britain.

About the situation in the United States I know almost nothing, since knowing for me is always practical experience, and until this visit I had only been in America for a fortnight—and that, technically (despite happy visits to the Children's Book Council in New York and to the Children's Book Division here in the Library of Congress), was a holiday. True, the shelves of the garden room in which I work at home are lined with large volumes of erudite essays on children's literature from the United States. At one point, terrified of appearing before you ignorant, I was tempted to reread (or, dare I say it, in some cases read for the first time) these monuments of considered and considerable American opinion. Then I decided, no. You had, I think, invited me here to share with you my experience of working in the children's book sphere in Britain.

And here we are back again, with the word sphere, to the circular concept. Speaking in the Library of Congress, itself a massive encyclopedia of world knowledge, with its great circular Main Reading Room, the concept is apt. Particularly so because I intend to concentrate my remarks on one word—*audience:* This word *audience* will be the hub of the wheel; each line of thought will radiate outwards from the word towards what is necessarily, in so short a paper, a limited circumference. But surely I need not remind a people whose history and psychology are governed by the frontier and the covered wagon that wheels, once fashioned, roll . . .

Tonight you are my audience. In today's society the opportunities for listening quietly to words diminish year by year. We live in a world that is increasingly and obtrusively noisy. But even if it were quiet, the impact of the word is being eroded by other forms of communication. By the picture—electronic and printed —obviously; but also by the deductions of the exact and social sciences. If these are expressed in words at all, they are expressed in words that are only understood, only meant to be understood, by the small charmed circle of the initiated.

It is, I think, deplorable but understandable (because the children's book world is part of the real world), that in the discussions that go on year in, year out in journals either directly or indirectly concerned with children and reading, a thorny hedge of terminology (borrowed from psychological, educational, linguistic, political, and sociological jargon) has also grown up.

Inside that hedge of thorns, sad to tell, lies the Sleeping Beauty—children's books. Outside—even sadder to reveal— armed not with the gleaming sword of the handsome and determined Prince in the fairy tale but with heavy textbooks designed for college students or works of criticism for scholars, stand the bewildered teachers and parents, defeated before they begin. That there is a Sleeping Beauty—a rich children's literature that is the rightful heritage of every child—they know because they have heard rumours in the village. That they are the Princes whose privilege it is to mediate that literature to the children in their lives, many cannot accept. Do they refuse the undertaking because of, or despite, the specialist?

I am aware, acutely aware, that even those who know about the Sleeping Beauty and wish to wake her and share her gifts with the young have been made to feel so insecure by the outpourings of many of us that, rather than sample directly for themselves the children's books that abound, they take refuge in the safe, sad reading schemes. About these the commercial world, having conducted its market research, speaks out plainly. Back to basics: You Need These. The result? Children today call their reading scheme pamphlets their 'books', and teachers talk about picture books and children's novels as 'supplementary reading material'.

Shame on us! It is our sophistication that has cut us off from the very audience we, as critics, reviewers (*commentators* is the word I honestly prefer in this context), need to reach: the audience in a working situation. For though there is a good case for stretching the intellectual faculties of the university student with academic treatises on various aspects of children's literature, we cannot expect any but the exceptional practising teacher in primary education to keep abreast of current theory.

The sad aspect of this dichotomy is that the student, lacking practical experience of children with books, will not find it easy to absorb in a creative way the academic treatises he reads, whereas the teacher with that practical experience only has time, generally speaking, to read straightforward comment if he is also to sample at least some of the new books. If we care deeply, can we not learn to speak plainly? Great thoughts have been expressed in Haiku. It is the spillover of academic parlance and lengthy argument into comment directed at teachers, among others, that is the thorny content of the forbidding hedge.

In any case we have yet, I think, to devise good criteria for examining an art form brought into being by the existence of a group—the children in our society—of which the critic is not part. As long ago as 1906, a lady called Eveline C. Godley, considering this situation in the course of looking back on the books she read as a child, remarked: 'Our attitude towards what we read is so entirely changed: there is all the difference between surveying a country from a height, and exploring it in detail.'

That the terrain as Eveline Godley envisages it should be there, stretched out before all child explorers, is our main concern. For once children have flown on the gander's wings with Mother Goose, walked in the forests with the Brothers Grimm, or plunged into the Golden River kingdom with John Ruskin, attained with our guidance the literary foothills, Parnassus, should they desire it, is theirs.

But how can we help to ensure that the child audience for children's books is wide, lively, and abundantly served with the huge variety of stories that can alone give children the confidence and experience they need in order to begin to climb?

Let us now leave the audience for children's book *criticism* —vital to our subject this evening, for without informed adults in the field there is little hope that we shall have entranced children—and begin to think about the child audience for children's stories.

We have, in Britain, a radio programme called *Listen with Mother*, an old-fashioned title which embodies a sound (in every sense of the word) idea. You need, if you are of pre-school age (which for us is under five years old), to sit comfortably with an adult in order to listen—to the radio, to a cassette, or to a story being read directly to you from a book. Listening effectively at any age is an active, not a passive, occupation. The audience for a story read aloud must work far harder than the viewer who has the same story told with moving pictures on television. The audience for a story told in words—the way stories have come down to us since time immemorial—must be a weaver of dreams, a painter of pictures, a creative artist akin to the film-maker. Every child born with normal faculties is naturally all these things, internally. But batter that child with crude, flickering images from morning till night and he will lose the great imaginative gifts that have been bestowed on him. Secondhand images will vie with, then vanquish, the self-generated.

Why, then, do we value the picture book so highly? At its most basic, the picture book offers the child a rare commodity: a still picture that he can look at for as long as he is able—which is often no time at all, until one has helped him to slow down his expectation for constant movement and replace it with the excitement of discovery in depth.

The great picture books of the last twenty years are great not because they confine the child's vision to the limits of the story but because they invite the child *in*, to roam about inside the picture—of Max's room, perhaps, 'in which a forest grew and grew—and grew until his ceiling hung with vines and the walls became the world all around.' Sometimes, the pictures give the listening child an altogether different facet of the story from the text. Anyone reading the purposely pedestrian thirty-two words of Pat Hutchins's *Rosie's Walk* to a group of children is made fully aware by the audience that the excitement is in the pictures; for Rosie the hen, all unknowing, is being followed, in those *pictures*, 'across the yard, round the pond, through the fence . . .' by a red-brown animal with crafty eyes and a bushy tail whose species is not so much as hinted at in the text. But clamouring children insist that the reader-aloud should know what is *really* happening in *their* story.

Their story. Involvement is all. Involvement and sharing the excitement of involvement, in the early years and to some extent the later ones, with a parent, a teacher, a librarian, or another child.

Reading aloud to children seems to me to be the key to children's pleasure in books at all ages. There was once a time when families were natural reading circles, and a few such families still exist, but the clock will not be put back. We have now to use the classroom and the library—less cosy than the fireside—as the minstrel's hearth.

In the primary school where I work just once a week as librarian (Britain does not have professional librarians in primary schools, generally speaking), reading aloud to each class once or twice a day has become established by the teachers as a valuable activity for the audience.

Sometimes it is my privilege to read aloud, to tell stories, or to talk about books with children of any age from five to eleven. I have been at this school for almost three years now, and I am sure that I have learned more about what we are all doing—or trying to do—with children's books from the children I now know so well, than ever I've learned from reading theses.

If you listen to children talking about stories and pictures, you begin to approach, for the second time in your life, children's books at ground level. And once your rheumaticky knees have bent, if you are prepared to follow along the children's own paths in a kind of healthy partnership, you will arrive with them at their personal crossroads. Then you can decide together that they should take the road to *Green Knowe*, to *Narnia*, to *Elidor*—to *Tom's Midnight Garden*, to *The House of Wings*, or to the *Shores of Silver Lake*. So often, it seems, the adult approaches the child's crossroads from the North and meets head-on, or at best, sideways on, a reader travelling from the South, East, or West. Being on the same road, even if (as is most likely) it is a road bordered by comics, sports papers, and Scarry, and paved by Nancy Drew, the Hardy Boys, and The Famous Five, establishes, among your travelling companions, the confidence they need to have in you (as someone who at least recognizes the landmarks in their terrain) if you are going to act as guide. If you consistently take the high road, while they take the low, it is quite probable that you will stay at different levels for ever.

It was Richard Hoggart who made the seminal observation that the 'strongest objection to the more trivial entertainments is not that they prevent their readers from becoming highbrow, but that they make it harder for people without an intellectual bent to become wise in their own way.' Children always read for the story, and the trivial, accessible writers like Keene, Dixon, and Blyton are simply providing what children like (a fast-moving story with a heroic hero or heroine) without also providing the vitamins they need but do not know they need.

What happens next in a story written by a mature writer for a child of any age depends not on the author's whim but on the inter-relationship he has built up between the characters, their attitude to circumstance, their reasoning, their quirks of personality. It was no mere accident that Peter Rabbit landed up in that watering-can, nor was it luck that enabled Karana to survive on the *Island of the Blue Dolphins*. A child of eleven (do you remember the age of Robert Louis Stevenson's American gentleman?) will, in the right conditions, draw nourishment from both these stories, but it is quite likely that that child will either not have access to, or not recognize, these diverse sources of pleasure and growth unless there is an informed and involved adult around who keeps the classroom stocked with a wide range of nourishing books. It is from among books of this quality that the teacher carefully selects those he or she will read aloud. The reading aloud of such books ensures that not only the able reader but the faltering reader too is all the time in contact with stories at his own emotional level.

But at about eleven, children need to range freely—among rubbish if they enjoy it, for even rubbish has its value: it provides something against which they can measure other stories, it is entertaining, and it is ephemerally anarchic. I asked a group of ten-to-eleven year olds if they would make a list for me of what they read *to themselves* in the course of a few weeks. The results were illuminating, heartening, and funny. Science fiction, joke books, family stories, adult detective stories, adventures, comics, information books about hobbies or projects, of course; and the sly reference to 'my sister's diary' or 'a letter to Mum that I wasn't meant to see'. Not a single adolescent novel, I noted. *But* Charlotte Zolotow and Maurice Sendak's *Mr Rabbit and the Lovely Present*, Raymond Briggs's silent book *The Snowman*, Dick Bruna's *Miffy Goes Flying*, Arnold Lobel's *Frog and Toad Are Friends*, and John Burningham's *Would You Rather?* also appeared. These picture books were on the same lists as novels by Philippa Pearce, Nina Bawden, Betsy Byars, J. R. R. Tolkien, Joan Aiken, and Beverly Cleary. This may surprise some of you but not shock you, I hope.

It has taken me a couple of years to break down, in that school, the artificial barriers which publishers, booksellers, and less aware teachers erect between books that look as though they are for the very young, and those that, as blurbs tend to say, 'ought to be found on every ten-year-old's bookshelf'. If a story told in pictures or simple words is more than a 'what-happens-next', if it subtly indicates why events occur and how they affect the characters of people (or animals), then that story can fruitfully be read by a child or adult of any age. The advantages to the less able reader of seeing all his peer group handling what might otherwise bear the stigma of baby stuff is, of course, immeasurable. It implies that it is OK for him to look at and read it—and that his teachers recognize the value of books of all shapes and kinds, at all levels.

I would love now to regale you, as a reward for listening so patiently, with some refreshing anecdotes. But time is short. I promised at the beginning of this paper to bring children with me into the Library of Congress and indeed they have been hovering about giving me guidance all the evening. But because we do not grow out of our love of stories, let me tell you a short tale about our friend Peter Rabbit who has already, I think, scuttered through one sentence tonight and now insists on reappearing.

On one happy morning, a little girl called Sophie brought her pet rabbit to school. He arrived, amid some excitement, with an entourage of thirty stroking, 'ah-ing' five-year-olds in the library at story time. Of course, I had quickly to substitute *The Tale of Peter Rabbit* for whatever I had prepared: a faculty for quick substitution is, I have discovered, one of the linchpins of good teaching. The rabbit was soporific throughout, whether from too many lettuces or too much stimulation, I do not know. But I was grateful. As you may remember, but in all probability do not, right at the beginning of the story, Mrs Rabbit 'went through the woods to the baker's. She bought a loaf of brown bread and five currant buns.' An insignificant statement you and I might think, one quite overtaken in interest and excitement by Peter's daring adventure and his thrilling escape from the pursuing Mr McGregor. But it was these five currant buns that were the most important element in the story to one listener. That child asked a question which I knew I wasn't supposed to answer. 'Do you know why Mrs Rabbit only bought five currant buns, Miss?'

'You tell me.'

'Because there should've been six, because of Mr Rabbit, but because he had been put in a pie by Mrs McGregor, Mrs Rabbit *decided* [note] to buy only five. One for her, one for Flopsy, one for Mopsy, one for Cottontail, and one for Peter.'

Now, I am not a great believer in the school of thought that presses for stories to be written for this or that therapeutic purpose, though I understand, and sympathize with, the motives behind the pressure. I go along with Ezra Jack Keats on this matter; he once said to me that 'what we must do is reveal people to one another and hope.' There speaks the creative man who realizes that implicit in many stories not specifically tailored for any group need is the very comfort and reassurance looked for by the politically active. *The Tale of Peter Rabbit*, on that morning in my library, was many things besides a good story: nature study, an arithmetic lesson, an occasion for juvenile logic, and an introduction to the rudiments of good housekeeping. You don't go buying a currant bun for a father who is already in a pie. (Beatrix Potter would have liked that.) But has the group that puts pressure on us to provide stories for single-parent families or tales that help children come to terms with death discovered *The Tale of Peter Rabbit*, I wonder? I have no doubt that any child with only one parent listening to the story would, if his situation bothered him, have derived comfort from the security of the rabbit-hole 'in the sandbank underneath the root of a very big fir tree.' Children are so much better than we are at sensing connections—and the less we investigate the way they digest and build on what they hear, the better, generally speaking. Which is why it is the children's right to be the audience for a story and to be left in peace to work out for themselves its relevance to their inner lives.

So children listen—either to an author's voice at one remove through the reader-aloud or directly, through words read silently, words which fall like snowflakes on the mind. Authors' voices are many and varied, like those of friends, family, people in the street. Children make bonds with the author, creating, as many critics have pointed out, the 'other end' of the relationship that the author offers. No one is an uncle unless he has a niece or nephew; consequently C. S. Lewis in *The Lion, the Witch and the Wardrobe* depends, for his existence as a storyteller, on a willing extended family of nieces and nephews, receptive to his unquestionably avuncular tone. Lucy Boston, austere, dependable, wise-with-age like 'Green Knowe' itself, must have families of great-grandchildren she has never met, the children who experience the sacred house and garden along with Tolly in the books. Philippa Pearce, remembering so exactly the workings of a ten-year-old's mind, the total absorption in the passing minute, the quick association of clue with problem, simply needs friends along the street, and of these she has an abundance.

The voice is important, and distinctive voices often spring from a circumscribed locality. A great deal has been written in the past about the vernacular and its place—as vital colour or barrier to comprehension—in children's stories. I can remember reading *What Katy Did*, *Little Women*, and *A Girl of the Limberlost* as a child and being vaguely aware that they weren't British, but far from being troubled by the occasional strange (to me) turns of phrase, I was, I think, excited by the new cadences. Fluent readers can take on stories from overseas with no trouble at all. We should not underestimate them . . .

On the radio, a few weeks ago, I heard Sybil Marshall talking about children's reading development. There are, she said, three stages: the on-the-lap stage, the over-lap stage, and the lap-it-up stage.

I have concentrated purposely on the audience for children's books that is still on-the-lap, and the audience at the over-lap stage, where reading aloud to children is still important even if they are already, in Russell Hoban's term, 'self-winding'. If we were to direct such resources as we have to these two stages, the third, the lap-it-up stage would become the norm. Then the child whose reading at between ten and eleven ranged freely among *real* children's books, you will remember, would emerge from the chrysalis stage, where heroes and strong narrative are necessary, into a butterfly ready for the extended demands of adolescent and adult fiction.

If we fail, as I fear we largely do, at the first two stages, we can be sure that the politicians will throw their resources not into the early years of education, in which adult expertise in profusion might create healthy caterpillars (Very Hungry at this juncture), but into fixing some sort of artificial wings on to the disabled butterfly, the illiterate or antiliterate adolescent who is in their terms a blot on society.

Prevention is better than cure. Believing this so strongly, I have limited my remarks tonight to what may seem to those of you who publish for the teenage market or teach adolescents to be a foreshortened interpretation of the subject.

But the Library of Congress, in its wisdom, astutely chose as the title of the International Year of the Child Symposium 'The Audience for *Children's* Books.' What an opportunity! Mr Chairman, I thank you most sincerely for inviting me to participate.

THE DREAM AND THE REALITY:
A Children's Book Critic goes back to School

If Memorial Lectures are meant to be sober occasions, this one was an exception. But because Sidney Robbins' great passion had been books in the classroom I think he would have laughed with the audience. Like most critics I had been able to theorize airily on books and children—until a stint of week-by-week practice as a primary school librarian with the real things in juxtaposition brought me down to earth with a bump. That the bump was improving my performance as a commentator on children's books was the theme of the 1980 Sidney Robbins Memorial Lecture.

It is an irony that this, the fourth Sidney Robbins Lecture, should take place in 1980, the year of the severest slashes in spending on books for schools ever experienced in this country. Without entering into the politics of central government's financial edicts or the social strategies of the local authorities' subsequent budgeting, one can categorically state that book services in general and book services to schools in particular have been subjected to a disproportionate and unjustifiable blow. The effects of this will, I am very much afraid, see the standard of the books we can offer our childen in mid decade reduced, and the choice decimated both by a fall in the number of new titles (no bad thing perhaps) and, much more serious, by a lack of the necessary cash to keep the staple picture books and novels of English children's literature in print. For what is now happening is that a traffic jam has begun to trail its way back, with increasing frustration, indeed desperation, from school library service to supplier, to publisher, to author.

It is, therefore, as something of an economic anomaly that I stand here tonight to talk about *The Dream and the Reality: A Children's Book Critic Goes Back to School*. As some of you know, on one day a week I work at an Inner London Education Authority primary school as a librarian. And yes, we do have plenty of books at Fleet, in the libraries (we have two) and in the classrooms. They are used and misused, talked about and experimented with, lost, but also found. For Fleet is an ordinary school full of rowdy children and often harassed teachers, but unusual in that its head, Edith Kahn, could see five years ago that there was a place in the back-up of teachers and direct contact with children for someone who knew about books. Primary schools in the ILEA were to be allowed, at that time, Media Resources Officers on a shared group basis; the Authority should also, surely, permit the appointment of a part-time librarian? There were those who knew the ILEA from within who said that the job of a part-time professional librarian in a primary school (a post unheard of in Britain) would never be offered to me. Doom-laden phrases like 'dangerous precedent' hovered on the air. Dangerous? No. Precedent? Yes, indeed—or so I hoped when the official offer finally came.

In 1976, when all this was taking place, I was only half-way through my projected ten-year stint of selecting the books for the National Book League's *Children's Books of the Year Exhibition*, writing its catalogue, being involved in the London summer showing. There was, as a result of this exposure, plenty of freelance work as a journalist, critic on radio, adviser on schools television series, coming in. What was it that drove me to pursue this new career as a 'dangerous precedent'?

The idea of trail-blazing is always attractive but, in retrospect, I think I was spurred on mainly by the invitations I often received to talk to groups of teachers, and the reluctance I felt to go among them as that odd animal called the 'children's book specialist'. Yes, I could talk about children's books all right (well, more or less all right) but only as one of *us* (the children's book people) not as one of *them*, the teachers who, I felt dimly, might resent with some justification the time we who never endured the hurly-burly of a classroom could spend on reading children's books and writing about them without much sense of the myriad responses these books could evoke (or not evoke), should they ever reach their intended audience.

Perhaps distance from the audience and specialism in a branch of literature is a good thing. I do not pretend to know anything at all about criticism at an academic level. I have no doubt, however, that 'we' could evolve a form of academic criticism the yardsticks of which could be applied to perhaps at most a dozen authors whose work, some of which is published for teenagers, appears on children's lists. But I think we must be careful, if we succeed in doing so, to avoid a danger that Valentine Cunningham pinpointed in his opening to a review in *The Sunday Times* a few weeks ago [3 August 1980] of Philip French's *Three Honest Men*:

> As literary criticism proliferates it tries to shed its embarrassing similarities to what ordinary people do with books. Increasingly the academic hireling 'reads' rather than reads . . . [implying] that the unprivileged common reader is short of the right union cards.

That sums up exactly my fears about reviewing children's books without being associated with a wide cross-section of children and with plenty of teachers. Teachers. Do '*they*', in '*our*' opinion, have the right union cards? Should 'their' voices (those few who wish to raise them on the subject of children's books) be listened to? Or do 'we' know all the answers? Although I was one of 'us' I had the, albeit remote, dual qualifications for also becoming one of 'them'. Finding out about daily life in a modern primary school, having teachers as colleagues and children as constant challengers, might improve my performance both as a commentator on children's books and a speaker at teachers' courses. If these activities mattered, and it seemed to me that they mattered very much, for teachers are the open highway along which books can travel to children, it was worth a try. Especially as Fleet School, with which I already had some links, wanted to be involved in this revolutionary experiment.

I wonder what those of you who are not teachers imagine life is like for a teacher in the primary school—how those of you who are librarians would envisage your role not in a well-ordered children's library but in a school? Certainly, despite my keenness to sample life among lost shoes and quartered apples, grazed knees and punch-ups, I had only the remotest idea, a view through rose-coloured spectacles, of the place of the book in the spectrum of really pressing priorities.

You mustn't laugh, but those of you who are teachers may smile indulgently when I describe to you how I foresaw my role as a one-day-a-week librarian in a primary school.

First of all, there would be the library to organize. I had visited it on a quiet evening or two and could see that it represented an earnest attempt at order by a series of unqualified librarians (either teachers with a brief holding of the library responsibility post or ancillary workers) who had been slavishly following their own necessarily quirky interpretations of the ILEA's professional rules. Professional librarians may not realize that few lay people have any idea at all of the difference between accessioning, classifying, cataloguing—that, given the job of 'librarian', most of them are likely to see their duties in terms of stamping, labelling, bandaging and counting books, guarding their upright soldiers-on-the-shelves from the marauding hands of the enemy, the none too careful children. This view is entirely the opposite of my own: *The main function of a librarian in a primary school must be to know the books, simplify the procedures and ensure that children and teachers use such books as there are fully and freely*.

Such books as there are: a quick look round the shelves did not impress me greatly. I had been promised what seemed a fairly generous amount of money to top up the stock and I had heady visions (soon to become deadweights) of quickly despatching orders to an eagerly awaiting local authority Supplies Department who would gather together all that I needed from a large stock-holding warehouse and send the consignment by return.

Once I had the books I needed, I would ensure that teachers came regularly into the library to familiarize themselves with what was available, and filled the book corners in their classrooms not only with books relevant to the current topic for that half term but with stories, poetry, folk tales that would once and for all demonstrate by their very presence the dreariness of the reading schemes which I knew were used because the shelves on the corridor between the two libraries were crammed with them.

And on Wednesdays—every Wednesday—I would make sure that as well as looking after the libraries (one was known as the Language Room, the other as the Resource Room) I would visit each classroom. Perhaps, like Little Red Riding Hood, I would bear with me a basketful of goodies (book goodies, of course). These would be received with delight by hungry teachers and starving children.

And also, naturally, I would be *in* the library, an accessible, smiling, patient, peaceful presence, awaiting the arrival of children who wanted to change their books or talk about them, find books on worms or stamps, astrology or fishing. Each would go away satisfied, stimulated, eager, even those members of the anti-book brigade. At playtime and lunch time I would be able to discuss books with the relaxed and communicative teachers. And after school they would volunteer to help me run the school bookshop, about the inauguration of which, needless to say, there would be not a murmur of dissent.

Where had I been all my life?

Imagine my dismay when, before term started in September 1976, I was handed a timetable from which it was clear that I was expected to take classes in the library from 9 a.m. to 2 p.m.—or was it 2.30? Administration (to include reorganization, reclassification, some kind of catalogue, book selection, ordering, processing and stock control) was allocated a whole forty-five minutes a week—but, luxury of luxuries, a teacher would help me and so would non-swimmers! There would be fifteen minutes to set up the bookshop (if the violin teacher had remembered to vacate the music room) and half an hour in which to sell books. And yes, playtime and the lunch break should be used for fruitful contact with the staff.

Fantastic—on paper! But when reality struck, what would happen to my dream? Was it better to go in quietly, test the situation and if I couldn't swim—which seemed quite likely—sink? Or should I protest at once that a week's work couldn't be done in a day and put forth my own visionary plan?

I am not a protester by nature, so I jumped in at the deep end determined, because the experiment was exciting, to spend the first year looking, listening, thinking, planning—always imagining, because I am an optimist, that I would survive physically to put a more reasonable plan into practice. For it was surely better to be expected to be an active book promoter for 375 minutes of a 420-minute day than to be thought of as a passive custodian of dead stock. There were imbalances in my Wednesday timetable certainly, but they were very heavily on the side of the angels.

So my life at Fleet Primary School began. Like any new girl in an Angela Brazil story—particularly one rumoured to have some kind of pedigree—it was lonely at first. Did I 'live' in the library—or in the staff room? If a staff meeting happened to be called on a Wednesday, did I attend it—or tactfully bury myself in the withdrawal of outdated stock? Did one pay for coffee? When was lunch? Anyone who has been a supply teacher knows this feeling. In no way is it calculatedly unfriendly, but the ambience for discussing the merits of Burningham's *Mr Gumpy's Outing* as opposed to Ladybird Book 3, of introducing the latest Alan Garner and evolving a policy over *Tintin*, of discussing whether we should spend money on poetry books or pottery books, who was doing which projects and what back-up they would like from the library, was clearly light years away.

I crept into the staff room in those early weeks to listen—not to talk. Gradually I came to realize that every teacher in a reasonably good school has his own approach to his classroom and to the relative importance within it of topic work and direct teaching, reading schemes and library books, swimming and singing, testing and serendipity. So there would not be, for me, one way in; it would be a matter of discovering very gradually where everyone stood and somehow or other *if they wanted it* offering them *the* story they would enjoy reading aloud, a collection of books for a certain topic, even perhaps one day periodicals or books about children's books to help them acquire a base in the subject from which they could experiment with books new and old for themselves.

I know now, in my fifth year, from some of the staff who have been at Fleet throughout the same period, that at the beginning they felt apprehensive—very—about having one of 'us' among 'them'. Could I ever, fresh from my ivory tower, become the sort of colleague who could help them? Good teachers all, they knew they could do with some back-up. But, cautious, they too would look and listen.

So, yes, it *was* a good idea at the start to have that horrific timetable. For only by experiencing the utter bedlam of a library period during which thirty-five children try to change thirty-five library books in thirty minutes could I begin to have the least notion of the pressures under which teachers constantly work, the range of problems, educational, administrative, disciplinary, that they face.

Because it is impossible to go into full detail, let us take a class of nine-year-olds (11.15 to 11.45)—as I did in those early years—and follow it up with an infants storytelling session (11.45 to 12.15). If you can hear the distant roll of thunder, it is the pounding thirty-five pairs of intimidating feet running, jumping down the stone staircase from the classroom above where a teacher has just said 'Go down *quietly* to the library'. Thirty-five kids—and only ten chairs, the little upholstered ones, so comfortable for those who actually sit and read. Nobody needs chairs in order to change library books, but the class nabobs bag them immediately and thenceforward glide on the chairs' iron runners towards the lowest shelves, unless forbidden to do so. When you suggest a Betsy Byars to a good reader who likes humorous books and get the reply 'Can't reach the Bs, miss, they're on the top shelf and 'e'll take my seat', you either have to become conspiratorially involved in gang politics (by handing him *The Eighteenth Emergency*) or (time, oh time!) break it up.

Once the chair problem is sorted out and the terrible business of getting the right tickets back in the respective books despatched (a system now mercifully circumnavigated to great advantage) what do these nine-year-olds read? The answer is anything from *I'll Teach My Dog 100 Words* (how good at the Beginner Book stage to have a dog who knows less words than you do) to *Lord of the Rings*.

Soon I begin to recognize the postures of kids at the bottom of the ladder ('Books is good to 'it 'im over the 'ead wiv') and at the top ('Which one comes after *The Children of Green Knowe*?'). I realize that a tactful reorganization of the library could result in a useful physical mingling of slow-learners with high-flyers—absolutely essential if those in the middle, who are seldom given the attention they deserve, are not to fall into a tempting but destructive habit. That habit, induced by a wish to identify with the good readers in the class rather than with the strugglers, is for the child quietly to choose an impressive-looking novel that he has no hope of reading because it is far too difficult, but that he believes gives him a certain status.

What are the possible answers to this very common, very unhappy condition? If you colour-code every story, make no mistake you are also colour-coding the children among their peer group. If your library consists of low-down shelves of picture books for the infants, high-up shelves of novels for the juniors, you might as well, from the prestige point of view, colour-code, for picture books become spurned as baby stuff and Picture Book = Baby, QED.

What was lacking at Fleet five years ago was a large, bright, clean collection of in-between fiction—Beverly Cleary's *Ramona*,

Catherine Storr's *Clever Polly*, Alan Coren's *Arthur* books—that could be read *to* some and *by* others, that were potentially common coin, a unifying force in a competitive world. That was a section of the library we built up, to the great advantage of almost everyone in the school. And the experiment of creating a high-on-the-wall Gold Star picture-book section (for Tintins and Asterixes as well as the more sophisticated picture books by Michael Foreman, Raymond Briggs, Anthony Browne, Anno and others) subtly undermined all kinds of artificial barriers, among staff and children alike.

I have described this experiment in some detail elsewhere (see p. 124) so I will step right off my favourite hobby-horse and back to the timetable at once. For that half-hour is of course over, and (11.46) the infants, hot and excited from apparatus in the hall, are waiting to be trampled underfoot at the door by the torrent of out-rushing nine-year-olds, some of whom I simply haven't had time to speak to, let alone help. I warn them that there are thirty-five five-year-olds outside.

The exchange of nine-year-olds for five-year-olds takes place without loss of life: the nine-year-olds are actually rather careful and respectful of the infants, some of whom are their own little ones. It has been possible and immensely gratifying sometimes to invite some of the bigger kids to stay on for a storytelling session. They begin by helping; then sit at the back looking faintly superior until the moment in, say, *Garth Pig and the Ice Cream Lady* when Madame Vulpina sings her song to pignapped Garth—the lip-smacking song that was not, as you may remember, about ice cream. Having rendered the song rather unmusically and shown them the picture of AWFUL TRUTH DAWNING ON GARTH PIG I look up and see not only enrapt five-year-olds, but the nine-year-olds now engulfed in the story. When the spell breaks they say they'd better go now, and thank you; very polite, very quiet.

Now I am alone with thirty-five five-year-olds, some of whom are amazing listeners, others only beginners at the art because never before has anyone read to them. The gulf that we saw among the nine-year-olds to some extent already exists at five, but with nursery rhymes and Eileen Colwell, Diana Ross and John Burningham, Eric Carle and Pat Hutchins to hand, there is a chance to narrow it.

It is midday. They have heard one story. Let's sing *The Grand Old Duke of York*. We do. A valiant soldier who will be five next week springs up from the carpet and begins to march smartly up to the top of the hill and down again. Before I can stop him—what *is* his name, I feel an attack of the Joyce Grenfells coming on—he has marched on Ninka's little finger and she is in tears. She comes to sit on my knee to help me turn the pages of *Rosie's Walk*. All is quiet, all is forgiven. 'Rosie the hen went for a walk across the yard, round the pond . . .'—Yes, Li-ming, you may go to the toilet, quickly—'. . . through the fence, under the beehives . . .' —Well how lovely; what a dear little tooth, Smita! Here's a tissue—'and got back in time for dinner.'

Very discursive all this, I know. But that is merely the message reflected in the medium. Even after five years of gradual change in my role at Fleet and the creation of what I hope is an organic library working for every member of the staff and every child to some degree, each Wednesday produces a large crop of astonishing and stimulating encounters. The seven-year-old who describes Maurice Sendak's *The Moon Jumpers* as 'all drifty'; the philosophical discussion initiated by a perceptive eight-year-old on the true meaning of Oscar Wilde's *The Selfish Giant*; the twins who are sure they've seen a ghost and want to do a mini project on 'real' hauntings; a very poor reader who has made a sudden leap into the *Ramona* books and has taken her mother to the local children's library to make *her* join so that she can read them too.

Then there is the outsider, Paul, who can unerringly create every voice in the Tintin bubble talk but who, says the Ed. Psych., mustn't be encouraged in his fantasizing, must get to grips with reality. I remember, but keep silent about, Mary Aswell's story, quoted in *Signal*, about a child who drew a horse and coloured it purple. His parents asked, 'Why did you make the horse purple?' and the child said, 'Why not?' '*We've* never seen purple horses,' commented the parents, disparagingly—and the child sighed, 'How sad for you'. It would certainly have been sad for Paul if some of his teachers hadn't been prepared to accept *his* purple horses, encouraged him to read, read *to* him. Here is part of a poem he wrote about a budgerigar that a classmate brought to school:

He's likc a eagle on a mountain
He's like a telephone
He looks into a mirror
All alone

(At this point in the poem Paul becomes one with the caged bird.)

He thinks about food and stories,
About *A Trip to Panama* and *Follow that Bus*,
He's *like* a Budgerigar
In a cage . . .

This transference may worry the educational psychologist, but is it not the losing and finding of self in another being, the vicarious experience, deeply felt, that is the fire in the heart of literature?

There are visitors to Fleet on Wednesdays now (another small factor that has to be accommodated in that administrative hour) who come and look at the libraries. Some heads (they are mostly heads) express more than a little surprise that we spend money on fiction, 'which' as they proudly inform me 'could just as well be borrowed from the local library.' Because this blinkered view of the school library is one of the main factors that make horrendous cuts in services thinkable to the unenlightened, it is worth pausing here to look for a moment at the true value of a large and varied fiction library as an integral part of the primary school.

Through this invaluable resource, teachers can become familiar with the stock, borrow books easily, replace them if the stories seem not quite right for individual children to read to themselves in the silent reading period, or for reading aloud to their class. In each classroom there are children's novels being read aloud, term in, term out. One of my functions is to channel books I love into the classrooms for communal reading; and my great pleasure is to discover through the teachers how unifying this practice of reading one book aloud to children of very varied personal reading standards can be. The enthusiasm generated by *Moonfleet*, *The Machine-Gunners*, *Bridge to Terabithia*, *Grinny* among the older juniors, by *The Midnight Fox*, *Little House in the Big Woods*, *The Summer of the Dinosaur* among the younger ones, carries over not only into the children's art work, drama, and writing but also into their motivation towards becoming fluent readers.

The same visitors who find me a profligate spender on fiction also, I discover, consider that the reading of novels aloud to ten-year-olds is a waste of valuable time. What are the children *doing* while you read? Do they just sit there listening? *Just?* Polly Devlin, comparing the medium of radio with television, has commented:

> One has only to hear *Wuthering Heights* being read to shiver again on the cold and elemental moors, whereas no sooner has Laurence Olivier or some other rough beast come slouching across the same moors on film than one realizes that the equivalent distance from Haworth in the other direction brings one to the municipal library in Keighley. (*The Listener*, 14 August, 1980)

And David Caute, reflecting on his childhood experience in the pre-television era, waxes polemical on the same theme:

> We learned through books and radio to *translate* images from one medium to another, to visualize in private metamorphosis scenes, faces, confrontations that are today served up ready-made—and hence pale—by round-the-clock barbarism. (*Bookmarks* edited by Frederic Raphael, Jonathan Cape)

So although lunch time at a primary school, where last night's episode in *Star Trek* or *Angels*, *Grange Hill* or *Dallas* shares the menu with fish fingers and baked beans, might induce one to believe that television feeds the story-hungry to repletion, it is important to recognize that today's children are, on the contrary, starved of the opportunity for that flowering of the personal imagination that Caute called 'private metamorphosis', and that therefore these children *need to be read to as never before*.

Once again, in education, the demand for products to be seen, measurements to be taken, records to be kept is growing. The less confident new teacher therefore feels uneasy about the justification for reading aloud to his class—but is carried towards it at Fleet by colleagues who discuss over coffee (nowadays) their particular chosen novels, the potential of new ones lying on the staff-room table. A project on survival accompanied by Scott O'Dell's *Island of the Blue Dolphins*, a project on insects with *Charlotte's Web* or *The Borrowers* running alongside, both are infinitely more attractive than they would have been without the stories. Yes, there are plenty of books on camping and edible fungi, ants and caterpillars in the Resource Room (I do also spend money on these) but the spur to the imagination which triggers off the personal response to the project in hand and makes it memorable resides, I believe, in these stories.

Again, for the sacrosanct record, there is some vague feeling that children who experience a book should spew out, in the form of a so-called review, what they have just taken in even before it is digested—or perhaps, horror of horrors, complete worksheets on it (in other schools, let me hasten to add). Such compulsory exercises seem to me to be totally counterproductive—'If you read a lot you'll have to write a lot. Don't be daft.' There are some children, however, who enjoy commenting on books and whose comments are revealing: I have a huge sheet of paper in my study bearing a collage of assorted criticism by ten-year-olds on a children's prize-winning novel. I won't say which—because the same fate might as easily have befallen many—but salutary reading for judges it certainly is. This exercise—'Do I agree with the judges?'—was optional and fun, very different from writing book reviews as a routine *task*.

Are there no educational administrators left who recall the pure joys of voracious childhood reading, reading with no purpose other than sponge-like to soak up experience, maybe only half understood and if so, so what? David Benedictus recaptures this heady happiness, followed by the loss of literary innocence, brilliantly:

> I read everything. Didn't care. Dickens, *Pooh*, *A Warning to Wantons*, *The Wooden Horse*, Jane Austen, schoolboy annuals, *Lost Horizon*, Lewis Carroll, Gulliver, Enid Blyton's weekly *Sunny Stories*, the *Eagle*, of course, with the ineffable Dan Dare and Harris Tweed—and to this day I'm confused as to whether he was an advertisement or a feature . . . Books were magic, they were urgent, their words had hooks on them that grabbed you. But now that I write them and, forgive me, review them, it's as though I'd crawled behind the conjuror's table and seen the rabbit waiting there with red astonished eyes for his startling appearance out of thin air . . . I didn't want to see all that. Why did they let me? (*Bookmarks* edited by Frederic Raphael, Jonathan Cape)

The astute teacher will allow picture books, storybooks, folk tales, poems, novels to be considered quietly, will not issue challenges in the form of reviewing or worksheets, will wait—gardener-like—and watch: the development of a child's style of writing is probably the best indicator we can hope for at this stage of the value of reading.

When our ten-year-olds made picture books—the classroom having been flooded with all kinds of picture books for weeks beforehand—the results showed clearly their likes and dislikes, their ability to absorb form and content, the extraordinary grasp by children of all abilities of the essentials of literary style. It is tempting to quote from the best. But I will content myself with the opening paragraph of Elizabeth Spencer's *The Girl, the Boy and the Bin* because Elizabeth was one of the children, four years before, who could not read when she came up into the junior school. She only became enthusiastic about books when, in one of the small library groups that eventually came to replace the more lunatic book-exchanging sessions, we began to use (spurred on by Frank Smith via Margaret Meek) textless picture books, then nursery rhymes that she half knew, building up towards *Frog and Toad*, the Haviland/Briggs *Fairy Tale Treasury* and on to Judy Blume, then Nina Bawden and anywhere . . . Elizabeth's story began:

> On a hill lived a little girl and boy with their mother and father. One day Tom and Sarah, for those were the children's names, went into the forest.

A classic opening that would never, I contend, have been written if Elizabeth had been kept on *Janet and John* until (if ever) she became fluent. A commentary, too, on all that had been read aloud by perceptive teachers in the intervening years.

Two large questions that cannot be sidetracked now face me on *my* worksheet. What have I, a commentator on children's books, learned from going back to school while still active in selection, journalism, reviewing? And, the $64,000 question which I have had to have help in answering, how has the school benefited from *investing* (one mustn't be squeamish about terminology in these cost-conscious days) in a one-day-a-week librarian?

To answer the second question first: the following points were randomly listed by three teachers to help me find a perspective, something that's difficult because I am still immersed in the job, actively trying to alter and improve the service, to get the reality closer to what I now see as Dream Mark II. Having a one-day-a-week librarian with knowledge of children's books has, they said:

—Given them security and support in their use of books in the classroom: books feature more in all areas of the curriculum than they once did.

—Saved them time because information about books is, as they put it, sieved for them.

—Given them an insight into the authorship, illustration and publishing of books that has been stimulating to them and through them to the children.

—Provided them with an attractive, well-stocked, sensibly organized library with open access and no fuss. (The only record of borrowing occurs when a book is removed from school: borrowing from the library for the classroom is unrecorded.)

—Ensured quick supply of books to meet instant enthusiasms: there's nothing like striking before the iron has gone dead cold.

—Convinced some of the teachers that it is possible for children to learn to read and to grow as readers without using reading schemes; other teachers who use reading schemes also have in their classrooms a kinderbox full of real books to provide a balance.

—And here I quote because this is a fragment of my dream that has apparently become reality: 'Your knowledge *transferred to us* has enabled us to select the right book for the 10–15% of children who present difficulties when offered the free range of all books in the library.'

—One day a week is a good idea because Wednesdays have become the day on which we all focus our attention on books.

If all that is true, it is because at Fleet I have kind, receptive, enthusiastic colleagues—as hard pressed as any other primary school teachers who would benefit in the same way from a similar service. In fact, the scarcer the funds to be spent on books the more important it becomes to have someone, perhaps one of the new teachers-with-library-diplomas trained at this Institute, who knows the books, the teachers and the children, intimately involved in the selection.

And what have *I* learned? A great deal about how children become readers; something of the craft and patience and intuition needed to help a child who has failed to become a reader to discover not only that the task is within his capacity but that it is well worth mastering. I know more than I knew before about the kind of books that *help* this child—and the well-intentioned ones published for the purpose that are, as they say, a right switch-off. ('Try *The Dittany Bush*, dear.' 'The wot?') I know about picture books that work with groups (the ones where the text is in type large enough to be read upside-down from right to left while the pictures face the audience) and the ones that are essentially private and none the worse for that; I know that a good teacher can turn a passable book into a goldmine, and a poor teacher reduce gold to dross—a tragedy.

I have learned also that 'we' generalize too much. For example, we say that reading homes make reading families. Sometimes: but the most reluctant reader I've met at Fleet had, his father told me, 'hundreds of books in his bedroom'. Two, in this instance, would have been better. We say that children need to be told stories from infancy if they are to become good listeners; on the whole this is true, but the most avid listener to stories at Fleet at the moment is a child who has never been read to at home. We say blithely, 'Teachers don't read children's books'; some don't, others do: I have to confess that I felt a twinge of unease the other morning when a young colleague arrived triumphantly in the staff room declaring she had just finished reading *The Eyes of the Amaryllis* on her motorbike!

We press for better school libraries implying that, if the libraries are properly stocked, the children will automatically become readers; I've seen some impressive school libraries now, and learned not to be impressed by anything other than the children's enthusiasm for books they can read, channelled to them by teachers who care. Most of all, I have learned to respect the committed teacher who is on the receiving end of often conflicting pressures from the Inspectorate, the head, the governors, from his own conscience, from parents and from every pupil in a mixed-ability class of up to thirty-five children.

Are we to expect this teacher, at the end of a wearing day, to go home and familiarize himself with the vast numbers of children's titles that pour from the publishers? What efforts must he make even to *see* the books that pour through *our* letterboxes as early copies? He knows about them, if at all, through those notoriously unobjective publishers' catalogues, and through 'our' reviews. These are often too early (it takes at least six months for new books to seep through into libraries), mostly too literary (we tend not to write about the books that most children between seven and ten need to read), often downright unhelpful because we are unable to accept that our role as mediators of children's books to those who will bring them to the child is for the most part far more important than either our status as critics or the status of a children's author as a literary figure. But, as I say, we generalize too much, and here am I, generalizing wildly, irresponsibly even.

So what has happened to the Dream—and the Reality? Five years ago they were, like colour separations in printing, meaningless on their own but recognizable as potentially part of a single image: the image was a school in which books played a seminal role in every branch of the curriculum as a matter of course. Nowadays I dare to place the Dream separation on top of the new Reality. Here and there the picture that I see is what printers and publishers call out of register. There will always be some out-of-register areas, for these are the vital challenge spots which provide the necessary forums for argument, disagreement, discussion—*for learning from each other.*

A SENSE OF COMMUNITY
Zen and the Art of Librarianship

Loughborough University of Technology, which has a lively Department of Library and Information Studies, hosts the annual Woodfield Lecture on Children's Literature. As the fifth Woodfield Lecturer in 1982 I seized on the opportunity to talk about the importance of the interaction of adult and child in a library world becoming dominated by a technology that threatens to drive them apart.

In thanking Mr H. J. B. Woodfield for endowing these lectures and the University of Loughborough Department of Library and Information Studies for hosting them and inviting me to be the Fifth Woodfield Lecturer, I am embracing my subject instantly by running counter to the tide which threatens to turn us all into zebras. Yes, zebras.

Now before you begin to ponder on the wisdom of the decision to hold this lecture after an excellent lunch instead of, as in previous years, at the sober hour of eleven o'clock in the morning, let me explain about the zebras. It is good, very good, to talk by NAME both of Mr Woodfield and his practical services in the selling of children's books, and of Loughborough University whose Department of Library and Information Studies has been the pioneer of many fruitful ideas about using them. But it seems sad to me that if Mr Woodfield were to borrow, say, *Only Connect* from Huddersfield Public Library the issue would be recorded by the passage of a magic pen over two sets of stripes representing the code for the book and the code for the borrower: the temporary mating of a zebra with a zebra.

The tide of technology will never recede even before an army of Canutes, so I shall certainly not attempt to raise a futile standard on this foreshore, a platform in a University of Technology. But that a University of Technology should play host to a lecture on Children's Literature I find encouraging—a recognition of the fundamental needs of human beings in a world dominated by electronic wizardry.

There are still *people* in the library service, people whose role, if the art of librarianship is not to be swallowed by its science, must be strengthened, supported. In the children's library service particularly, gargantuan efforts must be put into not just maintaining but developing the human relationships which are so vital a part of the mating not of zebra with zebra but of child with book. Adults in libraries may be able to cope, may not want the involvement of other adults however knowledgeable or helpful (though a report on some research to which I shall allude later suggests that this is not the case). But at the colt stage there is no doubt at all.

Children coming into any library need a certain amount of help. They may be looking for books on a certain topic, they may be looking for stories of a particular kind. Quite often they are not sure what sort of book they are looking for or even whether they are looking for a book at all. 'Mr Jones sent me,' they may say as they come sidling into the school library—and one glance tells me exactly why!

Helping children find their way in the morass of books that exists is probably the most demanding task in education today —so demanding that it is often not tackled at all. Knowing the child, knowing the books and knowing yourself are the three vital ingredients for even partial success. In school, teachers will often know the children but seldom the books. In public libraries, librarians will know the books, but only a few of their regular borrowers intimately. My preamble about zebras was directed against those library services who have allowed efficient administration—in the shape of a cancelling point in the entrance hall—to take precedence over the inestimable value to all concerned of a child bringing the book he has read or not read into the children's library in his hands, giving it to the librarian who is then in a position to discuss it with him naturally.

But not every adult who chooses to be a librarian or teacher finds talking about books with children easy. It isn't easy. And there is, I am glad to say, no equivalent of the Ladybird Key Words Scheme that claims it can unlock the door to success. Fortunately, though, the key to success is within every one of us; and the lock we must oil is one that we may have allowed to rust over our own artistic sensibilities.

I truly believe that if we are alive at our own level of artistic experience, we shall more easily be able to enter into the child's perception of literature, share what he enjoys, help him to extend his range—and sense the private places where even the most skilled professional must never tread.

Who we are, how we feel about books, is probably more important than all the technical skills we learn in library school or teacher training college.

One of the most successful programmes in the Thames Television Education series that used to be called Writer's Workshop arose in response to the question 'Who do you think you are?' That question is almost always rhetorical; but in the context of this programme it was asked seriously and with the hope that the children's answers in paintings, writing, conversation, would reveal their self image, their attitudes, their interests, their ambitions. Because the children approached were around nine years old the subjective view, which is the unique gift of childhood, came naturally.

If I were to ask that same question—'Who do you think you are?'—of each one of you I very much doubt whether the response would make an award-winning programme. Yet true self-knowledge and a capacity for self projection are essential characteristics of a good primary school teacher, or children's librarian.

So who are *we*? How strong is our sense of community with poets, authors, playwrights? For upon this, I maintain, depends our success in helping the young fully to realize and develop their own identity through experience of the written and spoken word.

Let us not minimize the importance of the task that confronts us. This decade, with its rising toll of unemployment, its headlong rush into cybernetics at the expense of human involvement in manufacturing crafts, brings the kind of problem Nigel Dennis foresaw in his fifties fantasy *Cards of Identity* into the forefront of *our* reality. Man *has* to be part of his world if he is to survive. His sense of community is his strongest link with reality. But whereas imaginative literature, painting, sculpture, music, drama, draw him in, make him an active partner, illuminate his life, television comes close to offering him not just the occasional escape from the giant problems with which he is confronted (no bad thing)—but a total substitute life. (Did you know that the BBC decided to scrap a scriptwriter's idea that one of the Archers should have a baby because the secretaries in the department concerned knew they wouldn't be able to cope with the muffled march of the thousands of pairs of bootees that would arrive from kind listeners? I find this terrifying because the line between fantasy and reality, healthily flexible in childhood, should be clearly defined by the time you are old enough to turn the heel on a sock.)

If the rising generation is to escape this death (for it is not a life in the true sense of the word) the cultivation of a personal language and with it the nurturing of a genuine response to literature must surely become a central plank in education policy. This is my plea.

You will notice that I put language before literature and I will tell you that ten years ago, before I incautiously leapt backwards into the world of the inner city primary school from the ivory tower that then housed a coterie of literary critics, I might not have done so. Although I still belong to the now healthily growing and more diverse group of people who write about children's books, I also have a sense of community these days with teachers who try to use those books and the children who do or do not read them.

And I know it is language—command of language, sensitivity to language—that opens the door.

I should have known anyway, for my first teaching job at the tender age of 21—we were rushed through university and training in those days because of the shortage of teachers due to the war—was in a residential school for children who were the flotsam and jetsam of Europe. A few of these had been caught in Britain in 1939; most were refugees from Nazism; but in 1945, into my special but naïve and inexperienced care, came the survivors of the concentration camps.

My brief was to teach them English—quickly. We would sit around a table in the little library that looked out over the Surrey heathland and we would try to communicate. Czech, Polish, German, French, Dutch were their mother tongues; and their ages ranged from 7 to 25 (for the school had a farm attached to it on which older boys worked). That in the course of a year that group developed a sense of community within its disparate self, that it stretched wary tentacles into the school, the little town and into the country of its adoption was nothing short of a miracle; the resurrection of the human spirit, hope springing from nightmare.

But if those links were to be made at all, *the new common*

language, English, and something of its literature, had to be absorbed. I remember weird things about those sessions. Telling Bible stories in English because the children knew the stories in their own languages. Looking desperately for a nursery rhyme book with action pictures for each line—in vain because Raymond Briggs was yet to produce his *Mother Goose.* Trying to understand why a Polish boy, talking about his new shoes, said 'Cadbury good'. (It was because of the advertisement for milk chocolate which ran *Cadbury's Means Quality*.) And I remember, too, reading aloud to the older ones *The Cataract of Lodore* by Southey so that its music, the music of the English language that they couldn't understand, should wash over them pleasurably.

They learned a kind of English from me, and perhaps something about innocence—for, comparatively, I was very innocent. Looking back on that period I believe I owe to them what I have since become—the kind of fool that rushes in where angels fear to tread.

There are two courses open to one in life, I suppose: to see need and to do what one can, always on a very limited scale as an individual, to minister to it directly: or to see need, draw away from it to gain perspective, study it objectively, write about it, influence the world. Both courses are valid, for without the thinkers the do-ers would have no base, no back-up. As I grow older I realize more and more the vital relationship of fool to angel. All my working life in the field of children and books I have needed angels badly—and they have always been at hand, ready to elucidate, illuminate, formalize, debate, encourage. And it becomes clear to me as time goes on that they need the feedback of us fools.

But to return to the place of language, in our case the English language with its rich regional variations worldwide, in the growth of the whole person's perception. At the University of London Institute of Education angels and fools work closely together trying to break down the age-old beliefs about 'correct' English for all, and to replace them with the potentially explosive idea that each child's natural mode of expression is the right vehicle for the projection of himself. Developing the philosophy formulated by Sybil Marshall in *An Experiment in Education*, her heartwarming and persuasive account of teaching single-handed in a village school in the 1940s, Professor Harold Rosen points out that 'not to recognize an individual's language is to make him effectively mute'. It is largely thanks to him and his apostles that the lifeless kind of school essay topic—'Write anything about something for anybody'—is giving way to the encouragement of personal reminiscence for the satisfaction of the young writer and his friends. A kind of embryonic *Akenfield.* The beginnings of literature.

'The young writer and his friends.' Those of you who are conscious of sex politics must already have noticed, with satisfaction or horror, that I have not succumbed to the pressures of non-sexist polemics on what I am tempted to call the neutering of language—with all that this term implies, both linguistically and zoologically. Latin has become a dead language; but English is still gloriously alive, and into its mainstream will flow the vivid metaphors of all those who use it freely. Brigid Brophy, no less, believes that the attack on language is merely a soft option of feminists who cannot successfully bombard the chairs of multinational companies; and that, should they succeed in toppling those thrones, language would then be permitted to live its own meandering life in peace. Reviewing Millet and Swift's *Handbook of Non-Sexist Writing for Women* Brophy remarks, 'With their tin ear and insensibility to the metaphorical content of language which is what makes it the vehicle for literature, M & S are inept arbiters of linguistic change.' I wholeheartedly agree; and I find it interesting to observe on the one hand the move towards freeing language from the restraints of élitist modes, at the Institute—whilst on the other there is the feminist assault upon its very nature.

Let us stop to consider for a moment two images. The child and his—or her—book. Children and their books—the non-sexist preferred usage. The intensity of the singular vision, the aura that it carries of an alchemy between the reader (of either sex) and the author, is extremely potent; whereas 'children and their books', the plural version, conjures up, for me at any rate, the confusion of a particularly fraught library period. So I will use the singular, unrepentant. Literature is, after all, a singular activity. If thirty children listen to the same story, there will be thirty minutely differing perceptions of it—a singular activity engendering a sense of community within a group.

For common ownership of story—as the Bible, the Koran, the Ramayana make manifest—is one of the most powerful bonds in human society. Myth is the oldest kind of literature known to man. It is peopled by archetypes whose *doppelgänger* rides in each one of us and it provides perhaps our strongest links not with *other* worlds as many people believe, but with the here and now, our feelings about family, friendship, death, love, ambition, riches, work. That literature, ancient or modern, should act upon us as an axe that smashes those frozen seas within us—Kafka's concept—was the theme of Aidan Chambers's lecture on this occasion last year. The picture that metaphor conjures up for me comes in several frames: I see first the author whose passion drives him knifelike into our deepest most icebound emotions; and then I see the reader (you/me/us) drawing back to begin with, but gradually submitting to an assault that can be painfully responded to, worked with, and finally embraced.

In a recent review article in *The Times*, Michael Ratcliffe remarked that the second most important character in any story was the reader, the author being given pride of place. And although we don't normally think about literature in that way, it is the truth. The author is a shipbuilder; but unless the reader knows how to sail the kind of ship the author has constructed *there will be no voyage*.

In using picture books as well as strip cartoons, Wordsworth's *Lyrical Ballads* beside Roger McGough's serio-comic explorations of the plight of modern youth, Roald Dahl's stories and Philippa Pearce's (both fantasies, but how different!) with children, we are helping them to navigate for themselves all kinds of *craft* (what a lucky word) that will *transport* them (another one) on personal journeys from which they will return to a private haven.

I am reminded, as I complete that sentence, of Maurice Sendak's *Where the Wild Things Are* and of Max's private boat, his own fantasy story that took him to the land 'where the Wild Things are', there to come to terms with his temporary disgrace and sail back 'over a year and in and out of weeks and through a day and into the night of his very own room'. Max achieved catharsis from within. The experience is exquisitely caught by Sendak's perfectly modulated text and by his paintings that magically transform Max's room (so constricting a small space) into a forest (more space there, but not everyone's idea of a comforting place to be) from which he is borne away over the open seas (aha!) on his private boat to the land where he is proclaimed king—and from whence he can return at will to protected small boyhood.

Here, in this much loved, liberating picture book for children we have, expressed in the simplest yet most potent manner, an essential message for adults: that story, offering us 'a sea change into something rich and strange', brings us back into ourselves refreshed, renewed, subtly altered by experience, our experience as we travel within it. In *Where the Wild Things Are* we find the essence of Bruno Bettelheim's *The Uses of Enchantment*—in picture strip.

And as some of you may know, that comment from me is no belittlement, for I believe quality picture strip to be a genuine art form. Reading strip is a juvenile skill that adults have to reacquire. If you find it difficult, as I used to, persevere. You will learn a lot about learning to read—if you watch yourself carefully . . .

So here we are, at YOU. First, you the primary school teacher. In the course of your one, two, three or four years of professional training you have studied child psychology and child development, the history of education, art and craft in the classroom, number work, topic teaching and, I suspect, the *problems* of teaching reading. You the children's librarian have studied cataloguing, book selection, stock control, reference work, and the classification schemes which are designed to order knowledge in such a way that visitors to libraries can find the book they want by themselves.

The content of courses of professional studies always seems to me to be overconcerned with *how*—to the detriment, sometimes even the exclusion, of those much more important 'serving men', *why* and *what*.

Thus, in education courses, a great deal of time will be spent studying theories about how children should be taught to read, looking at machines for this purpose, comparing one cheap horrible reading scheme with another expensive horrible reading scheme, all with the purpose of helping young children to become fluent readers fast. Only the exceptional course will come to reading by the route that asks first '*Why* should children learn to read?' That is not as simple a question as it sounds. But having exhausted it at the level at which it deserves to be considered (functional literacy is only the beginning, though many believe it to be, so to speak, the 'end') the course will naturally proceed from 'why' to 'what'. *What* books, real books, should teachers have around the classroom so that reading is seen to be such a pleasure that no one in his right mind will want to be precluded from joining in?

Similarly on most library courses, whether for teachers or librarians, techniques take precedence over a study of the purpose for which they were originally devised—the reader's pleasure in reading, delight in finding out.

There is very little point in having a perfectly organized, well-maintained bookstock if the atmosphere generated by it is such that ordinary mortals, especially children, feel intimidated.

In daring mood I bring to your attention, here in a Department of Library and Information Studies itself concerned with what is known as user research, a delicious report I came upon early one morning when, only half awake, I was scanning my morning mail in which there was the latest issue of the *Library Association Record*. Suddenly I found myself spluttering with mirth (I was drinking coffee at the time) because for a moment I thought that the LAR was indulging in a parody. I should have known better! What I was reading was a report of a real piece of research, funded by the British Library, into, and I quote, 'Non-usage of Library and Information services in Industry and Commerce'—a perfectly serious and important subject, for, as I have said, unused services might as well not exist. But listen to the analysis of the data 'supplied in the form of 173 answers to a questionnaire sent to a sample 460 industrial-commercial services.'

Analysed, the data shows that:

a) a problem of under/non-usage would appear to exist
b) that many librarians/information officers are concerned about this
c) that there is some agreement as to the type of under/non-user
d) that there is a wide divergence of opinion as to ways of dealing with the problem if indeed it can be dealt with
e) that further research into the subject might be useful.

Doris Palmer, the LAR's reviewer, remarks, less caustically than perhaps I would have, that 'perhaps one can be forgiven for wondering if the cost of the exercise might not have been better employed in promoting a greater awareness of library and information services in the community at large.'

But by what methods? Immaculately Letraset labels, hails of arrows, yards of notices of explanation—or by the personal direct approach of the librarians in charge of books and pamphlets and microfilms and microfiches? If those librarians who preside over mountains of material impregnable to the ordinary information seeker would use their personal skills instead of their professional techniques they might succeed in transforming seekers into users.

That does not mean that I consider professional skills to be expendable, only that to me they can never be an end in themselves. I once heard Michael Marland, Headmaster of the new North Westminster Community School and spokesman on many aspects of the provision of books in schools, say that when he was in America he got fed up with having Principals say to him, 'You must meet our librarian. She has so much charisma.' He didn't, he said, feel that charisma had anything to do with being a good school librarian. For a hundred reasons that I won't list but that I hope are becoming apparent I totally disagree with him. The art of book promotion, *for that is what librarianship really is*, is highly personal.

Charisma, of course, is not enough. Neither is charisma plus techniques. What we need is a genuine enthusiasm for books, and the only way we can acquire that is by reading widely *for our own pleasure*. Jane Austen and the Brontës, Tolstoy and Dickens, Nadine Gordimer and Patrick White, Malcolm Bradbury and David Lodge—these are the teachers who will answer for you, each in their own way, the perhaps unformulated question that lies at the heart of our subject, children and books. Why bother?

If you are able to respond—because every child with whom I come into contact professionally deserves the opportunity to enrich his life through reading *as I have enriched mine* you will find that those children and such books as you have in your library in these hard times are just so many potentially active parts of a complex electrical circuit. Once switched on it will yield for all of you a kaleidoscope of intriguing human patterns, unexpected reactions, exhilarating results. You, my friends, are the dynamo. If *you* are not charged, action will be sluggish.

Now that we have, I hope, established a sense of community with one another may I invite you to come along with me on a personal voyage of discovery through reading, a voyage that gave rise to much that I have said this afternoon?

When I was on holiday in Cornwall last year I began to read Robert M. Pirsig's celebrated novel (if novel it is—where do you librarians place it in your libraries?) *Zen and the Art of Motorcycle Maintenance*. What Pirsig is saying throughout that long and exciting journey of the mind illuminates brilliantly the dilemma of modern man who, in the technological age, is offered all the answers but often isn't even within striking distance of asking a question. Hence his growing isolation which is compounded by the desire to surround himself with electronic gadgets, in the mistaken belief that they will keep him in touch.

But really these gadgets separate him from his fellows, if meaningful two-way flow is what he is after—and who is not? Television, for instance, is going to the theatre alone. Ansafones enable us to avoid speaking to people. We are informed, by manuals whose language is totally impersonal, how to operate such machinery. 'When red bulb lights, dial may be set at 3.' But never a hint is given that we might like to understand what we are doing, that the nature of our input might have the slightest relevance to the smooth operation of the machine. This divides us from the things we use in a way that nullifies both ourselves and them, for we should have common cause with everything that is a part of our lives. In the simple life this is so.

Pirsig devised the Motorcycle as the vehicle that would best carry the Zen philosophy that the man and the task are one, and at the same time the story of his gruelling trip over mountain passes and along mile after mile of prairie road—towards self-discovery.

The book is not really about motorcyles as such—though Yamaha and Honda maniacs will find much in it to feed their enthusiasm. Pirsig uses the idea of his total rapport with the machine that carries him—or fails to carry him—through life as a searchlight to illuminate philosophical truths of universal significance.

When I was half-way along the road with him, begrimed with oil, listening for the telling click in a piston, it occurred to me that we were rushing through country and past sign-posts that were by no means unfamiliar. Indeed they had a particular application to my motorcycle—which is fired by books and children.

When Pirsig spoke about suffering a short between the ear-phones as he tried to fix his bike, I knew what he meant. It was writer's block, for me. Or alternatively it was the moment when, faced with an enquiring young reader, the right book had eluded me.

When, contemplating the whole art of explaining motorcyle maintenance to his son, Pirsig commented: 'That's the problem all right, where to start', I saw myself in relation to a young teacher enrolling on a short course on children's literature, innocently believing that he was going to get all the *answers* served up on a plate. But listen (I quote): 'To reach him you have to back up and back up, and the further back you go, the further back you see you have to go, until what looked like a small problem of communication turns into a major philosophical enquiry . . . I repack the tool kit and close the side cover plates,' says Pirsig, 'and think to myself HE'S WORTH REACHING THOUGH.' That's it exactly.

If he's worth reaching, and he certainly is, we who are further along the road have a duty, in Pirsig's terms, to 'back up' to where he is, help him ride pillion. To do this effectively, to bring what we know (which is part of us) to another person, be it child or adult, we have to absorb that person on our journey on his terms. That subtly alters our journey, takes us on detours, yields us new perspectives of oneness with the task; and that is all to the good.

An amazing new perspective of just this kind was revealed to me not so long ago by a teacher who was totally unwilling to ride pillion with me, but was nevertheless, I now realize, a vital component in my motorcycle.

She specialized in mathematics. When she took over an infants class in the school where I ran the library, she was adamant about the advantages of structured reading schemes, and totally resist-ant—yes, totally—to the delights I offered her from across the corridor. 'Terrifying', 'boring', 'too difficult', 'a waste of time' were the arrows she shot into my balloons of enthusiasm about Sendak, Faith Jaques, Keeping, Quentin Blake—in that order.

So all I could do was shut up—and use every second of my storytelling time with her structured little six-year-olds positively. This was some years ago. She left to teach in a village school in the back of beyond. I suppose I must have given her a booklet as a leaving present, but I don't remember doing so.

Anyway, imagine my surprise last Christmas when I was shown a letter that she had written to one of our dinner ladies in which I read 'Please tell Elaine that *Learning to Read With Picture Books* is working a treat with my 5- to 7-year-olds. Our official Infant reading scheme is Dominoes but I have a very free hand so most of the reading is done from Jill Bennett's suggested list.'

How extraordinary! Why had this change come about? The other teachers, themselves committed free range addicts, were as astonished as I was. And here, I think, is the clue we so often miss. We had probably, as a group, practised overkill. But now that Miss Smith had arrived in her village infants school where no one had heard of Quentin Blake, let alone Jill Bennett, she was the expert, enjoying her role, spreading not the schemes but the word and the image. Miss Smith had found herself in Jill Bennett's *Learning to Read With Picture Books* ('I could do that,' she must have thought) and the sense of community once established, she had ventured forth into that 'terrifying, boring, too difficult, time-wasting' world of picture books—and found it to be, indeed, the promised land. Her perception of her role has changed simply because she has climbed the mountain *for herself*. Now she has arrived I hope she will behave better up there than some of us do.

You do not need to be a meteorologist to know that a belt of hot air from above meeting cold rising from the ground is inclined to produce fog—not fog on the mountain top where all is crystal clear to the Olympians, but fog on those life-sustaining slopes in the valley where the real work has to be done. If we fail thoroughly to warm the air in the valley, if we cannot dispel the fog so that would-be climbers find the maps we make *for their journey* stimulating rather than daunting, they will not venture forth. Safer by far to retreat behind their classroom doors with their structured reading schemes.

But as we come to the end of *our* journey today, perhaps we should glance in our rear mirror to catch a glimpse of the road we have travelled together.

When we set out on this excursion its purpose was defined as a bid to defend the rising generation from being engulfed in the tide of computerization with its depersonalizing, isolating, anti-life force. With this end in view we have examined the vital place of language in the individual's view of himself and his links with society; we have touched on the way literature, with its myths and archetypes, strengthens people in their relationship with their fellows, reveals the individual to himself. We have stressed that only adults who are alive and aware, able to experience what Dame Helen Gardner recently called 'an enlargement of their being' through literature, will be in a position to mediate books to children since for them children's literature will be an extension of personal pleasure in story—not the terrifying mammoth closed book it is, alas, so often, to the non-reading teacher. We have thrown down the gauntlet, in friendly fashion I hope, to those professional training courses in our field that neglect, or lose sight of, the true life-endowing purpose of their technical disciplines. We have used Robert Pirsig as a tour leader who throws light on our central theme: the oneness, the sense of community that must exist between *who* we are and *what* we do if *that* is to be organic.

As teachers, librarians, parents, it is our task personally to ensure, through our own joy in books and skill in communication, that the children in our sphere catch the spark of enthusiasm that can ignite their own fires, enable them to blaze their own trails. The angel in me (for I suppose these days it is there somewhere) would like to believe that it is possible for all children everywhere to enjoy the best that our extraordinarily rich children's literature can offer. But the fool in me knows, from much experience, that this is not possible because so many adults haven't even seen the light, let alone felt the fire.

What makes me approach 1984 with less fear than otherwise I might, however, is the proof I now have, after six years in close professional association with teachers in a primary school, that every child, of whatever background, who comes into a class whose teacher is a word wizard is capable of being transformed into a book-addict even if he can't read. For such teachers know that it is reading aloud to children from a wide range of stories and poems—reading, reading, reading—that fans the latent flame.

It is my belief that if the fire of language burns freely, fiercely, and if literature becomes the food and drink of our children, then computer technology, the brainchild of human beings, may take its rightful place in the world of the future as the servant, not the master, of mankind.

It all depends on—US.

CRITICAL DECISIONS:
Reflections on the Changing Role of a Children's Book Reviewer

If I have learned one lesson over these twenty-five years, it is that those of us who are privileged to spend all our working days in the field of children's literature should, if we really believe that children's lives are enriched by reading, give practical support in what we write and say to those parents and teachers whose many other concerns make it hard for them to know enough about children's books to feel confident about helping the children in their care to become readers.

In 'Critical Decisions', a lecture given at the 16th 'Loughborough' International Seminar on Children's Literature at Aberystwyth in 1983, I tried to re-trace the steps that had led me away from pure criticism in the 1960s towards this pragmatic eighties viewpoint.

I have called this talk 'Critical Decisions' because what I am going to describe to you this morning is a series of decisions I found I had to make in the course of about twenty years in the field of children's book reviewing. I subtitled the talk 'Reflections on the changing role of a children's book reviewer' because, looking back, I can see that I started out the way most people do start out: receiving books for review—and reviewing them. But whether it was my temperament or the challenge of getting books to children in a largely indifferent world or a mixture of the two, I don't know—but for some reason, conventional reviewing alone became not enough for me. I might have become what is commonly known as a critic. But I don't think I did.

The title 'critic' with which I am lumbered here—and there, and everywhere else it seems—is one I shun. Largely because it has about it a negative, cutting-down-to-size kind of ring—and I am, I think, a positive, praising-where-it's-due, promotional animal.

Indeed, my fellow critics, some of whom are real critics sitting in solemn judgement on the work of the aspiring author or artist, have long ago given me up as lost. I have begged to be considered a commentator rather than a critic, not because I believe I really lack, as someone once said, 'critical grasp' (there's the snap of the dragon's teeth for you!) but because I am happy, very happy to leave literary criticism to those who work in universities or polytechnics and who write for a committed and learned audience in respectable specialist journals. That is where real criticism belongs. That is where it is (dare I say this?) *useful.*

Oddly enough I think I could perhaps do what they do, and that when I retire from a very active life in children's books I might even become a critic of a sort. Because now that I begin to reflect on my life I discover that my early training as an historian helps me to assemble, categorize and order material (which can as well be on the crusade for children's reading as on that First Crusade in the 11th century). I made this discovery when Nancy Chambers asked me to write a long essay on 'The Seventies in British Children's Books' for *Signal*'s 10th anniversary collection. I sat in the Goldsmiths' Library of London University inhaling that pungent smell of rarely opened heavy tomes of reference, savouring the quiet, watching the 'real' scholars and having a very self-indulgent ball. But then I came out and began all over again the rough-and-tumble practical activities in schools, in magazine offices, on platforms—advising, interviewing, selecting, talking, writing that I enjoy so thoroughly, but that have made me more of a commentator than a critic.

But I have been given the critic's slot in today's programme, and that is right in a way. After serving my apprenticeship as teacher, librarian, publisher's reader and mum (the last was the most important by far) I did start my more public life in children's books as a newspaper critic—on *The Times*. But with the parlous state of adult knowledge about children's books that existed then—and that still exists now—newspapers hardly seemed to be the place for 'in' discussions of children's book trade issues or for academic style criticism. But both began to creep on to that *Times* page. The space that is given to children's books should surely be used positively to help parents and teachers to get a grasp of the basic principles of choosing with children the books they will enjoy.

So I began to ask myself, as the months passed, what *The Times* page was doing, and why? Who was reading what was written? What was the effect? Were the hordes of children 'out there' a jot better off because of it? Or were they, possibly, marginally worse off because of the widening gap between critics' books and what real children want to read? Did these children get books? If so, what—and how? If not, why not? With questions like this assailing me I couldn't settle for the quiet (well, relatively quiet) life of the so-called quality press critic. I began to look at aspects of the children's book world, to learn by experience and to use what I discovered as an integral part of what I wrote. The historian in me, I now suppose, thirsting for fieldwork.

The first step was to leave *The Times*, a 'prestige' newspaper, and take over an occasional column in *The Sunday Mirror* which is anything and everything *but*. Here was a massive, and massively indifferent, if some people were to be believed, audience. Certainly the readers of a tabloid have to be written for quite differently from those who read *The Times*. It is really very easy to write about books for the quality press, for you are talking in the main to people of your own background and education about something that should be, even if it isn't always, of automatic interest.

But for *The Sunday Mirror* you have to think about hooking your readership, stimulating people, sending them off not to a bookshop but, in all probability, to a large multiple stationers and booksellers like our W. H. Smith where, hopefully, they will find the right books for their families. You have to write simple but arresting prose—no room for convoluted subsidiary clauses in an opening sentence that mustn't exceed nine words! And above all you have to guard against disappointment and disillusion on the part of the book-seeker—for the first steps in using books with children are hard and people are easily discouraged. So, unlike my predecessor in the job, who had written sparkling throw-away little pieces on the current new children's novels submitted for review by hopeful publishers (but unlikely to be found in 90% of the book outlets in this country because hard-cover fiction is hard to sell) I decided to work backwards. Ever pragmatic, I went to a large W. H. Smith and made a list of the best of the new books (paperback fiction and colourful information books) that they stocked. And it was from these that I chose my books for review: the James Reeves *Golden Land* anthology, then new in Puffin; *Mrs Pepperpot; The Naturalist's Handbook*. I did not prostitute myself I promise you—but I sallied forth into this new world under banner headlines such as 'Paperbacks to Keep 'Em Quiet' or 'Bloomin' Christmas Here again' which might make you blush unless times have changed—which I rather suspect they have.

Anyway, it was at this period, in 1973 I think, that by great good fortune I was invited by a group of social workers and teachers in London's Dockland to help them set up a children's bookstall, Stepney Books, in the Saturday market. There was no bookshop in that vast area, nowhere children could even *see* new books, let alone *buy* them. We proved on that stall, through blazing summers and perishing rainy winters that if the right books are easily accessible and you are prepared to stand around between the eels and cauliflowers regularly on Saturdays you make friends, influence people, sell books. Some books. Which ones? Why? You begin to value the best of the Ladybird series; the easy reading series that critics never write about; the paperback classics like that *Alice in Wonderland* for which one child saved up for a month. You know you need multicultural books not because activists say so but because not to have them is an offence to many of the families who come up to look at the books—and a limitation on your ability to reach them with stories. And you learn the value of knowing what's inside a book if you want to sell it.

I was already at this time embarked upon the ten-year marathon of *Children's Books of the Year* so I knew what was inside the books all right. No 'real' critic, I fancy, would have taken on *that* job. I didn't actually 'take it on', though; it just happened. The National Book League had, for some years, chosen what it called *New Children's Books* each year for a travelling exhibition. The choice could be arbitrary and haphazard really, because there was no annotated catalogue through which the selectors had to justify their choices, balance their selection. When I was called upon to assist the NBL in the choice of fiction (3 weeks in which to choose 200 titles as I remember) I began to ask awkward questions to which I received very dusty answers. Finally, someone said in exasperation, 'Well, if you want to be responsible for the whole selection *and* write an annotated catalogue, go ahead!' That, they thought, would silence me. Instead, it opened the way for me eventually to turn the *New Children's Books* touring exhibition into the catalogue and exhibition which came to be known as *Children's Books of the Year.*

It is not for me to evaluate that exercise. It provided a service I think in presenting busy teachers and librarians with a personal, (and fallible) choice of about 300 new books from a publishing year producing about 3,000. The catalogue provided annotations for each book which, because they explained why it was included, evaluating plot, style and likely readership, could not be thought of as criticism in the intrinsic sense. My aim was to be helpful to those who bought books for children's libraries—or for families—by offering them what I hoped was informed comment. In order to be able to offer such informed comment I suppose I thought it was my duty (though really it was my pleasure and delight) to broaden the base of my experience of children's books through every opportunity that came my way.

The first opportunity that making the selection afforded was to meet the public through a static, rather than a peripatetic *Children's Books of the Year* exhibition in the Albemarle Street gallery of the National Book League. But would anyone come? The opening exhibition was very low-key, experimental. The books on trestle tables; myself, or any of the N B L staff hovering discreetly. But it became immediately obvious to us all that a selected annual exhibition for professionals, parents and children (with storytellers, artists, competitions and a bookshop) would draw the crowds. It did. August, far from being a wicked month, was of course the tourist season in central London and to our surprise and delight we discovered that many of you began to key your holiday in to 'our' fortnight. Soon, study groups also became part of our programme.

Now my brief, I know, is to talk about critical decisions—not exhibitions. But, in retrospect, I can see how much the ten years I was responsible for *Children's Books of the Year* gave me in my education as a commentator. It was a thrilling opportunity to be in that gallery every day, not only watching people looking at books (often with the catalogue in their hands—rather daunting!) but answering, or trying to answer, a million-and-one questions on every aspect of using books with children.

I remember the large, silent, patient-looking Ghanaian who came in two days running and spent hours in the picture book section—before introducing himself to me as Ghana's Minister of Education and asking advice about starting a Ghanaian simple picture book programme. (Two years later at Bologna on one of those heart-rendingly empty Third World stands, I saw his first books.) Then there was the teacher-librarian from Prince

Edward Island who told me I was her 'best friend'—though we had never, until that moment, set eyes on each other; and the Head of a Comprehensive School in Hong Kong who greeted me with the words, 'the two ends of the lifeline come together at last'. Each had a story of book-life in other places to tell, as had a missionary from India, a teacher from Mexico, a delegation of Colombian printers (would pop-ups ever catch on? they wanted to know), and mothers and fathers of English-speaking families from Italy and Iceland, Singapore and Malta.

Then there were the specific requests. Books for deaf children—which put me in touch with a scheme for adapting the texts of ordinary picture books for children with impaired hearing. The problem of the child of 8 with a high IQ and reading age who needs 'more difficult material but is not emotionally ready for 10+ novels'. The younger child in a family who has overtaken the older one. And inevitably the child who is brought remonstrating to a book exhibition: he doesn't read; his mother thinks he should; here he is; make him! That was the only situation I would gladly have ducked because with both parties present and books silently protesting that forced feeding will result in permanent disability on the part of the fed, there is nothing one can do.

Of course many of the conversations were about broken pencils (we ran competitions), how to get lunch, the best way to the British Museum from Piccadilly, where was the loo? And hundreds and hundreds about finding just the right book to give to someone special. When you think about it this is really the end to which all practical children's book criticism is directed—through librarian, bookseller, teacher, parent. So I won't apologize for having chosen for you my favourite *Children's Books of the Year* story which, like Wanda Gág's *Millions of Cats*, is about the agony of choice—a choice of cats, too, as it so happens.

A very serious 9-year-old started to talk to me about picture books with cats in them. She was, she said, trying to choose one for her sister who adores cats. She was sure, very sure, of the kind of book she was looking for. In her words, 'They must be lovely cats, and the story mustn't be sad'. It was the year of Graham Oakley's debut with *The Church Mouse*; I thought she might find Samson appealing. But no. 'My sister wouldn't be able to stand the picture of Samson the cat tied up in all those cords by the mice.' Understandable. So what about Bolliger-Savelli's *The Knitted Cat*?—no dramas there—but 'He isn't REAL!' The Yeoman/Blake *Mouse Trouble*, then? 'But the farmer tries to be *cruel* to the cat!' So, at my wits' end, I suddenly thought of *Orlando*, a new edition of which had appeared that year. 'How about Orlando?' I asked hopefully. She looked carefully through Kathleen Hale's enchanting, untidy pages, then said with a sigh of relief, 'Yes, yes; that will do.' I was delighted. And as she walked towards the book sales point to buy *Orlando* I asked casually, 'How old is your sister?' She smiled, looked up at me trustingly and said, 'Promise you won't laugh if I tell you? She's twenty-one!'

It is tempting to imagine that my interest in picture books for older readers stemmed from that conversation—but I must be honest with myself—and you. I don't think it did. I think that in writing the annotations for the *Children's Books of the Year* catalogue, and above all in setting out the books as physical objects in the exhibition, I became acutely aware that lumping picture books together as the first fiction category automatically implied that they were for the early years only. I began, therefore, to scatter them through the fiction categories as appropriate—placing *A Walk in the Park*, Anthony Browne's humorously surrealist masterpiece about snobbery, in fiction for 8- to 11-year-olds, and Russell Hoban and James Marshall's delicious teenage frolic, *Dinner at Alberta's* where it truly belongs, and is now appreciated in daring schools, with fiction for 11 to 14.

Arthur, you will remember, is an adolescent crocodile whose behaviour is the despair of his long-suffering family:

> That evening at dinner Arthur chewed with his mouth open, felt the saltcellar, and diddled with his spoon again. He also knocked over the milk jug while reaching for the beef stroganoff instead of asking Father to pass it. Then Arthur wiped up the milk with a sponge, dropped the sponge into the beef stroganoff, was sent to finish his dinner in his room, tripped over his music stand, cleaned the beef stroganoff off the rug, and played his electric guitar very loudly, very late.

But everything changes when pretty little Alberta Saurian comes along—and Arthur falls helplessly in love.

A Walk in the Park is picture flat in size and shape. *Dinner at*

Alberta's looks like any easy reader for 7-year-olds. Were we really to allow the physical form of a book to cut it off from its best potential readership? It seemed a pity.

This, as it so happened, was the moment that at the ripe old age of 52, in the middle of my ten-year stint with *Children's Books of the Year* and busy as always with review articles for the *Times Literary Supplement* and other journals, a now-or-never opportunity to get a worm's-eye view of children and books presented itself to me. Would I like to be the Inner London Education Authority's first Chartered Librarian in a primary school, just one day a week as an experiment? I have to confess that like the proverbial fools of which, as you will doubtless by now have observed, I am truly one—I rushed in. Why else I asked myself, looking for pattern as always, had I qualified both as a teacher *and* as a librarian in my twenties? Was it not so that I could bring children and books together to their, I was going to say, *mutual* advantage? I will say mutual—for it doesn't do books any good to stand silent on the shelves gathering dust. They need to communicate like the rest of us.

That children from 7 to 11 need, enjoy and profit from picture books was proved beyond doubt in that school. In two articles called, 'Them's for the Infants, Miss', I have described that picture book project in detail; and in *Picture Books for Young People 9–13* (a Signal Bookguide) I extended the articles into what with some trepidation I venture to call a work of simple criticism—though being mine it is, I now realize, criticism of a positive, practical and promotional kind. I mention these pieces of writing for two reasons. In the first place they were the result of direct experience giving rise to theory, the practical running alongside the formulating principle. So much that is written about children and books is either hatched in the isolation of the academic incubator or written by librarians in retirement during that pleasant afterglow, when blinkered teachers and disruptive children are memories one can smile over, not frustrations that make one despair. I tend to write as I go, journalistic pieces really.

And this is the second reason for mentioning them. If they *do* have any value for readers then you have to thank Nancy Chambers for them, not me. When I first saw the infant *Signal* the one thing I was sure of was that here was a professional and academic critical journal of high standard to which never in my wildest dreams could I aspire as a contributor. But Nancy, in her wisdom or unwisdom I cannot judge, thought otherwise. My debt to Aidan and Nancy Chambers is immeasurable, because but for *Signal*, which made me stop in my tracks, think, write, I would not now have the faintest idea of how I felt about all kinds of experience over the years. And, almost certainly, you would have had a 'real' critic standing where I stand at this moment.

But that is not quite the end. There is an epilogue. In his new novel *Deadeye Dick*, Kurt Vonnegut comments, 'We all see our lives as stories . . . If a person survives an ordinary span of 60 years or more there is every chance that his or her life as a shapely story has ended, and that all that is to be experienced is the epilogue. Life is not over, but the story is.' Shapely or not, you have had the story.

The epilogue began in 1980 when I gave up *Children's Books of the Year* in the tenth year of its life. I was invited by two young enthusiastic business men, both of whom had served their companies in remote parts of the world and had felt deprived of books, to join them as Children's Books Adviser on their exciting new venture called *The Good Book Guide*. This is a full-colour magazine featuring current books that people will want to know about. Each section, be it Health or the Arts, Biography or Sport, Detective Fiction, Cookery or Children's Books is selected with the help of a specialist adviser. But the remarkable feature of this magazine is that its editors, Bing Taylor and Peter Braithwaite, have set up a warehouse on an industrial estate in Battersea in which they stock multiple copies of every book reviewed.

The idea of being able, through *The Good Book Guide*, not only to promote the children's books each season that I thought parents would want to know about, but in addition to be sure that every book written about was accessible to families at the drop of a—well, credit card or postal order—was thrilling. I *had* to say yes.

And what has resulted from Bing Taylor and Peter Braithwaite's commitment to children's books, a field that most 'adult' editors and booksellers regard as a necessary thorn on the stem of a beautiful rose, is a paperback that would appear to be a real breakthrough for children's books. This is *The Good Book Guide to*

Children's Books—the first colourful wide-ranging and broad-based guide for parents and children to in-print children's books.

The Good Book Guide to Children's Books was originally to be produced independently by the Good Book Guide team for its subscribers; but because Penguin thought the idea so worthwhile they became co-publishers, with the result that *The Good Book Guide to Children's Books* is now available in bookshops all over the world where British books are sold.

Perhaps epilogues should be gentler, quieter, more reflective and dignified. Mine, however, is embodied in this lively, cheerful-looking pioneer venture—a torch from the past (me) borne by the next generation (Bing and Peter) for their children's contemporaries. It makes me happy; but it doesn't I'm afraid bring me any nearer to being a critic.

But wait!

In an article in the *Times Educational Supplement* last year, Neil Philip, a young and respected critic, surveys the world of children's books and remarks on its ever widening range, its disparate audience, the diverse ways in which children's books are used and the 'hotly contradictory' perspectives from which they are viewed. His is a distinctive voice of the 80s, recognizing that children's books will only survive in their rich diversity if they are seen not only in relationship to the *literature* of their day but also to the idea that all children need to be catered for.

Reading his piece I began to wonder whether, all unawares and following my own instinct, I hadn't, after all, been a children's book critic—of this new strain, but working away in the decade before it became respectable.

I shall watch new developments from my armchair with interest.

INDEX